Christian Mueller-Roterberg

Handbook of Design Thinking

Tips & Tools for how to design thinking

Copyright © 2018 Christian Mueller-Roterberg

All rights reserved

ISBN:

978-1-7904-3537-1

Preface

Another book about Design Thinking?
Yes, and this book is different in that it presents all the knowledge about Design Thinking from a business perspective in a comprehensive and straightforward way. In this sense, this preface is also short and concise.

How can you benefit from this book?
You will find countless tips, recommendations, checklists and tools in this book. If you can only implement a few of these tips, your time and financial investment in this book has paid off. And you'll definitely get more than just a few tips, guaranteed!

The symbol indicates further literature tips following some chapters. Recommendations for interesting internet pages are marked with the following symbol:

What awaits you in this book?
The contents are structured along the Design Thinking process as shown in the figure below. This process is described step by step, but it is iterative with many feedback loops.

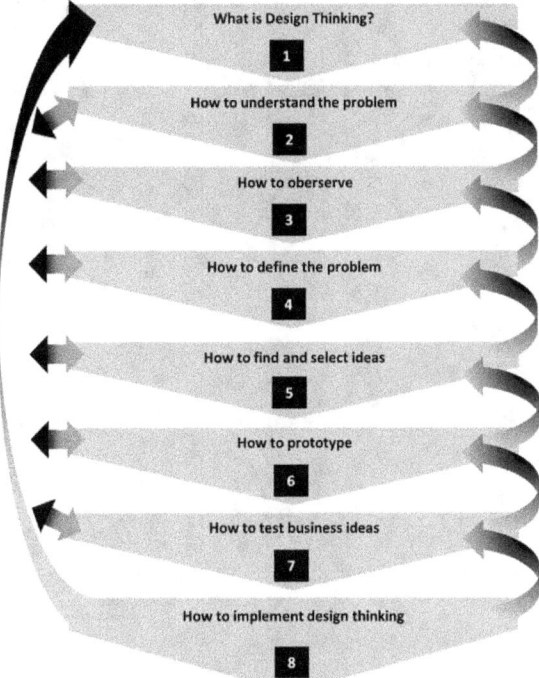

PS: Results from the Design Thinking are never perfect. This book is not perfect either, but lives from your feedback, dear readers. With this in mind, give me your feedback and make this book better with me: **feedback@innovationsratgeber.de**

For Gertrud und Bernhard

For Kerstin, Leonard and the little miracle that's on its way.

Thank you for the way full of happiness,
whom you go and will go with me.
Thank you for the loving hands,
who are always so helpful to me.
Thank you for your love and support.

Table of contents

	Preface	V
1	**What is Design Thinking?**	**1**
1.1	Principles of Design Thinking	3
1.2	The process of Design Thinking	4
1.3	How to plan a Design Thinking project	7
2	**How to understand the problem**	**11**
2.1	Search field determination	12
2.2	Problem clarification	12
2.3	Understanding of the problem	15
2.4	Problem analysis	16
2.5	Reformulation of the problem	28
3	**How to observe**	**33**
3.1	Observation Phase	33
3.2	Empathetic design	34
3.3	Tips for observing	34
3.4	Methods for Empathetic Design	40
4	**How to define the problem**	**61**
4.1	Point-of-View Phase	61
4.2	Characterisation of the target group	61
4.3	Description of customer needs	64
5	**How to find and select ideas**	**79**
5.1	Ideate Phase	79
5.2	The creative process and creative principles	79
5.3	Creativity techniques	84
5.4	Evaluation of ideas	132
6	**How to protoype**	**143**
6.1	Prototype Phase	143
6.2	Lean Startup Method for Prototype Development	144
6.3	Visualization and presentation techniques	160
7	**How to test business ideas**	**177**
7.1	Test Phase	177
7.2	Tips for interviews	179
7.3	Tips for surveys	185
7.4	Kano Model	188
7.5	Desirability Testing	194
8	**How to implement Design Thinking**	**199**
8.1	How to conduct workshops	199
8.2	Requirements for the space	205
8.3	Material requirements	206
8.4	Agility for Design Thinking	207
9	**Glossary**	**209**
10	**Bibliography**	**213**

1

What is Design Thinking?

1	**What is Design Thinking?**	
1.1	Principles of Design Thinking	3
1.2	The process of Design Thinking	4
1.3	How to plan a Design Thinking project	7

1 What is Design Thinking?

„The future has many names.
For the weak it is the unattainable.
For the fearful it is the unknown.
For the brave it is the chance." – Victor Hugo, French poet and novelist

Design Thinking is a comprehensive customer-oriented innovation approach that aims to generate and develop creative business ideas or entire business models. Essentially, Design Thinking attempts to project designers' approaches and methods onto business processes.

The approach is ultimately applicable to all kinds of business ideas – whether they have a product or service character. The first mouse for the Macintosh computer was created after a similar approach, or the first toothbrush with a wider ergonomic shaft.

The features of Design Thinking can be summarized as follows:

Design Thinking ...

- is an **integrative approach**: This means that for problem solving, the process of problem solving is considered together with its framework conditions. The problem analysis and solution development are considered systematically and holistically in the form of a process (see below). The various experts necessary for problem analysis and solution development (see below) are involved and enter into exchange with each other.

  The working environment for this process is designed to promote creativity. One also speaks here of the **three Ps of Design Thinking** (see Curedale (2013)): **People** (the human being), **Process** (the problem solving process) and **Place** (the working spaces) must be considered for a successful idea development. A fourth P can be **Partnerships**, since a large number of partners must be involved in the development and implementation of ideas.

- focuses on **early customer orientation**: Design Thinking starts with people and not with a technology or a business goal. Ultimately, the customer should have a decisive influence on the "go/stop" decisions in the process. It is no longer sufficient to question customers about the classic market research instruments. Traditional methods of (testing) market research often only deliver disappointing results in the search for innovations.

- emphasizes **Empathy**: The central element is to put oneself in the position of the customer/user and to observe him in detail. Empathy can create distance to the innovator's own person on the one hand and proximity to the customer on the other. In other words, this approach creates customer orientation. Developments can thus be better aligned with the customers and, if necessary, prioritized to what extent they can satisfy the needs and wishes of these customers.

- strives to make ideas tangible at an early stage: **Prototypes** must be created as quickly as possible – this also applies to immaterial services. It is not a question of testing a quasi-finished (perfect) product, but quite the opposite: individual functions/features/characteristics or activities of the product/service offer are to be checked by the customer. The maxim when creating or selecting a prototype is: **as simple as possible, as meaningful as necessary**.

1 What is Design Thinking?

- consists of frequent **iteration loops** between the development phases. The return to a previous phase is not a mistake, but shows the learning success in this process. Failure is an integral part of this approach and should be tolerated, accepted and even expected by all participants. The motto is: "**Fail fast to succeed sooner**".

- Pay attention to the **diversity of the participants**. Design Thinking combines interdisciplinary breadth and technical depth: The knowledge, experience and perspectives of a team of engineers, natural scientists, humanists, social scientists and economists, etc., who have the ability for multidisciplinary cooperation, are put to good use.

  Furthermore, differences in age, gender, affiliation to the company (long-time/for the time being short in the company), experience with the topic (intensive, little, not at all) and/or personality type (introverted, extroverted, etc.) should be taken into account.

- creates **team-oriented, creative working spaces**: "Me"-spaces (for individual work) and "We"-spaces (for group work) are flexible and inspiring to equip for individual, group and plenary work. It can be advisable to choose different locations, rooms or furniture arrangements for the different Design Thinking phases in order to create new atmospheres (suitable for the respective work) again and again.

- combines **analytical phases** (collecting, organizing, evaluating information) and **synthetic phases** (developing, testing, improving solutions). In the first part, the problem is analysed in detail (so-called **problem space**), where the focus is on what? and why? (what is the problem? why is it a problem?). Only in the second part concrete solutions are developed and tested (so-called **solution space**): Here the question is asked about the "how (something can be solved)".

  In addition, one can differentiate between **divergent phases**, which lead to an expansion of the perspective by collecting information or generating ideas, and **convergent phases**, which lead to a focusing of the field of vision by making decisions between alternatives.

  These divergent and convergent phases alternate, so that the Design Thinking process is framed by a **double diamond** (Design Council UK (2005)). The description of the procedure in chapter 1.2 explains this process in more detail.

1.1 Principles of Design Thinking

When carrying out the Design Thinking process described below, the following principles must be observed, quasi the "Ten Commandments of Design Thinking":

❶ Leave titles at the door!
There is no hierarchy during a Design Thinking workshop.
Chef and other rolls are hung on the coat hook.

❷ Encourage wild ideas!
Let your imagination run wild. Any (supposedly) crazy idea and every idea should be treated equally.

❸ Go for quantity!
Quantity before quality. Selected, analyzed and evaluated later.

❹ Build on Ideas of others!
There is no copyright. Ideas from others should be taken up, supplemented or changed.

❺ Think human centered!
Design Thinking is first and foremost thinking about people and not about technology or business goals.

❻ Be visual and make it tangible!
Use drawings, illustrations, photos, videos, prototypes, etc.

❼ Avoid criticism!
Idea generation and evaluation must be strictly separated.

❽ Fail early and often!
Failure means learning. Often failure means that you have learned a lot.

❾ Stay focused!
Set yourself limits, stick to the concrete tasks in the Design Thinking process**.

❿ Let`s have fun!
Developing new ideas in a team should be fun. Creativity needs this fun.

These rules should be written in large letters on a flipchart in a Design Thinking workshop for all participants to see all the time. The participants are to be reminded of these rules again and again by a moderator.

The rule "Stay focused! appears at first contradictory to the rule "Encourage wild ideas! Experience with creative processes has shown, however, that setting clear boundaries or limitations, in which the imagination should be given free rein, is a target-oriented approach for the idea generation and, in particular, development phase ("necessity makes invention!"). Such limits may include, but are not limited to, the broad direction set by the vision and corporate strategy, specific time and cost objectives (e.g. product/service offering to be launched within X months), a specific regional focus, number of new features, compliance with regulatory constraints or limited resources available. Boyd/Goldenberg (2013) speak here aptly of "Thinking Inside the Box" in order to add a counterpoint to the "Thinking Out of the Box" mainstream approach (see chapter 5.3.4).

In individual cases, a balance must be struck between, on the one hand, the danger of stifling unconventional ideas with potential and, on the other, pursuing utopian spinning.

Staying focused also refers to the Design Thinking process described below. Limits here can mean setting clear time budgets for the individual phases or specifying for whom, how and where the solution is to be used. Used to the right extent and communicated in a challenging way, these limitations can promote creativity and have a motivating and inspiring effect on the Design Thinking team.

1.2 The process of Design Thinking

"Some people think design means how it looks. But of course, if you dig deeper, it's really how it works."
– Steve Jobs, Apple

According to Plattner et al. (2009), the Design Thinking process consists of six process steps with iteration loops: Understanding, observing, defining problems, finding ideas, developing prototypes and testing. The initial three phases, the so-called **problem space** (see Lindberg et al. 2010)), describe the problem and its causes (what is the problem and why is the problem there?). The subsequent three phases, the so-called **solution space**, describe which solutions there can be and how these can be implemented.The process steps are described briefly below and then explained in more detail step by step (see also Figure 1).

Even if the following process representation is shown sequentially, the process is strongly iterative, i.e. there are numerous feedbacks to the previous phases in each phase. The individual process steps should be completed quickly in order to learn fast through iteration loops according to the "**fail early and often**" principle or, if necessary, to be able to terminate the process completely. It is helpful to define concrete time budgets for the individual phases (in agile project management, this is referred to as Timeboxing, see chapter 8.5).

Phase 1 "Understand" (Understanding the Problem):

In the first phase it is first about developing an understanding for the challenge/the problem/the need or the requirement (problem understanding). It must be clarified who has to be integrated into the process and, in particular, which technical perspective (process organisation) is necessary Finally, it must be clarified how the question can best be formulated so that the customer need/problem is defined in concrete terms.

Phase 2 "Observe":

In this phase, detailed research and on-site observations are carried out on the customer's need/problem. Numerous methods can be used for this, such as interviews, written surveys, observations with recordings through photos or even videos. The results are the clarification of the general conditions, the exact definition of the target group and a comprehensive understanding of the customer and his needs and behaviour.

Phase 3 "Point-of-View" (Define the problem):

After the observations, the findings should next be condensed to a single prototypical user whose problem/need is to be summarized in a clearly defined question.

Phase 4 "Ideate" (Finding and selecting ideas):

It is only in this phase that the actual brainstorming process takes place. Here the creativity techniques mentioned in chapter 5.3 can be used. Strictly separated from this, the ideas can then be analysed in a customer-oriented manner in order to identify weak points, and a selection decision can be made on the basis of an idea evaluation.

Phase 5 „Prototype" (Develop the prototype):

In this very important phase, ideas should be visualized as quickly as possible, made tangible, sketched, designed, modelled/simulated, etc. Following the technical field one can speak here of "Rapid Prototyping", whereby the prototype development applies decidedly not only to products, but also to services. A variety of methods for prototype development are available for this purpose.

Phase 6 "Test":

In this final phase, the ideas are to be further developed and tested through further experiments and customer feedback. In addition, important development, production and market issues have to be clarified.

In the process flow presented here, the actual implementation phase with the development of the idea to a marketable product/service would only follow afterwards.

1 What is Design Thinking?

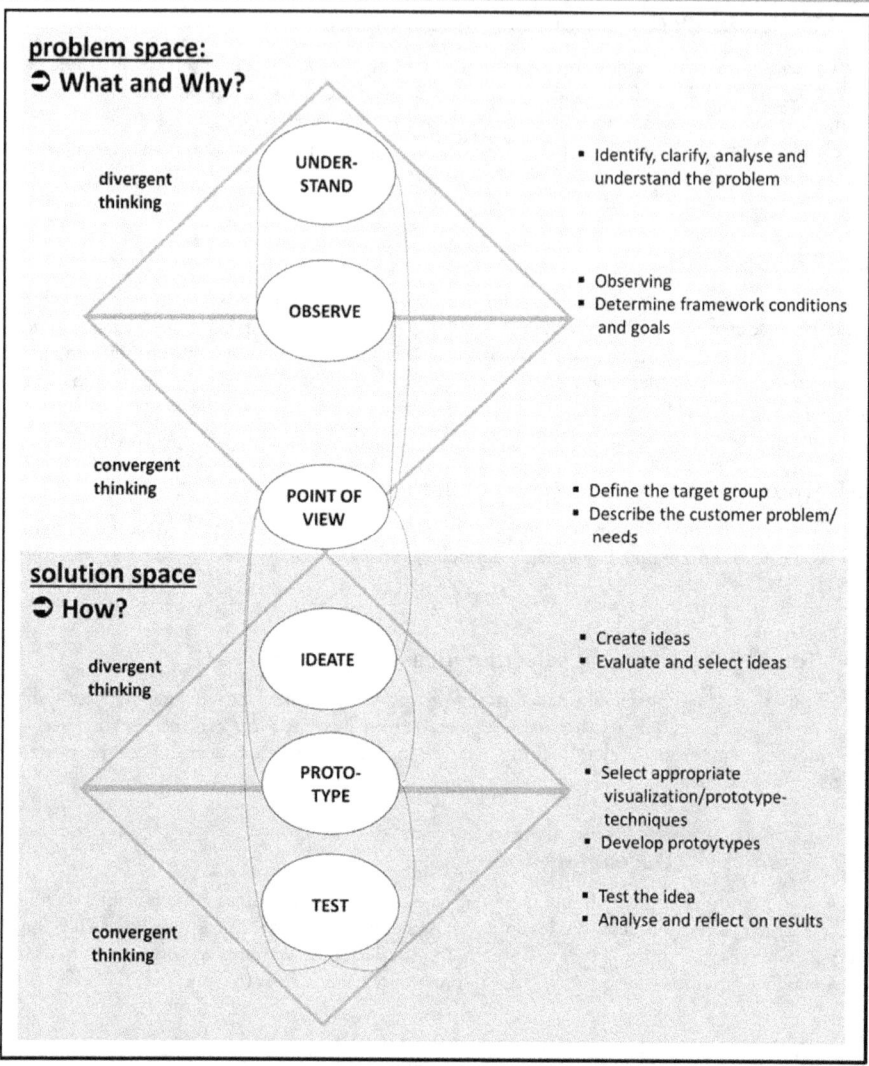

Figure 1: Process of Design Thinking supplemented with the Double-Diamond model
Source: Plattner/Meinel/Weinberg (2009), Lindberg et al. (2010) and Design Council UK (2005)

Overall, Design Thinking is a very comprehensive, user-oriented approach that systematically applies methods for observation, questioning and brainstorming as well as other moderation techniques in the individual phases in a process with numerous iteration loops.

1.3 How to plan a Design Thinking project

First, the goals for the Design Thinking project are to be defined derived from the company/innovation strategy and the expectations of all participants are to be clarified:

- Should new ideas be found? If so, for what or for which search field (see chapter 2.1)?
- Should concrete customer needs and/or certain patterns or trends be found among the customers in a specific subject area?
- Which goal is to be achieved by when?
- Which priorities are to be set in terms of content and time for the achievement of the goal?
- Which employees or which external participants (experts from practice and research, customers, suppliers, external parties from outside the industry) are to be involved from which areas/disciplines?
- Who will be responsible for project management or moderation?
- Where are the interfaces between the required disciplines?
- Which project budget is available for Design Thinking?

Once the goals have been clarified for all those involved, it is certainly necessary to critically review whether the method is at all suitable for the goals.

A decisive success factor for the Design Thinking project is the project organization. In the vast majority of cases, Design Thinking is carried out as a project that involves internal staff as well as external participants from different disciplines. The project team should consist of six to a maximum of nine representatives from different areas (R&D, production, marketing and sales) or disciplines who contribute at least 50% of their working time (and are open to external ideas). Different experience horizons and characters are also helpful to get the diversity necessary for Design Thinking (see chapter 1.1 introductory to the characteristics of Design Thinking).

Not to be neglected is also the internal support in the company for the later implementation of the results from Design Thinking. The support of top management, which can be a decisive success factor, is also very helpful here. The support can be seen concretely in the following activities:

- Adequate resources for the project
- If applicable, taking over patronage for the Design Thinking project
- Desire for continuous reporting on the progress of the project
- Permanent internal and external communication about the strategic importance of Design Thinking
- Member of the steering committee, if any
- Personal participation in workshops
- Recognition of the employees involved

In the case of a more extensive project, a steering committee consisting of managers from the above-mentioned areas must also be set up. Overall, the tasks, competencies and responsibilities must be defined by all project participants.

For the implementation of the project, the explanations in chapter 8 must be considered.

1 What is Design Thinking?

Brown, Tim (2009): Change by Design – How Design Thinking Transforms Organizations and Inspires Innovation, Harper Collins, New York/USA.

Curedale, Robert (2013): design thinking – process and methods manual, Design Community College, Topanga/USA.

Gray, Dave / Brown, Sunni / Macanufo, James (2010): Gamestorming: A Playbook for Innovators, Rulebreakers, and Changemakers, O`Reilly Media, Sebastopol/USA.

Kelley, Tom / Kelley, David (2014): Creative Confidence: Unleashing the Creative Potential within us all, HarperCollins, London/UK.

Kelley Tom / Littman, Jonathan (2001): The Art of Innovation, Random House, New York/USA.

Kumar, Vijay (2012): 101 Design Methods: A Structured Approach for Driving Innovation in Your Organization, John Wiley & Sons, Hoboken/USA.

Lewrick, Michael / Link, Patrick / Leifer, Larry (2018): The Design Thinking Playbook: Mindful Digital Transformation of Teams, Products, Services, Businesses and Ecosystems, John Wiley & Sons, Hoboken/USA.

Liedtka, Jeanne / Oglivie, Tim (2011): Designing for Growth: A Design Thinking Tool Kit for Managers, Columbia Univers. Press, New York/USA.

Martin, Bella / Hanington, Bruce (2012): Universal Methods of Design: 100 Ways to Research Complex Problems, Develop Innovative Ideas, and Design Effective Solutions, Rockport Publishers, Beverly/USA.

Silverstein, David / Samuel, Philip / DeCarlo, Neil (2012): The Innovator's Toolkit: 50+ Techniques for Predictable and Sustainable Organic Growth, 2nd edition, John Wiley & Sons, Hoboken/USA.

Stickdorn, Marc / Schneider, Jakob (2013): This Service Design Thinking, BIS Publishers, Amsterdam/The Netherlands.

https://hpi-academy.de/design-thinking/uebersicht.html

https://www.ideo.com/

http://www.designkit.org/

https://dschool.stanford.edu/resources/

https://designthinkingforeducators.com/

2

How to understand the problem

2   How to understand the problem

2.1	Search field determination	12
2.2	Problem clarification	12
2.3	Understanding of the problem	15
2.4	Problem analysis	16
2.4.1	Clarifying the framework conditions	16
2.4.2	PESTEL -Analysis	16
2.4.3	Trend Impact Analysis	20
2.4.4	Delphi method	22
2.4.5	Analyzing the cause of the problem	23
2.4.5.1	Ishikawa Diagram	23
2.4.5.2	Root-Conflict-Analysis (RCA+)	24
2.5	Reformulation of the problem	28

2 | How to understand the problem

„*A problem well stated, is a problem half solved.*" – Charles F. Kettering

„*You can tell whether a man is clever by his answers. You can tell whether a man is wise by his questions.*" – Naguib Mahfouz, Nobel Laureate in Literature

"*You can't fix a wrong problem.*" – Rupert Platz, UX Designer, prsentation at the WUD Berlin, November 2015

In this first phase, after defining the search field (chapter 2.1), the aim is to clarify what the problem is, i.e. what a solution must be sought for at all (chapter 2.2). On this basis, a deeper understanding of the challenge/problem must be developed (problem understanding in chapter 2.3). This requires an analysis of the problem in order to examine the framework conditions and causes of the problem. It is helpful to think about reformulating the problem (see chapter 2.5) before, during and after the problem analysis. The further steps of the observation phase, the final problem definition and the problem solution are the subject of chapters 3 to 5. The individual steps are summarized in the figure below.

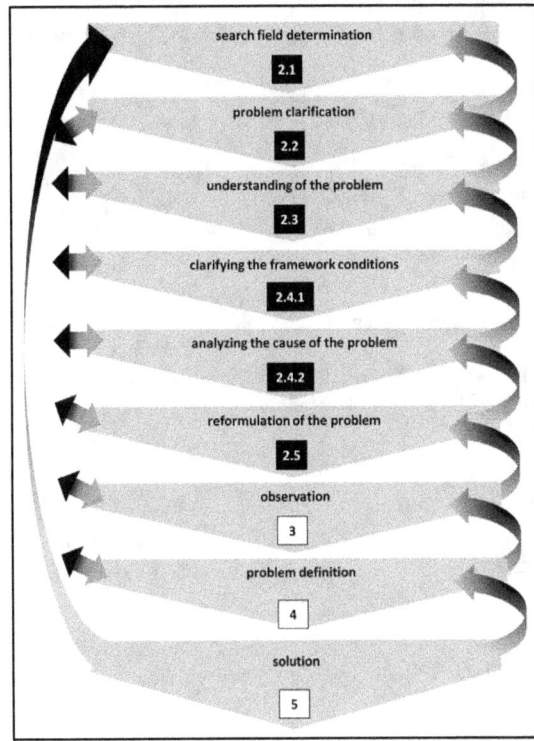

Figure 2: How to analyse problems
   Note: Numbers refer to the chapter number.

2 How to understand the problem

You should take the time for this basic understanding of the problem, because only then can the further steps be carried out in a meaningful way. On this basis, you can also first decide which technical perspective you need to integrate in the further steps and which expert knowledge is relevant (see chapter 1.3).

2.1 Search field determination

The determination of the search field serves for orientation, in order to analyze more purposefully and/or to find more effective and/or more efficient ideas. In order to define search fields, there are basically three different variants available:

- **Market-oriented search field determination**

    The focus here is on customers and competitors with the following questions:
    - What needs or problems do our customers currently have or will they have in the future?
    - Are there any developments that could awaken new needs?
    - Which offers are currently and in the future offered by direct, indirect or potential new competitors, and how could one differentiate oneself from them?

- **Technology-oriented search field determination**

    The focus here is on new technologies with the following questions:
    - Which technological developments are relevant for the company? Which interesting applications could result from this?
    - Which technological challenges will have to be solved in the future?

- **Competence-oriented search field determination**

    The focus here is on your own (core) competencies with the following questions:
    - For which products and services could one's own competences, abilities or resources be of use?
    - In which market and technology areas are (similar) competencies important?

Derived from the corporate vision/strategy, a suitable search field should be defined for Design Thinking. Not too narrow to limit the scope for radical ideas. But also not too broad, because otherwise the focus becomes too vague and makes the next step of the problem analysis more difficult. The search field becomes more and more concrete also by the following steps.

2.2 Problem clarification

In order to develop a better understanding of the problem/situation, it is advisable to go through the following catalogue of questions with the 5-W+1-H-questions (Who? What? Where? Why? When? How?) for a structured clarification of the problem (see table below).

Table 1: Questionnaire to clarify the problem
Source: According to Andler (2016)

	problem	non-problem	solution
Who	has the problem? is indirectly affected? believes that they are affected? makes decisions?	is not affected by the problem?	could use the solution as well? can contribute to solving the problem? does not want the solution? could stand in the way of the solution?
Where	does the problem occur?	does not the problem occur?	has something similar already been successfully resolved? is the best place to solve it? could the solution also be used?
When	did the problem start? does the problem occur? does it become an even bigger problem?	does not the problem occur?	should the solution be available? will it improve?
What	Is the problem? do you know or don't know about the problem? is not understood about the problem? is different than it should be? is particularly noticeable? annoys you about the problem? are the individual aspects of the problem?	is not the problem?	has been made the solution so far? should the solution necessarily be able to do? are the constants that must not/cannot be changed? is needed for the solution? will be different in the future? is (or is not) important for the solution? are your goals for the solution? do you have to discover?
How	does the problem manifest itself? is it related to another problem? can it be formulated differently?	is it usually going?	should the solution look like? is it tried to be solved so far? could the problem be an opportunity?
Why	is it a problem? is the problem unusual?	isn't it a problem for others?	is the solution needed? do we want to solve it? won't it just solve itself? can it be solved? is it difficult to solve?

Based on this catalogue of questions, the following problem analysis according to Kepner/Tregoe compares the problem with a case in which the problem (surprisingly) does not occur. The problem as well as the comparison case have to be checked systematically for their differences. On this basis,

2 How to understand the problem

hypotheses are developed and tested that contain the cause of the problem or the cause of the missing problem in the comparison case.

How to do it:

The following table is filled in systematically. For this purpose, a comparative case is sought in which the problem (surprisingly) does not occur. This case can be very similar or can come from a foreign field (other scientific field, foreign industry). Other techniques, such as the fishbone model and root cause analysis (both see chapter 2.4.2), can also be used to analyse the causes.

Table 2: Problem clarification according to Kepner/Tregoe
Source: According to Andler (2016)

	problem	non-problem	discrepancy	Cause (why is there a discrepancy?)
Who	has the problem?	has not the problem?	differences?	assumption about cause
Where	does the problem occur?	doesn't occur the problem?	differences?	assumption about cause
When	does the problem occur?	does the problem not occur?	differences?	assumption about cause
What	Is the problem?	isn't the problem?	differences?	assumption about cause
How	does the problem emerge? extensive is the problem??	is it usually going? many parts/areas are not affected?	differences?	assumption about cause

In addition to the description of the problem, initial insights into possible solutions can also be gained. On the one hand, this includes the clarification of framework conditions: What is permitted? What is possible? What is available? Also consider what would happen if framework conditions changed, such as the available or necessary resources, the technical possibilities and/or the political/legal situation.

On the other hand, you should carefully analyse the current state of the art:

- Why are the existing solutions not sufficient?
- Where are their limitations or shortcomings?
- Why are there no adequate solutions so far?

2.3 Understanding of the problem

„*There are known knowns; there are things we know we know. We also know there are known unknowns; that is to say we know there are some things we do not know. But there are also unknown unknowns – there are things we do not know we don't know.*"
– Donald Rumsfeld, US Secretary of Defense

After clarifying the problem, it is helpful to reflect again on what we know or don't know about the problem. According to Gray et al. (2010), the following matrix with the so-called blind spot of knowledge is helpful for this. The next questions have to be answered in the individual fields:

- What do we know about the problem? Which means we're aware that we know it.
  (**known Knowns**)
- What do we know that we don't know about the problem? Which means we're aware that we don`t know it.
  (**known Unknowns**)
- What do we know without even knowing that this knowledge could help us with the problem? Which means we're not aware that we know it.
  (**unknown Known**)
- What do we know that we don't know we don't actually know? Which means we're not even aware that we don't know.
  (**unknown Unknowns**)

The unknown Unknown area is, so to speak, the blind spot of our knowledge and awareness, which we only get out through the exploratory discovery. This is where Design Thinking begins.

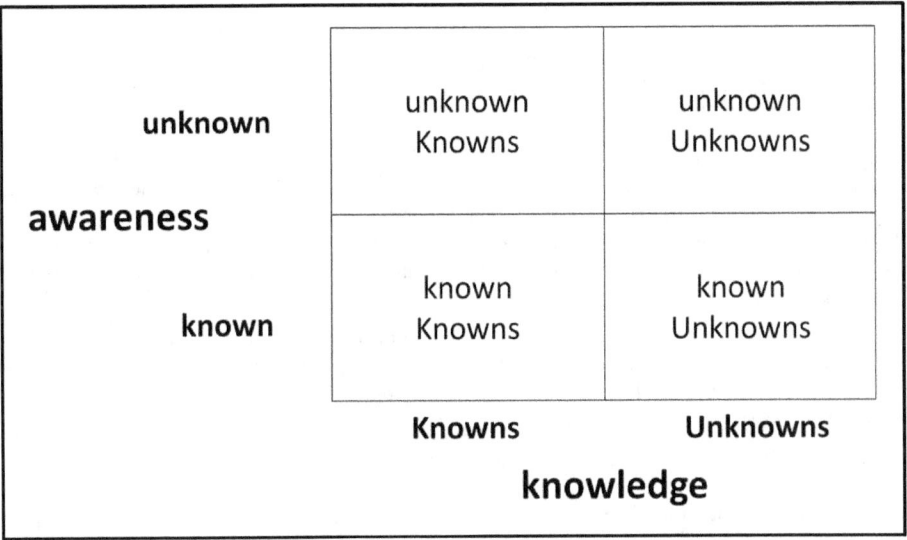

Figure 3: The blind spot of knowledge and awareness
Source: According to Gray et al. (2010) (with changes)

2.4 Problem analysis

The first step in problem analysis is to clarify the framework conditions of the problem area so that you get a general overview of the external influencing factors. Numerous methods are available for the systematic evaluation of the external influencing factors, which are explained in detail in the following section. In addition, the observation phase, which is described in detail in chapter 3, serves to clarify the problem from the customer/user perspective.

2.4.1 Clarifying the framework conditions

There are many factors that need to be considered in order to analyze a selected problem area. In order to identify trends and developments, scouting is helpful in the context of Design Thinking. Scouting is the detailed search for a specific selected subject area and thus project-related with a small but clear information task.

The first step is to better understand the search field and identify important market and technology trends. This information about the trends in the search field can be systematically evaluated using the following techniques. First, the so-called PESTEL method (chapter 2.4.1.1) can be used to analyse the external influencing factors/trends more precisely. The effects on the individual stakeholders and ultimately the effects on the company can in turn be analysed using the trend impact analysis (see chapter 2.4.1.2). Finally, the Delphi method (chapter 2.4.1.3) is presented as a method that allows well-founded forecasts to be made about the influencing factors or trends through multi-stage expert surveys. In addition, a look at other industries that either use similar technologies or face similar market challenges is very helpful. In order to find such analogous areas, creativity techniques such as synetics or bionics (see chapter 5.3.2.4 or 5.3.2.5) can also be used to help open the view.

2.4.1.1 PESTEL-Analysis

The PESTEL method represents an analytical grid for recording external influencing factors. It differentiates the factors into **political**, **economic**, **social**, **technological**, **environmental** and **legal** spheres of influence. Trends and developments in the influencing factors in turn have an impact on individual stakeholders of a company, which in turn have consequences for the company. This makes it possible to systematically identify the relevant influencing factors and to recognize patterns/directions of change at an early stage.

The development of these factors in the future can be estimated using methods that are the subject of the next section. It is important to understand the cause/origin of these trends, to trace their development from the past to the present, and to create a trend forecast that describes their relevance, probability of occurrence, impact (see below), and sustainability.

In order to obtain reliable information about trends and developments at an early stage that can have direct or indirect effects on the company in the short, medium and long term, it is helpful to evaluate the following sources of information:

- Publication/patent databases
- Newspapers/scientific or technical journals
- Technology/market/industry studies by associations, service/consulting companies, scientific institutions (universities, research institutes) or national and international government institutions (ministries/authorities, OECD, UN)

- Statistics
- Analyst reports, trend/market research reports
- Annual reports, sustainability reports, presentations, press releases and websites of other companies (competitors, suppliers, start-ups)
- General internet research, forums, blogs, social networks
- Conferences, trade fairs
- Customer surveys, observations, supplier surveys, workshops
- Personal networks of your own employees
- Expert talks/interviews, association work, associations
- Cooperation with scientific institutions and companies
- Employee surveys

Possible political, economic, social, technological, natural and legal factors that can influence a company are listed in the tables below.

www.trendwatching.com, www.trendguide.com

www.thecoolhunter.net, www.boingboing.net

www.scout.com, www.Engadget.com

www.gizmodo.de, www.mashable.com

www.techcrunch.com, www.trendsportting.com

www.springwise.com, www.coolhunting.com

www.trendwatching.com, www.trendreports.com

www.coolbusinessideas.com, www.ideaswatch.com

www.iftf.org

www.trendresearch.com, www.clubofrome.org

2 How to understand the problem

Table 3: PESTEL Analysis (I)

Political	Economic	Social
political Influencing Factors	**economic Influencing Factors**	**social (societal) influencing factors**
political climate/stability	economic growth/ economic development/ sector growth	values/norms
understanding of democracy, election results/	liberalisation of markets vs. protectionism/trade barriers	social justice, social cohesion
party commitment, party reputation	privatization	tolerance/justice settings
government expenditure on labour market measures, health, infrastructure/construction, education, research, environmental protection, consumer protection, foreign development aid	national debt	societal commitment
financial/tax policy	rates of inflation	social contacts (number, intensity)
health policies	interest rates	population growth
pension policy	unemployment vs. labour shortages in certain sectors	changes in the family structure
interdependence economy/politics, lobbyism	labour costs and productivity	fragmentation of society
bureaucracy	purchasing power of the population, wealth growth, income distribution, poverty/wealth gap	smaller private households
	influence of trade unions, collective	geographical migration of the population
	propensity to invest	regional disparities
	stock indices	ethnic changes in population structure, migrations
	company valuations	interculturization
	subsidies/nationalisation	religious and ethnic conflicts
	foreign exchange rates	spiritualization
	fragmentation and specialisation of markets	demographic change
	market saturations	school/university/training quality
	competitive activities	work mentality
	state of orders	career consciousness
	cost of living	attitude towards (lifelong) education
	housing costs	attitude to technology, image of science
	private health expenditure	technical expertise
	private vs. state pension plans	ownership rights (Sharing Economy)
	health enhancement	image of politics
	customer satisfaction	willingness to participate
	customer loyalty	image of economy
	migration rate	attitude towards foreign investments and profits
	propensity to consume, saving habits	leisure behaviour
	consumer behavior: Quality awareness, price sensitivity, individual desires, brand awareness, status thinking, need for consulting/information	environmental/sustainability awareness, consumer behaviour, health awareness
	growth of e-commerce, e-business	24/7-Society
	digital currency	acceleration of social change
		media influence / media image
		transport/mobility traffic, mobility pattern
		need for security
		corruption
		crime, violence and terrorism

Table 4: PESTEL Analysis (II)

Technological technological Influencing Factors	Environment natural environmental factors	Legal legal Influencing Factors
technological advances, dynamics of technological change	natural events (flooding, volcanic eruptions, tornadoes, drought, cold, etc.)	changes in civil rights (travel, people, media)
innovation rate	pollution, climate change, extinction of species, desertification	changes in the national and multinational legal situation (tax/competition/cartel law, patent rights, etc.)
product/process innovations	shortage of raw materials (crude oil, rare metals, etc.)	product liability
development times	water shortage	regulation
R&D-expenses	energy and raw material prices	enforceability of contracts
number of patents	recycling/disposal behaviour and systems	growing influence of interest groups on legislation (associations, environmental/consumer protection movements, non-governmental organisations)
inter-disciplinarisation	waste disposal costs	
convergence of technologies	epidemics, resistance development	
digitalization		
automation, miniaturization		
cyber attacks, proliferation of computer viruses		

In the next section, a checklist is added with table 6 that summarizes the most important questions for this step. On the basis of this identification of possible influencing factors (trends and developments) from the corporate environment, an initial assessment can be carried out with regard to relevance for the company, probability of occurrence and sustainability. A simple evaluation scheme is outlined in the following table. These results then form the basis for estimating the impact on stakeholders or on the company with the help of the trend impact analyses described below.

Table 5: Evaluation of external influencing factors

Influencing factor (trend/development)	signal/indicator	importance (0...5)	probability of occurrence at time X	probability of occurrence at time Y	sustainable development (permanent trend of at least 5 years)
growth in market XY	growth rate per year	2	20%	60%	doubtful
new technology Y	number of patents in the technology area Y	4	30%	90%	yes
...	...		...		...

2.4.1.2 Trend Impact Analysis

After identifying the trends (influencing factors) and an initial assessment of their relevance, probabilities of occurrence and sustainability, the final step is to specify the effects on the individual relevant stakeholders and then the effects on the company. For this purpose, an impact analysis is useful, which first assesses for each trend what effects there are on the individual situations, challenges, needs and/or problems of the relevant stakeholders of the company. In order to identify the relevant stakeholders, a stakeholder analysis of the current situation is helpful in advance.

Table 6: Checklist of trend analysis

Checklist of Trend Analysis
▪ What are the surrounding influencing factors today and in the future (in 5, 10, 15 years)?
▪ With which political changes is to be expected (and how likely with which effect and when)?
▪ With which economic changes is (how likely with which impact when) to expect?
▪ What social/social changes are expected (and how likely)?
▪ What technological changes are expected (how likely with what impact when)?
▪ What natural changes in the environment are expected (how likely and what is the impact of these changes?)? When is it to be expected?
▪ What legal changes are to be expected (and how likely with what effect and when)?
▪ Which of these factors will change when and how? How long-term and far-reaching are these factors?
▪ Are there interactions between different trends? Are there contrary developments?
▪ What effects do these factors have on the company and its competencies?
▪ What impact do these trends have on stakeholders?

The following table provides a comprehensive overview of such a trend impact analysis.

Table 7: Impact analysis to assess the influence of trends on individual stakeholders

stakeholder	situation, needs and requirements	trend A	trend B	trend C	...
customer	needs, problems and purchasing behavior of current customers	What influence do the individual trends have?			
	needs, problems and buying behaviour of new/potential customers	Which new customers do the individual trends enable? What influence do the individual trends have on them?			
	needs and problems of non-customers	Which new non-customers are responsible for the individual trends? What influence do the individual trends have on them?			
	customer structure	What influence do the individual trends have on the customer structure?			
competitors	current direct/indirect competitors	What influence do the individual trends have on their survival, number, strategies, products and behaviour?			
	new direct/indirect competitors	Which new competitors are responsible for the individual trends? What influence do the individual trends have on their emergence, number, strategy, products, behaviour?			
	substitute products/solutions	What influence do the individual trends have on existing and/or new substitute products/solutions?			
suppliers	current suppliers	What influence do the individual trends have on their challenges, importance, price expectations, negotiating power, strategy, products, quality and behaviour?			
	new suppliers	Which new suppliers do the individual trends enable? What influence do the individual trends have on them?			
	supplier structure	What influence do the individual trends have on the supplier structure?			
cooperation partner	current cooperation partners	What influence do the individual trends have on their challenges, importance, bargaining power, strategies and behaviour?			
	new cooperation partners	Which new cooperation partners do the individual trends make possible? What influence do the individual trends have on them?			
	fields of cooperation	In which areas will there be increased cooperation on the basis of individual trends?			
science	importance	What influence do the individual trends have on the importance of individual scientific disciplines/institutions?			
	willingness/ability to cooperate	What influence do the individual trends have on the willingness and ability of scientific institutions to cooperate?			
	diversity	What influence do the individual trends have on the diversity of content and institutions in science?			
investors	current investors/financial sources	What influence do the individual trends have on their strategies, goals, bargaining power, values and behaviour?			
	new investors/financial sources	Which new investors/financial sources enable the individual trends? What influence do the individual trends have on them?			
	investor mix	What influence do the individual trends have on their composition?			
interest groups	currently relevant interest groups	What influence do the individual trends have on their importance/power, challenges, strategies, goals and behaviour?			
	new relevant interest groups	Which new interest groups make the individual trends possible? What influence do the individual trends have on them?			
media	importance	What influence do the individual trends have?			
	quality/objectivity/diversity	What influence do the individual trends have?			
	relation to economic issues	What influence do the individual trends have?			
politics	labour market	What influence do the individual trends have on the design of these policy areas, with what possible effects?			
	taxes/interest rates				
	competition/trade				
	energy				
	environment				
	health care/consumer protection				
	infrastructure				
	civil rights				

The effects of the trends on the relevant stakeholders can then in turn have more or less strong short-, medium- or long-term consequences for the company. In order to estimate these effects on the company and to derive future needs for action from them, a further impact analysis is useful. In this impact analysis, the changes or requirements of the individual stakeholders are compared with the individual elements of a company and their effects and time frame are estimated.

For reasons of simplification, the trends have so far been viewed in isolation from each other. In practice, however, there may be a variety of interactions between the trends that reinforce or compensate each other. In order to identify these interactions and estimate their extent, a cross-impact analysis between the trends (influencing factors) can be carried out.

2.4.1.3 Delphi method

The Delphi method (derived from the oracle of Delphi) is a multi-level, highly structured expert survey on the estimation or expression of opinion of the future development of a topic or question. Iteration loops are possible so that the opinions of others can be addressed. Frequently, the survey is conducted in written and anonymous form. The method can also be used to generate new ideas (see chapter 5.2 Creativity techniques).

To prepare the method, a clear definition of the problem/topic is necessary (see chapter 2.2). On this basis, suitable experts can be identified through personal contacts, recommendations, participants in specialist conferences/trade fairs, publication and patent searches. In addition to possible monetary incentives, the results themselves can provide an incentive for the experts to participate. The further steps are summarized below:

How to do it:

① **Problem description**

Each expert is asked by a moderator to explain the question, the topic or a catalogue of theses orally, by telephone or in writing and to comment on them in detail. The PESTEL method (chapter 2.4.2) can be helpful in drawing up this catalogue of theses. Of particular interest is the question, which problems/needs can occur in XY in X years?

② **Evaluation by the experts**

Each expert fills out the form separately. Only questions regarding the understanding and delimitation of the topic are possible.

③ **Summary of contributions**

The moderator analyses the contributions of the experts and summarises them anonymously without commenting on them. This evaluation can be quantitative or qualitative, depending on the question. Differing opinions are also compared.

④ **Feedback from the experts**

The summary of the expert opinions will be sent back to the experts with the following question: Can they add/concretize/change the list of information? The experts should be asked to give reasons, especially in the event of divergent judgments.

⑤ **Iteration loops**

Steps 2-4 are repeated until the desired approximation of the results is achieved or the moderator cancels the feedback. Two to three rounds should be sufficient.

⑥ **Evaluation**

The average value or qualitative assessment of the last revision of the results represents the final assessment.

The advantages of the Delphi survey are worth mentioning:

- No one-sided expert opinion
- Mutual stimulation by the ideas of other experts
- No personal mutual influence
- Promotes consensus building among experts
- Can be used to generate ideas if necessary

However, the high time and possibly cost requirements due to the involvement of experts must be mentioned as a disadvantage, as well as in particular tendencies towards adaptation, which suppress deviant, singular – but quite interesting – assessments or ideas.

2.4.2 Analyzing the cause of the problem

The Ishikawa diagram (chapter 2.4.2.1), Root Conflict Analysis (chapter 2.4.2.2) and 9-field thinking (chapter 2.4.2.3) are three techniques that support the analysis of the causes of problems.

2.4.2.1 Ishikawa diagram

Ishikawa diagram (also known as fish bone diagram) is a simple scheme to clearly identify simple cause-effect relationships. For a better overview of the cause-effect relationships, the individual cause factors are written on the individual lines (= bones) in the Ishikawa/Fishbone diagram – either as the main cause or represented in the form of a branch as a secondary cause. In the sense of a system, the causes for the (problem) situation in the areas of people (activities/behaviour of the personnel), management (organization, planning, leadership, controlling), machine, material, methods (technical/organizational approach) as well as the "environment" (= environment; external factors) are searched.

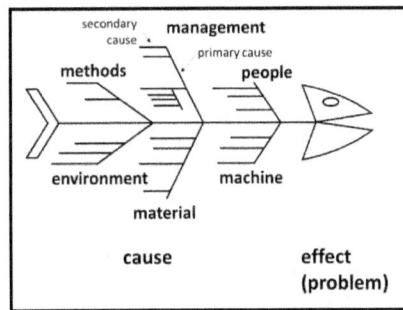

Figure 4: Ishikawa/fish bone Diagram

The Ishikawa/Fish Bone Diagram provides only a very rough overview of the cause-effect relationships. With the Root Conflict Analysis (RCA+) explained below, a more in-depth analysis can be carried out on this basis.

2.4.2.2 Root Conflict Analysis (RCA+)

Root Conflict Analysis (RCA+) is a detailed analysis to identify technical, physical (but also administrative, economic) contradictions in products/procedures/services. In principle, the analysis is based on a simple cause-effect analysis such as the Ishikawa diagram.

How to do a RCA+-Analysis
Example after Souchkov (2005):

Step 1: Problem description:

First the harmful, adverse, undesirable or insufficient effect is described. The description should be kept short in form:

Object in which the problem occurs, as a noun.

+ Harmful/negative function or activity as verb

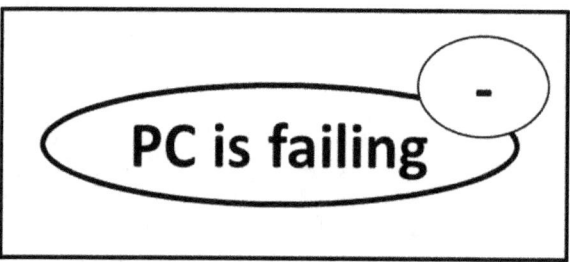

Figure 5: Problem description of the RCA+ method
Source: According to Souchkov (2005)

Step 2: Analyse the causes

With the question: "What causes this effect?" the cause for this harmful effect is briefly described on the next level. The formulation of the cause is to be structured as follows:

Object, which is the cause factor, as a noun (can be the state of an object, a situation or a behavior).

+ Function or action as verb

if applicable + condition/object/function/task/process step influenced by cause as noun.

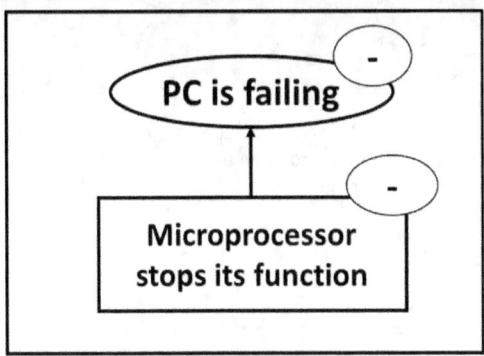

Figure 6: Cause analysis of the RCA+ method
Source: According to Souchkov (2005)

The causes can be negative but also positive (or both, see below).

The causes can also only be assumed at first. This is indicated in the diagram with dotted lines.

Step 3: Summarize the causes

When combining causes that have the same effect, a distinction must be made between the AND relationship and the OR relationship in cause analysis. AND relationship means that several causes work together. This means that only one cause would have to be eliminated and then the effect would no longer exist. In the OR relationship, the different causes are independent of each other and would therefore all have to be eliminated individually.

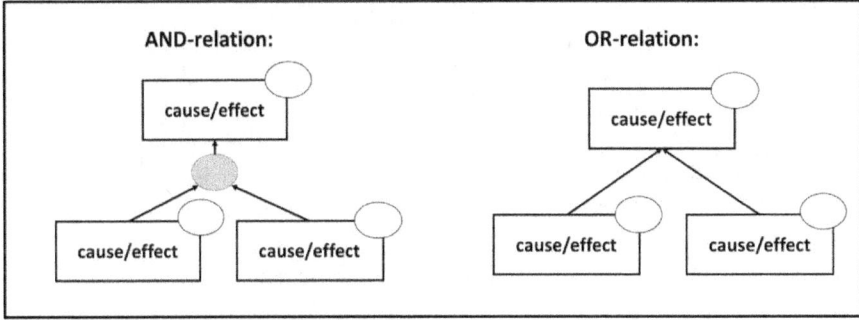

Figure 7: Cause summary of the RCA+ method
Source: According to Souchkov (2005)

Step 4: Evaluation of the causes

The causes (effect) can be positive (+), negative (-), both positive and negative (+-) or non-changeable (--). The latter is the case if the causes themselves cannot be changed because they are controlled by external variables (weather conditions, legal regulations, someone else's responsibility, external specifications, etc.).

2 How to understand the problem

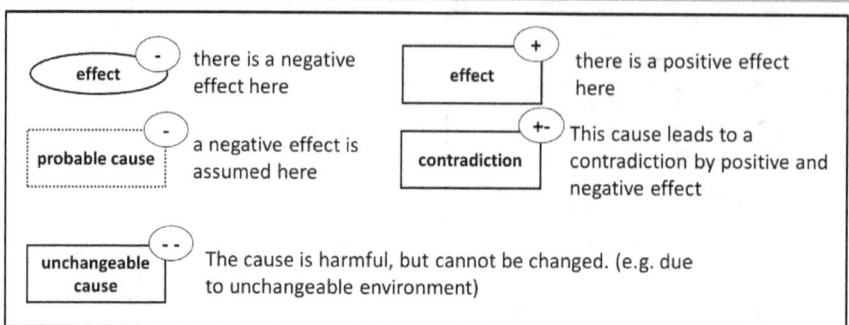

Figure 8: Notation of the cause evaluation
Source: According to Souchkov (2005)

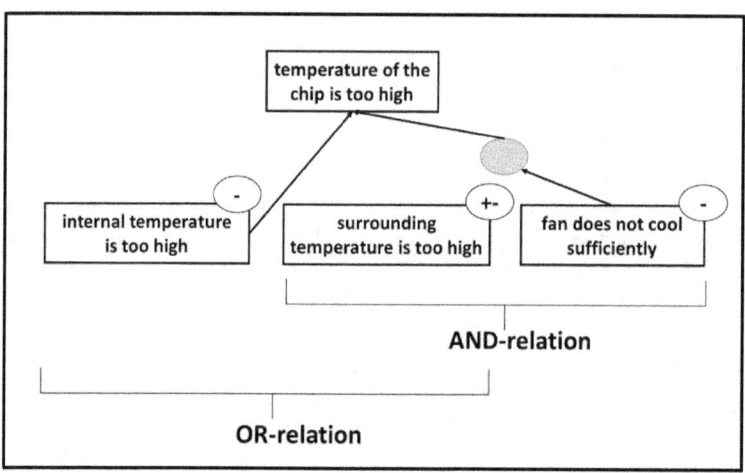

Figure 9: Cause evaluation of the RCA+ method
Source: According to Souchkov (2005)

Step 5: Identify and summarize deeper causes

Steps 2 to 4 are then performed level by level for each of the deeper causes. So the same questions are asked for each cause / effect: "What is the cause for this effect?" or "What is the condition for the state to occur?" or "On what is the state causally dependent?".

This type of cause analysis can be terminated if the cause cannot be changed (e.g. by a nature/law) or if there is a contradiction in the form of a positive and negative effect.

Finally, the created RCA+ must be checked for logical errors or incompleteness.

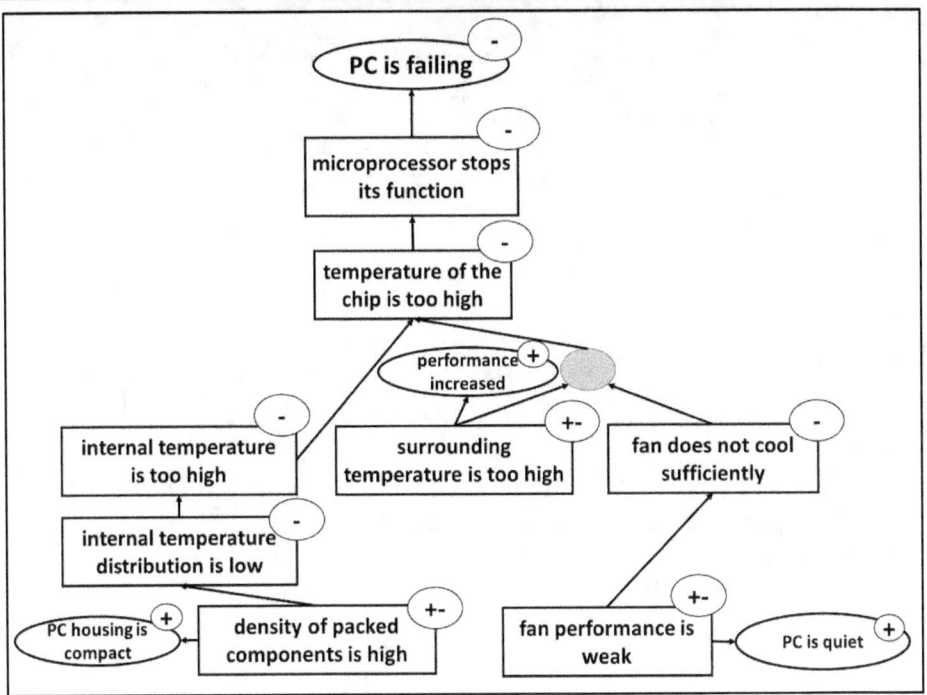

Figure 10: Levels of Cause in the RCA+ Method
Source: According to Souchkov (2005)

2.4.2.3 9-field thinking

The so-called 9-field thinking is to help along the figure below to grasp possible causes and effects of situations or concrete problems in their temporal and systematic contexts.

The 9-field map (see figure below) is spanned by a system and a time dimension: On the system level, starting from a certain situation, the view is directed to the focusing of details (sub-system) – such as individual components or process steps/activities – up to the context of the larger whole (sub-system) – such as the entire industry or the technical or economic infrastructure/environment. In the time dimension, development steps or usage processes of products/procedures/services can be considered.

These 9 fields are to be filled out in key words in order to overcome blockades of thinking, to analyse problems or situations holistically or to get suggestions for concrete approaches to solutions from different perspectives.

2 How to understand the problem

	the past What happened before? What was supposed to happen before that? (development/ prevention)	the present What happens now? What is the current situation? (situation/ problem)	the future What will happen?? What should happen? (Trend/ changes)
super system (Industry level/ Infrastructure environment)			
system product-/process-/ Service-level			
subsystem components/task/ process steps			

Figure 11: 9-Fields Map
Source: Gadd (2011)

2.5 Reformulation of the problem

A basic approach to analysing the problem is to try to reformulate the problem/situation in order to get a different view of the problem. According to Michalko, the following creative techniques can be used (partly taken from Michalko (2006)):

- Formulate the problem from the **perspective of all stakeholders** (in this context you should conduct a stakeholder analysis in advance): How do the individual stakeholders see/perceive the problem? How bad is it for them? Is it a problem at all? What would the solution look like from the point of view of individual stakeholders?

- Formulate the problem from the **point of view of foreign personalities**, a foreign company or a certain profession:
  Put yourself in the role of a foreign person or company and consider how these persons/companies would see or solve the problem. People can be famous sportsmen, politicians, artists, a preacher, a judge, a picture newspaper reporter, a psychologist, a child etc. Companies can be Apple, McDonalds, Microsoft, Google, Facebook, BMW, etc., who stand for certain strategies/business models and thus possibly encourage a new perspective on a problem.

- Formulate the problem **at different levels of abstraction**:
  Formulate more globally or more specifically (use different levels of abstraction): Find the right level of abstraction with Why-How questions (see also Why-How Laddering Technique, chapter 4.3.2 for the means-end approach and chapter 5.2 for the creative principles).

➲ Try to break the problem down into **several individual problems**:

Looking at the problem as a whole and then at its individual parts is a proven technique for reducing complexity at the same time. The Ishikawa diagram (see chapter 2.4.5.1) can be used to support this.

➲ **Rephrase the problem** in other words: Sometimes it is sufficient to reformulate the problem only linguistically in order to get a different point of view. You can do this as follows (see Michalko (2006)):

- Use the appropriate synonyms for the keywords in the previous problem description.
- Change the order of the words and look at the description.
- Use colloquial language to describe the problem or describe the problem to a layperson in simple words without technical terms.
- Change nouns to verbs and verbs to nouns.
- Replace the noun in the sentence with its opposite.
- Search lexicons or Wikipedia for the definition of the words used in your problem description. Does this give you a new perspective on the problem?

➲ **Alienate the problem or view of this**
(taken from Michalko (2006), p. 42):

- Try to view your problem as a living being: What would it look like? Make a picture of it.
- Consider your problem as something edible: what would it taste like?
- Look at the world from the perspective of the problem: How do you look yourself from this perspective?

➲ Increase or decrease **the size of the problem**: With the **Power-of-Ten technique**, you mentally try to reduce the problem or a frame condition by a factor of 10 or increase it by a factor of 10.

➲ Try to **visualize** the problem/situation.

➲ Change or **reverse** the problem:
If, for example, something is supposed to be improved, think about how you could make it worse.

3
How to observe

3   How to observe

3.1	Observation Phase	33
3.2	Empathetic design	34
3.3	Tips for observing	34
3.4	Methods for Empathetic Design	40
3.4.1	Artifact Analysis	40
3.4.2	Behavioral Mapping and Tracking	40
3.4.3	Empathy Map	41
3.4.4	Cognitive Walkthrough	42
3.4.5	Heuristic Evaluation	43
3.4.6	Mental-Model Diagram	44
3.4.7	Customer Journey	45
3.4.8	Service Blueprinting	51
3.4.9	Mystery Shopping	56
3.4.10	Critical-Incident Technique	57

3 How to observe

"See what everyone is seeing, but think differently!" – Buddha

3.1 Observation Phase

In this phase the focus is on the potential customer/user. In order to gain a comprehensive understanding of the person of the customer/user, a real target group should be selected. Essentially, one should concentrate on customers/users who have the same needs / problems and are looking for appropriate solutions. Christensen (2003 and 2016) speaks here of the so-called "Jobs-to-be-done" concept (see chapter 4.3.1 for details).

If the solution to the problem is based on a radical innovation, it is also helpful not to concentrate on the "average customer" but first to look for progressive customers, the so-called innovators or early adopters. They have a concrete awareness of the problem and are actively or urgently looking for a solution. They will therefore probably be very willing to provide qualified customer feedback. Also search for extreme users who use products in very specific (extreme) situations (cold, heat, permanent use, certain regions etc.), or search for so-called lead users who have already developed their own solutions for the problem. The methods Persona (see chapter 4.2) and Empathy Map (see chapter 3.4.3) are also helpful here.

After selecting the "right" target group, it is advisable to first put yourself in the role of the target customer in the next step, against the background of your own experiences and views: What are your own experiences if you put yourself in the role of the customer? What would you as a customer do, want, wish, expect, be able to do, etc.? How could the customer be? Appearance, age, gender, special behavioural characteristics, etc.

Next, various methods can be used to directly or indirectly obtain information from the customer about himself or his behaviour and emotions: Analysis of secondary data, written surveys, interviews, observing future users and taking photographs or even shooting videos.

Secondary data about the customer can be very diverse: Search online and offline for studies, news articles, newspaper reports about your target group and collect statements in social networks (Facebook, Twitter, Instagram etc.), contact data or other relevant information. Search for blogs from or about your target customers. Also use internal knowledge sources from marketing/sales and in particular from customer service.

On this basis, you will consider what information you have or still need and how you can best research it through written surveys, interviews and/or observations. For all methods, the two basic questions are the following: What do the customers do and what do they not do? What do they say and what do they not say?

You will find detailed information and numerous tips on the methods of written surveys and especially interviews in chapter 7.

3 How to observe

In the following, there are some tips on how to carry out an observation. It's about putting yourself in the customer's shoes, so that one also speaks of empathic design. Subsequently, in chapter 3.4 some methods of empathic design are presented in detail.

3.2 Empathetic design

"Innovation begins with an eye." – Kelley (2001), S. 23

Empathic design means that the (potential) customer is observed during his activities (e.g. the use of a product/service but also during his daily work/service on site), so that the observer can "empathize" with the role of the customer and the situation and thus better understand it. This is in contrast to so-called product clinics or usability tests in which an artificial observation situation is created in a kind of laboratory. If the observer takes part in the situation himself, this is also referred to as **"shadowing"**.

In addition to the use of a product/service, the situation to be observed can also include the use of prototypes ("Minimum Viable Products", see chapter 6.2) by the customer. The observation does not only concern the use of a product or prototype, but also the situation and environment of the customer, the general conditions or his daily routine. Also, knowledge about the customer's motivation and behaviour should be gained.

This approach offers numerous inspirations for innovations (observation of usage errors or hand-knitted solutions as well as latent or inarticulate customer needs) and is unfortunately too rarely used in practice. Observations are often only used in the context of usability tests, which, however, take place in a very late phase of the innovation process. Already in a very early phase – as described here in the Design Thinking Process – valuable customer-relevant information for problem solving and new ideas can be found.

In the following, we will first explain how to observe correctly. Subsequently, numerous methods of empathic design are presented in order to carry out observations or to systematically evaluate the observation results.

3.3 Tips for observing

Basically, it should be clarified in advance:

- Who should be observed?
- Who should carry out the observation?
- Which behaviour should be observed?
- How are the observations recorded?

In detail, the following further information should be observed:

During the observation one should become clear before about the place and the time of the observation, whom and what one will see there, which influence one exerts as an observer if necessary on the customers and/or environment. In this context, it is also necessary to clarify in advance how one behaves in the situation itself, where and how one sits, moves, what gestures and facial expressions one has, what and how one says something, how one wants to register the actions, etc. Recordings in the form of videos, photos or audio require the prior consent of the persons observed (preferably in written form). You should also always be aware of what expectations you have of the situation and the people involved. So one should try to let one's own prejudices become clear.

In this context, one should become aware of the numerous possible observation/perception and assessment errors. Above all, the interviewer effect ("observer effect" or also "Hawthorne Effect", see below) must be taken into account here, that a change in the customer's behaviour can be determined by observation alone. The individual observation/perception and assessment errors are explained below. These can falsify the results and their analysis.

It would be helpful if different persons with different knowledge were to carry out the observation or evaluate the recordings. So psychologists, engineers/computer scientists or design experts can pay attention to very different aspects of the customer.

The observations can be supplemented with a survey of the customer before, during or after the observation situation. For example, this serves to clarify why a customer is doing something or what feelings he feels during this activity. In particular contradictions and discrepancies between the answers and the observations are particularly interesting to investigate further. For this purpose, you should observe the recommendations described in chapter 7.2 or 7.3 for conducting oral or written surveys.

In preparation, you should ask yourself the following questions (you should also be aware of your own bias/prejudices or the possible observation/perception/judgement errors listed below):

- What do you think the customer is doing?
- Why do you believe that?
- Where do you think you will find the customer?
- What will the customer do?
- How often do you think the customer acts like that?
- When do you think the customer will do that?

Situations are very informative when a customer wants to use something for the first time. What problems do the customers have? What do the customers do?

What is observed at all and how this information is to be evaluated must also be clarified in detail in advance. There are numerous schemes ("frameworks") to structure the observations and not disregard any essential aspects. In the following the concepts "nine dimensions of descriptive observation" of Spradley (1980), the "AEIOU-" as well as the "POEMS-" schemes are presented.

The very differentiated scheme of Spradley (1980) comprises the following nine dimensions, which one should pay attention to during observations and make corresponding notes:

Table 8: Nine dimensions of descriptive observation
Source: Spradley (1980)

observation dimensions	Explanation
SPACE	Describe in detail the premises or outdoor area in which the customer is staying.
ACTORS	Write down the names and the relevant information about the persons observed.
ACTIVITIES	Summarize the activities performed by the persons.
OBJECTS	Write down the objects that the persons use or find in the situation (furniture, PC, special equipment, etc.).
ACTS	Emphasize special individual actions of the customers.
EVENTS	Describe the events or situations in which the customers find themselves (meetings, small talk, customer talks, etc.).
TIME	Make a note of the order in which the individual activities/actions take place.
GOALS	Describe which goals the customers want to pursue concretely with their actions.
FEELINGS	In particular, write down the emotions of the customers in the various contexts.

The observation scheme AEIOU of the Doblin Group (see Martin/Hanington (2012): 10) is structured in a similar way, with which, as an extension, the interactions between the individual observation aspects can also be visualized in the form of a matrix (see below).

Table 9: AEIOU scheme of the Doblin-Group
Source: According to Martin/Hanington (2012): 10 and
Lewrick et al. (2018): 21

Acronym	observation dimensions	Explanation
A	ACTIVITIES	What happens? Which targeted activities do the customers carry out to achieve something? Which tasks do the customers perform? What happens before/after?
E	ENVIROMENTS	What does the environment look like/is the atmosphere in which the customers act? What is the character and function of the room?
I	INTERACTIONS	Which interactions take place between which people? Are these routine processes or does each interaction take place differently? Are there interfaces? How is the operation carried out?
O	OBJECTS	Which objects/devices are consciously or unconsciously used or not used, changed, moved etc.? Who uses these objects, in which environment (see above)? How do these objects relate to each other?
U	USERS	Who and how are the persons (customers, employees) and what behaviour, preferences, values and needs do they have? What roles and relationships do they have with each other? Who influences them?

Table 10: Interactions of observational aspects

	A	E	I	O	U
A					
E					
I					
O					
U					

Similarly and somewhat more condensed, the **POEMS scheme** by Kumar/Whitney (Kumar/Whitney (2003): 50-57) can be used to combine observations with **People, Objects, Environments, Messages** and **Services**. In the latter case, messages mean the verbal and non-verbal (gestures, facial expressions, movement) messages that people send. Services mean the services used by the customer.

3 How to observe

Finally, the so-called Five Human Factors by Kumar (2012) are very useful as an analysis scheme describing the physical, cognitive, social, cultural and emotional factors of a customer experience:

- **Physical:** What is the interaction of the customers/users with their environment like? What do customers/users touch, open/close, press, pull, move, carry, etc. in certain situations?
- **Cognitive:** What meaning do the customers/users give to the objects/materials etc. with which they interact? What do they read, look at intensively, decide, execute?
- **Social:** How do customers/users interact with other people? Do they act more formally/informally, fun/seriously, distanced/narrowly etc.? How do they talk, decide, negotiate, work together?
- **Cultural:** Which values, norms and behaviours can be observed? How do these values and norms manifest themselves in interaction?
- **Emotional:** Which feelings and thoughts do the customers/users show? How do these feelings and thoughts express themselves?

When observing, you should pay particular attention to the following signals:
- Confusion, hectic or misunderstandings of the customer
- If the customer needs additional work for an activity or is overburdened with it
- Its "pain points", i.e. where was it uncomfortable for the customer, too slow, difficult, boring etc.?
- When disturbances occur (without/with influence of the customer)
- Has the customer used anything differently or incorrectly than expected?
- The customer skips steps or does not use something
- When the customer reacts emotionally: This can mean anger, anger, insecurity, resignation, curiosity, interest, enthusiasm or devotion.

Overall, the focus should be on the customer's actions and not on his attitudes, which can only be found indirectly through the method of observation. During the observation you can therefore also ask the person to explain his or her activities aloud or to say what he or she feels/perceives – this is the so-called think-aloud technique.

This think-aloud technique can occur at the same time when the customer/user is actually doing the job (**concurrent think-aloud**). Alternatively, a video can be recorded if the customer/user performs the activities silently and then the customer/user comments on his activities when viewing the video (**retrospective think-aloud**). This variant has some advantages, e.g. that the customer can concentrate on his activities and can subsequently articulate his intentions, thoughts and feelings in a calm atmosphere. With both you should always ask if something is unclear, and not only assume something.

3 How to observe

Errors during observation/perception/judgement:

- **Hawthorne effect (interviewer effect):**
  People change their natural behavior under observation.
- **Rosenthal effect:**
  The expectations, attitudes, beliefs, and stereotypes of the observer
  have an effect on the result within the framework of a self-fulfilling prophecy
  of the observation.
- **Halo effect:**
  Individual properties/activities outshine everything else.
- **Cognitive dissonance:**
  Observer seeks only confirmation of his expectations, since an incompatibility with
  is perceived as unpleasant according to its expectations.
- **Primary effect or recency effect:**
  The first (primary) or last (recency) impression outshines everything else.
- **Role effect:**
  Because of his role, one has a certain expectation of a person.
- **Contact effect:**
  The more often a person is observed, the more positive it appears.
- **Similarity/contrast effects:**
  Own characteristics (age, education, origin, etc.) and behaviors (hobbies, etc.)
  of the observer are transferred to the observed person. If
  similarities discovered create this sympathy. Differences are discovered,
  these in turn generate antipathy.
- **Attribution errors:**
  The characteristics, behavior and attitudes of the observed person will be
  systematically overestimated and external factors (situational influences) underestimated.
- **Logical false conclusions:**
  The "logical" conclusion of an observation is based on a false assumption
  or prerequisite. From a temporal relationship of events,
  a cause-effect relationship is falsely assumed (e.g. return of the storks in the
  spring causes an increase in the number of births in spring). From a
  spatial connection of events it is falsely assumed that a content-related connection between the
  of these events exist. If events (statistically) occur frequently,
  it is falsely assumed that there is a connection in terms of content.
- **Runaway effect:**
  The observed behaves in a similar way to persons (groups of persons) who are observed on the
  (supposed) winning side.
- **Show/liveliness effects:**
  Attention-grabbing images create more meaning.
- **Glue effect:**
  An observed behavior from the past is projected onto the future.
- **Peripheral effect:**
  The focus is not on the person being observed, but on the radiation of the
  periphery (environment, atmosphere, scenery, neighbouring objects, existing
  objects, other persons or other aspects) strongly influences the observation.
- **Selective perception:**
  Observation concentrates only on a few properties, characteristics, or behaviors.

3.4 Methods for Empathetic Design

3.4.1 Artifact Analysis

Artifact analysis is the systematic examination of objects, things and other objects that the customer/user owns, uses or wishes to have (so-called **Personal Inventory**). In addition to the haptic analysis of the object on site, video/photo recordings or drawings can be made for later analysis. The investigation can relate to the value, functionality, complexity/user-friendliness, materiality, aesthetic/color design, frequency of use, place of storage, brand character, etc. of the object. From this, conclusions can be drawn as to how the customer is, which habits and needs he has, if necessary which problems he could have with the use of the object and how the customer can presumably be characterised culturally or socially on the basis of the object.

The objects can come from the professional or private environment of the customer. The potential customer can, for example, be asked to name those objects that have a great (ideal) value for themselves. This also enables informative analyses of the use of competing products (cf. Martin/Hanington (2012)). The customer/user can also be asked about these objects, how and how often he uses/keeps them, what he associates with them, why he acquired them, how he would feel if he no longer had them or if they were damaged, etc. The customer/user can also be asked about these objects, how and how often he uses/keeps them, what he associates with them, why he purchased them, how he would feel if he no longer had them or if they were damaged, etc.

3.4.2 Behavioral Mapping and Tracking

In Behavioral Mapping, the movements and activities of customers are systematically recorded and examined. A distinction is made here between place-centered and individual-centered mapping, which can also be combined with each other. In **place-centered mapping**, people are observed at specific, predefined locations within a specific period of time. The number of persons, how these persons can be characterized (age, gender, habits), whether they are alone or in groups at the location, how they interact with each other at the location, how long they stay at the location overall, how long certain activities can be observed etc. can be noted. The notes can be drawn directly into a plan, floor plan or sketch of the place to be observed (e.g. shelf aisles and stands in the supermarket). During the analysis, different time periods can also be compared with each other to see whether the observations change as a function of time. Photos taken at different times in the same place can support the analysis.

In **individual-centered mapping**, a certain person is observed how he or she moves or what activities he or she undertakes at a certain location and over a certain period of time. The person's consent to this type of intensive observation must be present. The above-mentioned Hawthorne effect (interviewer effect) is particularly pronounced here, so that the person must be given time to get used to this situation. In compliance with data protection and personal rights, the situations can also be recorded on video with the consent of the persons observed.

3.4.3 Empathy Map

The so-called Empathy Map initially pursues the goal of putting oneself as comprehensively as possible into a person or a group of persons, e.g. potential customers. This involves imagining a specific person in a specific situation. This situation can be an everyday situation (e.g. shopping, use of a certain electronic device; household activities; surfing the Internet, travel/leisure/cultural activities, etc.), which the person should look at from different perspectives. Using the example of a concrete person in this situation, the following six questions are asked, which again have to be answered in keywords (on Post-Its) on a sheet of paper (see also following illustration).

➢ **What does the person think and feel in the situation?**

What does he/she want or what does he/she not want? What does she think of when she does the activity? Here you should try to find out what the person's feelings and thoughts are. This gives you an impression of what drives and motivates them. Which emotions often play a role?

➢ **What does the person say and do in this situation?**

A person acts actively with the outside world. What does this person say and do to other people? What could be observed? What behavior does he show? What are some quotes, keywords or statements that the person frequently uses? What behaviors and activities does the person do frequently?

➢ **What does the person hear?**

This involves analysing what the customer hears (noise, advertising messages, information) and how and by whom this person is influenced, e.g. through conversations with family members, friends, colleagues or information on the radio/TV/internet, etc. What do they say about the person? What should they do/not do? Which communication channels are relevant here?

➢ **What does the person see in the particular situation?**

Here one should describe the concrete environment of the person in the situation to be investigated (during the day, at work, at home, shopping, during a leisure activity): How does it look in the environment? What visual impressions does she get in this situation? What offers does he see or does he not see? What does he see, what do others do?

➢ **What frustration does the person have or get in the particular situation?**

Here it is necessary to consider what problems, worries, fears, obstacles and needs the person might be confronted with. What risks does the person face? What is the person trying to avoid?

➢ **What makes the person happy in the situation?**

This includes the other questions: What goals does he pursue? What does he want to achieve? What does she want to achieve? How does the person measure their success? How does he try to be successful?

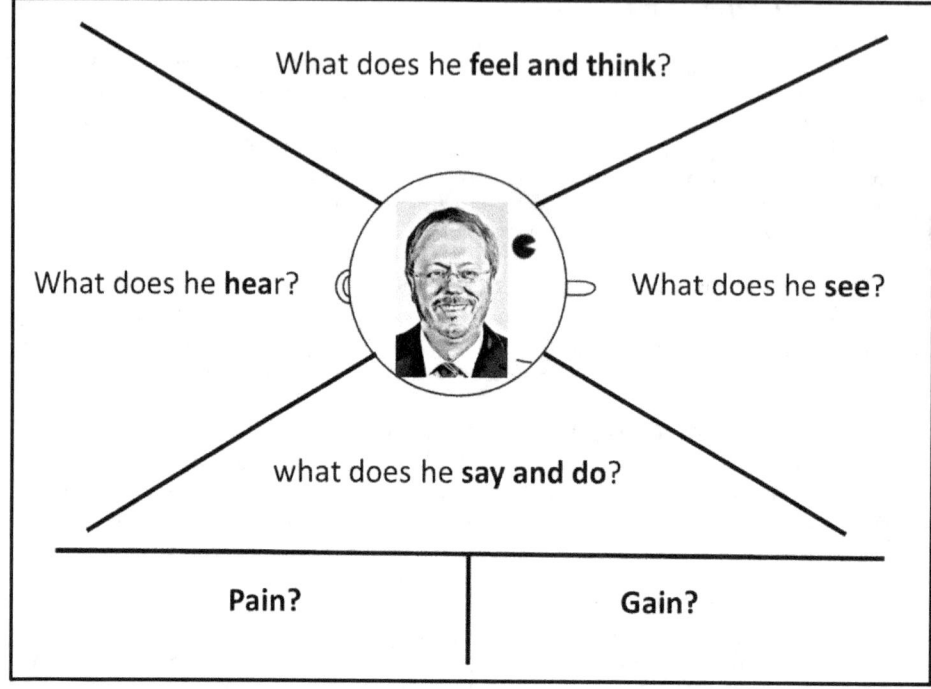

Figure 12: Empathy Map

3.4.4 Cognitive Walkthrough

In the so-called Cognitive Walkthrough, developed by Cathleen Wharton (cf. Wharton et al. (1994): 106), the cognitive behaviour of a user is simulated when he uses a product, uses a service, operates a system or generally accomplishes a task. In this situation general questions are: What would the user perceive and think or how would he act on this basis if he had to accomplish a task? Cognitive walkthroughs can be used in an early innovation phase to gain new ideas or to improve the idea in the prototype phase. All in all, the following goals can be pursued:

- Investigate how complicated an idea, a concept, a system, a product, a service, a process or a general task is for a person.
- Identifying barriers and opportunities for improvement
- Find missing information for the user
- Find difficulties for the user

How to do it:

A limited number of experts individually work the tasks with which a user/customer is confronted when using a product or a service. A step-by-step approach that is as realistic as possible is recommended. The experts should receive exactly as much information and as much time as the users/customers would have. For preparation, information about the potential user/customer should be available, what experiences he has and what knowledge he brings with him. For the analysis of user characteristics, the Persona method is particularly useful (see chapter 4.2). The experts should therefore put themselves into the role of a hypothetical customer/user as far as possible. A user/customer will (want to) perform actions without much thinking. The following questions should be answered at each action step (based on Wharton et al. (1994): 106):

- Does the user know what to do?
- Does the user see how to do it?
- Does the user understand the feedback he receives from the system in response to his action?
- Is the next correct step obvious to the user?
- Does the user associate the next step with his actual intention?

The execution of the cognitive walkthrough can be logged or even recorded by a silent observer. The actions of the experts are compared step by step with the ideal use of a product, service or system.

Approaches for new ideas or improvement measures would be e.g:

- Provision of additional information for operation
- Omitting too much information
- Reduction of complexity (number of required actions of the customer are reduced)
- Removal of unnecessary action steps (automate if necessary)
- Merging of action steps
- Use of a language appropriate to the user
- Improvement of layout/design
- Customer/user gets positive feedback from the system when correct action is taken
- Incorrect operations/incorrect entries are not possible
- Establishment of a customer service

3.4.5 Heuristic Evaluation

In the so-called heuristic evaluation, experts examine products, services or general systems by judging them with a list of heuristics that represent ideal principles for the user-friendly use of products or services. The dialogue with the (potential) user during the use of the product or service is in the foreground. The heuristic evaluation can also be used to support the above-mentioned cognitive walkthrough.

How to do it:

Independently of each other, experts should examine existing products or services or new ideas or prototypes. They try out the products, services, prototypes or ideas and compare them with heuristics that describe the ideal user-friendliness. An example of such heuristics, which should be set up in advance depending on the object of investigation, are the ten heuristics from Nielsen (1994). According to Nielsen (1994), these heuristics are the following:

1. Simple and natural dialogue: No technical terms or difficult to understand expressions, symbols etc. are used. The product/service becomes a human being and its use is like a dialogue between people.
2. The product or the persons in the service speak the language of the user.
3. The user's memory load is minimal: when using the product, the user should not have to think about the next steps (**"Don't make me think"**). It must be intuitive to use.
4. Consistency: The same action of the user always leads to the same result.
5. Feedback: there is a permanent feedback of the system to the user about the status of the usage.
6. There are clearly marked exit points, so that the user has the possibility to stop actions at any time or in total.

7. Shortcuts: There are "shortcuts" for frequently used operations, so that the user can interrupt and quickly rejoin later.
8. Good error messages: Errors of the user or the system are communicated clearly and comprehensibly.
9. Error avoidance: The innovation/idea or prototype is designed in such a way that errors do not occur in the first place.
10. Help and documentation are available, easy to find and always available for the customer.

Another helpful list can be found in Tognazzini (2014).

As a result, the found deviations from the heuristics are discussed, grouped, described and finally evaluated by the experts. For the evaluation, Nielsen (1995) suggests the following dimensions:

1. **Problem frequency** (is it a common or rare problem?)
2. **Problem impact:** can the user easily overcome this problem?
3. **Persistence:** is it a unique problem that users can easily overcome, or is the user permanently confronted with this problem?

The severity of the problem is ultimately a combination of these dimensions. In addition, the market influence should also be taken into account, as some problems can cause massive image problems in the market. These dimensions can be weighted according to their importance and used for evaluation (severity ratings). Nielsen (1995) proposes the following rating scale for this purpose:

0	I do not agree that this is a problem at all.	
1	Just a cosmetic problem:	Doesn't need to be fixed as long as there is no extra time available.
2	Minor Problem::	Fix gets minor priority.
3	Major Issue:	Fix gets high priority.
4	Catastrophic:	Should be fixed before introducing product.

3.4.6 Mental-Model Diagram

While the perspective of the Cognitive Walkthrough was still the insertion into a hypothetical user, the so-called mental models take on a real user view. Mental models describe the assumptions a person makes about how something should function or run (cf. Young (2008)). These assumptions can deviate from the actual course of action or how the provider of a product or service thinks it should proceed. This discrepancy can lead to operating errors, frustrations, annoyances, inefficiencies, superfluous actions, misunderstandings, etc. on the part of the user. Such an analysis offers therefore numerous starting points for the improvement and/or for the development of innovations.

A person's assumptions are based on previous experiences and knowledge, but also on wishes and expectations or free interpretations. On the basis of observations (see chapter 3) and surveys (see chapter 7.2 or 7.3) of specific user groups (see chapter 4.2), the actual action steps and behaviors of individuals can be analysed. Action steps and behaviour patterns can be physical activities, but also thought and feeling processes, which are broken down to individual activities or thoughts/feelings. It is important that these are concrete actual actions and not abstract wishes or expectations for the future.

The following figure shows a mental model diagram showing all steps of action with the individual activities or thoughts/feelings, how a person or group of persons wants to achieve a goal or accomplish a task. Similar or strongly connected activities or thoughts/feelings are grouped and provided with headings. These represent individual "towers" in the diagram. For example, the tower "Prepare" at breakfast would include all preparatory activities, such as making coffee, opening the refrigerator, removing and transporting food, fetching and cutting bread, etc. The level of abstraction depends on the objective of the study.

Below the line, concrete offers are visually compared to the individual towers by own or third-party products or services. From the comparison above (activities/thoughts/feelings) and below (offers) the line, weak points and gaps (the so-called mental spaces) can be identified in order to derive needs for action or approaches for new ideas. Individual service contact points (so-called "touch points", see chapter 3.4.7) can also be identified, which can support individual activities at the customer's premises. With this approach it is also possible to compare different user groups (e.g. differentiated with the Persona method see chapter 4.2), whether they differ strongly in the individual activities or thoughts.

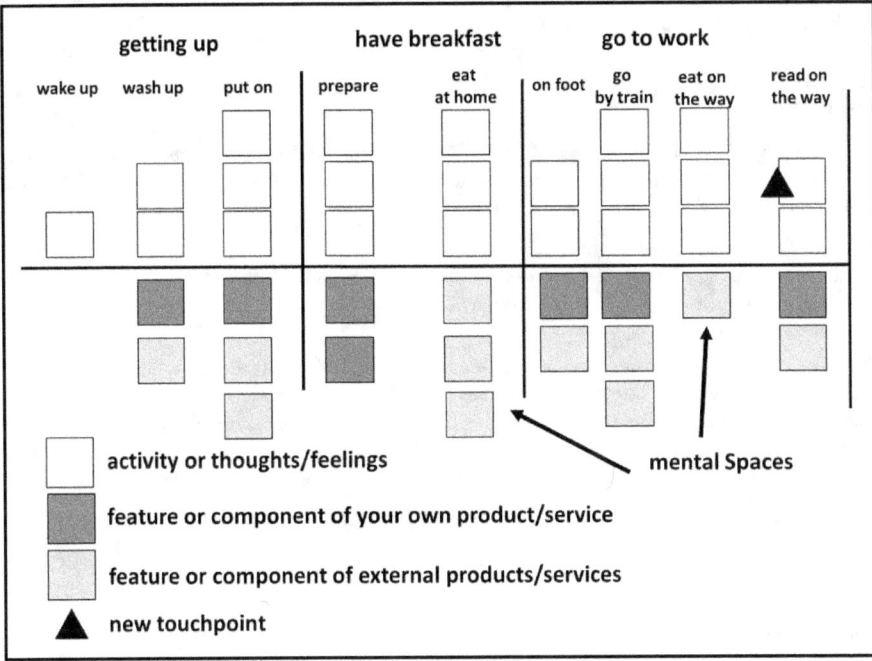

Figure 13: Mental-Model Diagram
Source: According to Young (2008) (with modifications)

Mental model diagrams are similar to the following Customer Journey (chapter 3.4.7) or Service Blueprinting (chapter 3.4.8).

3.4.7   Customer Journey

The so-called Customer Journey can be seen as a consistent further development of the methods mentioned above. With the Customer Journey it is presented which steps a potential customer (best in the form of a concrete persona, see chapter 4.2) goes through before, during and after he/she has used a product or service (see also following figure). The terms customer process analysis and customer process monitoring are similar (identical) approaches to a customer journey, which is described in detail below.

3 How to observe

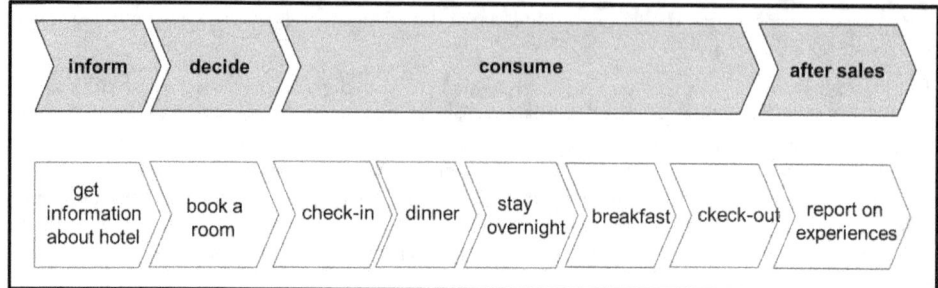

Figure 14: Phases of the Customer Journey with an example of a hotel stay

How to do it:

① First a persona must be created (see chapter 4.2) or selected and supplemented with an empathy map (see chapter 3.4.3). As already mentioned with the persona, different persona can also be used to work out differences and peculiarities in the Customer Journey. Possible persona could be:

Persona of a certain target segment, first-time buyers, extreme users (who frequently or under special conditions use products), non-buyers (negative persona), customers vs. user persona, decision-makers, influencers, possible saboteurs in the sales process, etc.

② With the help of information from surveys (see chapter 7.2 or 7.3 and the Lean Startup method in chapter 6.2), observations (see chapter 3), sales records or own experiences, customer satisfaction analyses or a brainstorming session (see chapter 5.3.1.1), the following phases of a Customer Journey can be summarised in key words (on Post-Its). At first, the phases can be described very roughly in order to describe them – especially the consumption phase – in more detail later.

In addition, there may be different customer journeys for a persona or different persona may have individually different customer journeys.

Phases of the Customer Journey:

Phase 1 – Attention:

How does the customer become aware of his need, his problem or an offer?

Phase 2 – Informing:

How does the customer inform himself about his wishes, a solution to his problem or an offer? How does he compare the offers?

Phase 3 – Decision:

How and by whom or by what is the customer influenced positively or negatively in his purchase decision? Why do customers make a choice?

Phase 4 – Consumption:

What does a potential customer experience step by step when he uses a service or a product? This phase should be described as concretely and in detail as possible. Virtually every step, every activity, every movement and every thought can be considered individually.

Phase 5 – After Sales:

What requirements/tasks/expectations does the customer have in the after-sales phase? How and by whom or what can the customer be encouraged to make another purchase? How and by whom or what can the customer be animated to report on his positive buying experiences or where can he report on them?

③ In each phase the following questions are asked:

- What does the persona want? What does she really want to achieve?

- What does he/she do/what does he/she not do (surprisingly)? How does she try to achieve her goals/wishes?

- What does she use for it and in what order? Who is the persona in contact with? Where are the contact points (points of contact) with the company? How long do the touches with the company last in each case? How long do the individual phases of the Customer Journey last in total?

    Of particular importance here are the contact points – the so-called **"touchpoints"** – which represent places/opportunities/moments where people come into contact with the product or the brand or the company in the broadest sense. Touchpoints can be controlled by the company, e.g. advertisements, TV or radio spots, brochures/catalogues, flyers, trade fairs and events, customer hotline/call centres, mailings, personal consultation/sales, point of sale, shop fittings (see chapter 3.4 as well as chapter 3.4.8 on Service Blueprinting, chapter 3.4.9 on Mystery Shopping or chapter 3.4.10 on Critical Incident Technology), Internet presence, online advertising (e-mail/newsletters, banners, e-shops, landing pages, company/product blogs), etc. In addition, touchpoints that cannot yet be influenced or only indirectly, such as family members, acquaintances, friends of the target group person, social media networks, reports in newspapers/magazines, forums, blogs, comparison/evaluation portals, etc., must be taken into account.

    The touchpoints should be as consistent as possible throughout the entire customer journey (by means of so-called **customer touchpoint management**). This means that everything the customer perceives (see, hear etc., see also the Empathy Map in chapter 3.4.3) should be coordinated with each other. This includes, for example, the visual and linguistic information presented to the customer at the touchpoints. The uniform and harmonious use of logos, images, fonts, messages with their tonalities etc. is part of this. In practice, this is by no means a trivial task, as various internal and (in part uncontrollable) external persons/departments/partners are responsible for the individual touchpoints.

    Each touchpoint (in particular the controllable touchpoints) must be analysed in more detail with the following questions, for example:

- Which touchpoints are particularly effective from the customer's point of view – which are not?
- To what extent does each touchpoint contribute to positively influencing the customer's experience?
- Are the possible touchpoints along the customer journey coordinated with each other?
- How do your employees evaluate the individual touchpoints in terms of effort vs. benefits? Are there touchpoints that offer little customer benefit but are very complex? Are there too many touchpoints that tend to confuse the customer?
- Which touchpoints does the competitor not have? Why?
- Are the touchpoints along the customer journey enough? Where are there gaps? Which additional contact points can be created for the customer?
- What can be automated and how?

The touchpoints must be analysed more closely, especially in connection with the moments of truth mentioned below.

↪ Which consciously/unconsciously/not (yet) perceived problems or negative emotions are/could there be?
> - Customer is annoyed.
> - Customer is unpleasantly surprised about price/cost.
> - Customer does not know what to do.
> - Customer performs activity incorrectly.
> - Customer tries to solve the problem himself.
> - Customer has to wait and loses time.
> - Customer performs useless activities (waste).
> - Customer is disappointed about the quality.
> - Customer perceives situation/activity as too complex.
> - Customer perceives situation/activity as too user-unfriendly.
> - Customer fears risks/feels insecurities.
> - Customer embarrasses himself in front of others.

These problems/negative emotions could be evaluated in their significance (extent, frequency of occurrence), selected and analysed with regard to their cause. Various techniques are available for cause-effect analysis (see chapter 2.4.5) or the critical incident technique (see chapter 3.4.10). The assumptions behind the causes could also be investigated in more detail (see chapter 6.2 on the Lean Startup Method).

④ For each phase and each step in a phase, the satisfaction of the customer is assessed (so-called **Customer Experience Map**). How does the persona feel? It is possible to work with simple symbols (☺ ☺ ☹).

⑤ Furthermore, the so-called Key Moments of Truth (Carlzon (1989)) can also be identified for each phase/step, i.e. moments/situations that are of particularly high relevance for the customer. Various "Moments of Truth" can be located along the customer journey:

- "**First Moment of Truth**", if the customer perceives the product/service at all.
- "**Second Moment of Truth**", if the customer is currently using the product or service and during this time evaluates the product/service on the basis of its quality requirements.
- "**Third Moment of Truth**" if the customer has a positive, neutral or negative perception/service after using the product/service.

You can also add more:

- **"Zero Moment of Truth"**, when the customer perceives his problem/need for the first time through a stimulus (e.g. advertising) and seeks or compares information about possible problem solutions.
- **"Ultimate moment of truth"**, when the customer reports on his experiences/sensations with the product/service to others (e.g. via social networks, opinion portals, virtual communities, etc.).

⑥ The Customer Journey combines very well with the **Customer Benefit Matrix**, developed by Kim/Mauborgne (2015), a methodology to develop improvement opportunities for each phase/step. Answer ideas for the following questions need to be developed:

> - Where can something be simplified for customers?
> - How can you create more benefits for your customers?
> - Where can their risks be reduced/minimized?
> - Is it possible to add more fun and entertainment?
> - What would inspire customers?

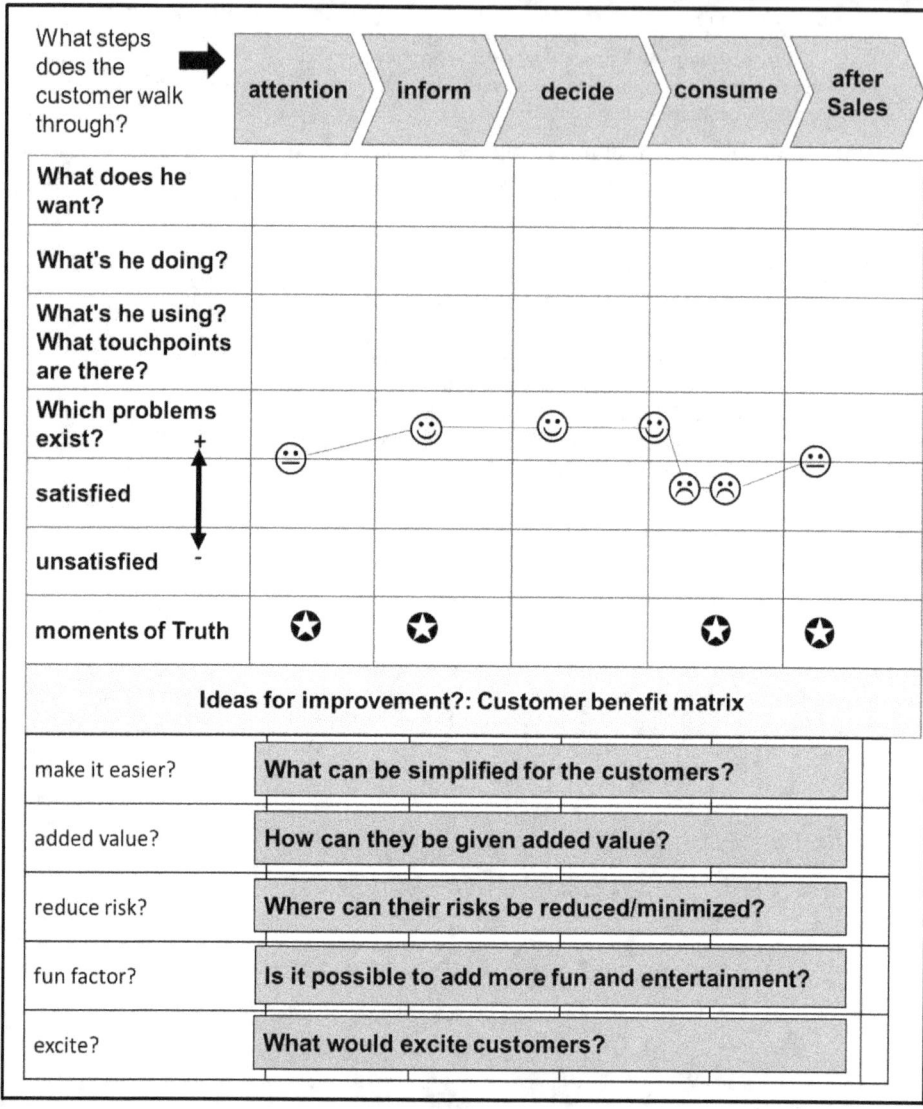

Figure 15: Customer Journey in combination with the customer benefit matrix

One variant of the Customer Journey is to outline a day in the life of a customer ("**A Day in the Life**").

In steps of 15 or 30 minutes, the following questions, for example, can be asked using the example of a concrete persona:

- How/where does the persona spend the day?
- What products/services does she use?
- How much time does she spend using the product?
- How would the persona's life change after receiving her product?
- How often is the persona online? Does she use a PC, laptop, tablet or smartphone?

- Which devices does the customer use, when and how often?

In addition to household and leisure activities, a typical working day can also be focused on.

The Customer Journey and in particular the variant "A day in the life of a customer" can be supplemented with pictures, comic drawings and even videos in addition to the keyword textual description in order to visualise the information and thus make it more descriptive (see also chapter 6.3).

3.4.8 Service Blueprinting

Service Blueprinting – originally developed by Lynn Shostack (1984) – represents service processes in a process diagram from the customer and company perspective, in which different levels are differentiated according to proximity to the customer. Service processes can thus be visualized, (newly) developed, analyzed, controlled and optimized. This method can help to increase customer satisfaction, improve the quality of individual steps or the entire service process, and save costs and time.

In the presentation of a Service Blueprint, five levels can be differentiated, which are first roughly subdivided between the (sole) customer and service provider activities and then differentiated according to different visibilities for the customer. In detail, there are the following levels:

1) Line of interaction:

Above this line, the customer journey takes place, i.e. all process steps performed by the customer. Below this line, the activities are carried out by the service provider. This line therefore determines the division of labor between the customer and the service provider.

2) Line of visibility:

Above this line, the activities are visible for the customer; these are the onstage activities (or front office activities) of the service provider with direct (face-to-face; verbal/written, electronic) customer contact. These customer contact points (touchpoints) are to be designed as concretely as possible. Below the visibility lines, the activities of the service provider are not visible to the customer, but in some cases are also carried out by persons with customer contact (backstage activities or back-office activities).

3) Line of internal interaction:

For further differentiation, an internal interaction line can be defined, which includes support activities below. These support activities are carried out by other persons who no longer have direct customer contact (in practice, these activities are also often referred to as back-office activities and not as support as in this differentiated system).

4) Line of order penetration:

The planning line distinguishes the service creation process from the planning activities below this line. These activities are not performed during service creation, but can be performed (in advance) independently of a specific sales order (for example, maintenance work).

5) Line of implementation:

Finally still the implementation line can be specified, below this line are the activities (Facility activities), which must be accomplished partially far before a concrete customer order like e.g. procurement procedures.

In addition to this very differentiated consideration of activities, an overview of components of the external appearance of the customer environment can also be integrated in the process diagram. One speaks here also of "**Physical evidence**". In connection with services this is particularly important, because the environment and (technical) equipment affect for the customer directly the perception of the quality. The external appearance is determined, for example, by customer parking spaces/lifts/seats, the internet site (including appearances in social networks, e-mails, blogs, etc.), the salesroom/customer lounge, offer folders, objects/equipment for the (self-) operation of the customer, etc.

Furthermore, the so-called **Key Moments of Truth** (see chapter 3.4.7) can also be identified for each step, i.e. moments/situations that are of particularly high relevance for the customer or the company. These "moments of truth" are often found at the points of contact between customers and companies, but do not necessarily have to be. Even situations on which a company has no (direct) influence can be significant for the customer's (purchase) decision (e.g. reading an independent test report).

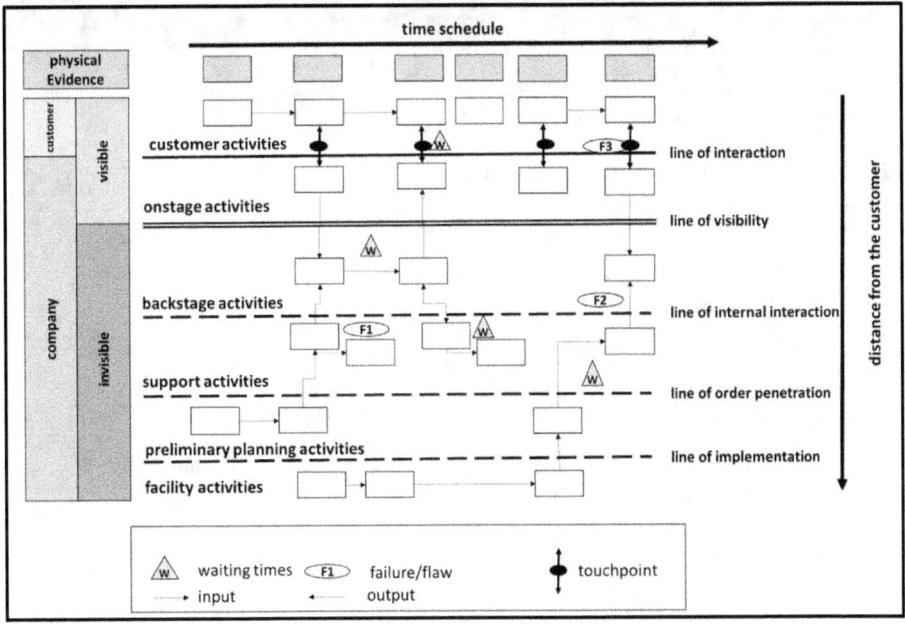

Figure 16: Structure of a Service Blueprinting

How to do it:

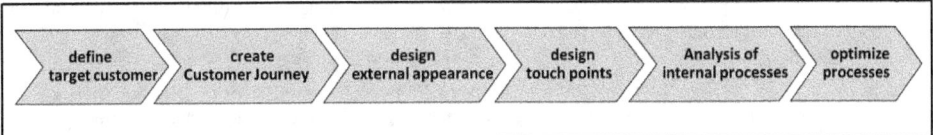

Figure 17: Procedure for Service Blueprinting

❶ Identification and selection of the target group

The first step is to identify and select the target group for which a Service Blueprint is to be created. Depending on the target group, the individual process steps can differ considerably. It is helpful to use the methods Persona (see chapter 4.2) and Empathy Map (see chapter 3.4.3) to get an accurate picture of the target person.

❷ Creation of an (ideal) Customer Journey

The next step is to create the Customer Journey, i.e. to outline all customer activities from the first perception of the problem/need to the after-sales area. The initial question would be here: What would be the ideal course from the customer's point of view? The problems or negative emotions for the customer mentioned in connection with the customer journey should be avoided. In addition, the question can be asked whether activities that the customer has previously carried out himself should be taken over by the service provider.

Here it is advisable to focus on one phase first, because service blueprints can quickly become highly complex and thus confusing.

❸ **Design of the external appearance:**
In order to improve the equipment and environment from the point of view of the customer's perception, the following questions must be addressed:

> - Where can the perception of the customer be improved?
> - What and how can the customer's perception be improved?
> - When (in which phase of the customer journey) should investments be made in particular in the equipment / environment?
> - What equipment can be added, renewed or removed?
> - Should the equipment/environment differ depending on the customer (group)? (average vs. premium customer)?
> - Which equipment devices/points need to be improved first, second, etc.?
> - What is the cost-benefit ratio for possible improvements?

❹ **Definition and design of touchpoints**

The connection and touchpoints (contact points) between the customer and the service provider must be defined. The following questions must first be raised:

> - Is contact established by the customer himself or by the service provider?
> - Why does the customer contact the company? His motivation/goals are to be identified.
> - In which situation does the contact take place?
> - What do both interaction partners know about each other? What should they (ideally) know about each other?
> - How much does the interaction at the point of contact cost the customer or the company? What added value does the interaction have for both?
> - Could the interaction be designed differently? Can the interaction at the touchpoint be automated, for example? Does a previously automated contact point have to be carried out by people?
> - Can the touchpoint be omitted? Do further contact points have to be added? Can contact points (in terms of time and content) be connected with each other?

This interaction at the touchpoints must also be described in its own way (face-to-face, by telephone, in writing, electronically, automatically). The service provider's persons are not necessarily involved in this interaction. The customer can first interact with the company electronically and automatically or read through the company's information documents.

The touchpoints can exist along the entire customer journey, individually or over a longer period of time, e.g. in customer advice, interaction during purchase, interaction during use/service, customer care, customer service/complaint management or in customer relationship management. To focus, the touchpoints can also be evaluated on the basis of their significance – from the customer and/or company perspective – so that one can concentrate on the essential (weak) points.

Derived from this, the requirements have to be defined in order to make the contact with the customer as satisfying as possible. Requirements can refer to the employees but also to the technology and the further (internal) processes.

❺ Process analysis of internal activities

The next step is a process analysis of the activities to be carried out by the company. These activities can then be arranged horizontally according to their chronological sequence and differentiated vertically according to onstage activities, backstage, support, pre-planning and facility activities. For reasons of simplification, support, pre-planning and facility activities can (initially) also be grouped together. Since this is ultimately a process modelling, the various software solutions with different display options can also be used for the analysis, development and optimisation of processes.

❻ Process optimisation

In order to define the ideal internal process or to optimize an existing process, errors/weak points and/or waiting times must be avoided or minimized.

The following questions can be asked for further analysis:

- ➢ What would the ideal process look like?
- ➢ Which process steps can be (how?) accelerated? Where can waiting times be eliminated?
- ➢ Which activities and internal coordination processes can be omitted/are redundant/not important for the customer or are not perceived by them?
- ➢ Where can process steps be parallelized or at least overlapped?
- ➢ How can the internal decision-making and coordination processes be improved?
- ➢ Can/should internal process steps be taken over by the customer (from operation to self-service)? Which process steps can be standardized?
- ➢ Which process steps can be automated?

Ultimately, all activities must also be subjected to a cost-benefit analysis (Shostack (1984)) to determine whether the process created/optimized in this way is feasible and economically viable at all.

A service blueprint can also be seen as a kind of prototype of a service. This prototype can be further improved through early customer feedback (see Lean Startup method in chapter 6.2).

3.4.9 Mystery shopping

With Mystery shopping (also called **silent shopping**), the quality of service with its shortcomings and potential for improvement can be assessed by systematic observation, in which an observer takes part in a real consultation or purchase action as a test customer. This market research method can also be carried out as a test call (**mystery call**) or customer inquiry by e-mail. With Mystery Shopping, the test persons must be trained so that they can behave like a real customer and can register in detail the environment and in particular the behaviour of the salesperson or consultant.

The testers should – if possible – be independent, objective persons and should have the appearance of a real potential customer. Alternatively, external experts or internal company employees, the so-called checkers, can be used. Exercises in the form of role plays or real pre-tests can prepare the testers for different situations and thus make the trained eye learnable in order to track down suggestions for improvement possibilities.

It is helpful to define in advance a standardised catalogue of criteria and guidelines on how, what and when to observe. The type of observation should be as representative as possible (place and time of observation) and preferably carried out several times with different test persons. In addition, it is possible to concentrate on critical process steps in consulting or sales. For this purpose, the Critical-Incident technique mentioned below (chapter 3.4.10) and Service Blueprinting (chapter 3.4.8) can be used in addition. The latter differentiates the creation of services into individual steps.

Theoretically, mystery shopping can also be used for hidden benchmarking with a competitor in order to obtain indications of improvement potentials or strengths and weaknesses of the competitors. Nonetheless, this hidden competitive analysis is ethically questionable and will therefore not be further elaborated here.

With Mystery shopping the following characteristics can be observed:

- Quality of the environment e.g. design and cleanliness of the premises, room atmosphere, discreet consulting atmosphere, seating, aids, appearance of the employees
- Meeting deadlines, availability, waiting times, opening/consulting times, delivery times
- Quality of consulting: scope and depth of analysis of the customer's problem/need
- Solution quality, e.g. correctness and objectivity of statements, individual advice, credibility and motivation of the customer consultant, presentation and comprehensibility of benefits
- Communication quality e.g. friendliness, politeness, empathy, helpfulness and discussion atmosphere
- Delivery qualities/flexibilities, return options, payment methods offered

In addition to concrete suggestions for product and, above all, service innovations, this process can also generally sensitize employees to consulting deficiencies and thus improve service quality. Furthermore, the customer's satisfaction can be determined objectively.

3.4.10 Critical-Incident technique

In the Critical-Incident technique according to Flanagan (1954), the survey of customers concentrates on particularly memorable experiences in connection with the consultation and use of a product or, in particular, a service. These critical events often live on as stories through mouth-to-mouth communication and thus also gain great importance for the company.

Through personal interviews with standardized, open questions (recommendations for planning and conducting such personal interviews, see chapter 7.2), customers should remember critical events and report on them at touchpoints with the company and its employees. These experiences may have led to the non-purchase/return of the service or product. The Critical-Incident technique can also be combined very well with Service Blueprinting, which is presented in chapter 3.4.8.

According to Bitner et al. (1990), the following basic questions are suitable for the analysis of critical events:

- Do you remember a particularly unsatisfactory contact with an employee?
- When did this happen?
- What specific circumstances led to this situation?
- What exactly did the employee say and do? What did they say, what did they do?
- What exactly happened so that they found the contact unsatisfactory?
- How did you feel before, immediately after, or a week after the event?
- Did you change your behaviour after the event?

In principle, it is also possible to query events that are perceived as particularly positive. However, particularly negative experiences are often better remembered by customers. This survey of critical events must encompass a concrete situation, have generated strong dissatisfaction, be sufficiently detailed and have taken place within a clearly defined period of time.

When evaluating the mostly qualitative statements, it is possible to identify minimum expectations of the customer, the level of dissatisfaction and the extremely perceived behaviour of the personnel or process, and to classify the events according to their cause in problem categories. The indication of the frequencies of the individual problem categories allows an initial quantitative assessment of the importance of certain problems in the service (or product consultation/use).

4
How to define the problem

4 How to define the problem

4.1	Point-of-View phase	61
4.2	Characterisation of the target group	61
4.3	Description of customer needs	64
4.3.1	Jobs-to-be-done	65
4.3.2	Means-end approach	74

4 How to define the problem

"If you don't know where you're going, you'll end up somewhere else"
— Laurence J. Peter (inventor of the famous Peter-principle)

4.1 Point-of-View Phase

After the two analysis phases of understanding the problem and observing the customer, the information gained is brought together – synthesized – in a condensed form. The information must ultimately answer two basic questions that are of central importance for solving the problem:

❶ **What is the specific target (customer) group that is at stake?**
❷ **What is the specific need/problem to be solved?**

All in all, you should observe the following guidelines when redefining the question:

- The search field should not be too broad (too vague), but also not too narrow to stifle creative ideas.
- Do not provide a solution at this stage.
- The question should be challenging and inspiring.
- It should be clearly formulated for all participants in the Design Thinking process.
- Make sure and ask the participants that they formulate the question in their own words.

In the following, the Persona method (chapter 4.2) and the Jobs-to-be-done concept (chapter 4.3.1) are two approaches that can answer the two questions. In addition, the means-end approach (chapter 4.3.2) can be used to characterize the customer's needs step by step in an overarching context.

4.2 Characterisation of the target group

The relevant information to describe the target (customer) group can best be summarized in a focused way with the Persona method, which is presented below.

4 How to define the problem

Persona

With the Persona method, the user is placed in a hypothetical customer/user who represents members of a real customer/user group. This method is universally applicable both in the development of ideas and business models and in the design of marketing activities.

The selected person represents a fictitious person with individual characteristics that represent the target group (or part of it) of the innovation. However, one should not put together an average persona, but rather concretize different personas with actual data. It is recommended to represent different persona with different functions in the buying process. For example: persona of a certain target segment, first-time buyer, extreme user (who frequently or under special conditions use products), non-buyer (negative persona) or customer vs. user persona. The method can also be used in the business-to-business area (so-called buyer persona), in which decision-makers, influencers, possible saboteurs etc. are differentiated between companies in the sales process.

On a DIN A4/3 page, the person with a concrete name should be described in the form of a profile with keywords or short sentences (on post-it). The persona should not be reduced to a single characteristic, as is often the case in classical market research in the context of customer segmentation, but should be described holistically in its entire lifeworld. A (fictitious) quotation or motto of this persona can introduce the description.

The following biographical information can describe this person, for example:

- Gender, age, origin, marital status (married/disabled; children? How many? How old? What style of parenting?)
- Occupation (job, position), educational background, special knowledge, expert on a specific topic
- Friends and social environment, Pets
- Living conditions, own house / condominium / rented apartment / industry / type, design, quality and equipment of the apartment
- Asset status
- Attitudes (values, interests, preferences), frustration tolerance, health awareness, life goals
- Hobbies and leisure activities, sporting? Which sport? How often?
- How much time does the persona have for certain topics/activities?
- Which media/information sources does she use for which topics?
- Attitude towards digital media, users of social networks or rather loners, sharing information generously with others?
- Consumption habits or factors that influence purchasing decisions: How quickly does the decision to buy take place? Is it a spontaneous buyer or more planned? Which information channels does it use? Price, quality or service-oriented? Brand conscious?

It would also be useful to analyse the problems ("Pains") and wishes ("Gains") associated with innovation: For example with the following questions:

- What annoys/frustrates the persona? What problems does she have? What challenges in life does she face? What does the persona find too expensive, too uncomfortable, too time-consuming, too inferior, too user-unfriendly, too complex? What makes them angry? What risks does she fear? Why would she be ashamed of friends? What mistakes does she often make? What can the persona not do? What resistance is she confronted with?
- What needs does she have? What does she want? Where does she dream of? What goals in life does she pursue? What (buying) motives does she have? What offers does this persona need? What would she expect from an offer? What will make her life easier? What would make her happy? What would inspire them? How would she be admired by others?

These questions can be specifically adapted to the problem at hand and extended if necessary. Nevertheless, one should really sketch the answers on one page. It is also helpful to describe the persona and her problems or wishes in a personal form and in an ego form. The persona should also be updated again and again, because needs and desires are variable in the course of an innovation project. The Jobs-to-be-done method described in chapter 4.3.1 is recommended to deepen these "Pains" and "Gains".

Benefits of the Persona technique:

Persona can be used to create distance to the innovator's own person on the one hand and proximity to the customer on the other. This means that this approach creates customer orientation. Developments can thus be better aligned with the person and, if necessary, prioritised to what extent they can satisfy the needs and wishes of this persona. In addition, persona enables employees in the company who do not have frequent customer contact (e.g. employees in research, development and production) to become more sensitive to the needs of customers. Everyone understands the descriptions of the persona. Everybody can better understand the person. Furthermore, the customer is no longer seen as an anonymous something in an undefined mass, but gets a real character and is "brought to life". Furthermore, this method is cost-effective and can be combined with the following other approaches.

Motto:
„Who says innovations are dangerous, should try it with routine: which is deadly."

C.M-R (age)
male, German, married,
has a son (age), family man, no pets,
Professor with a background in
business administration and technology,
is enthusiastic about innovations, is an
online and technology enthusiast,
formerly an active handball player,
wants to do more sport in the future,
prefers japanese and indian cuisine,
addicted to chocolate, etc.

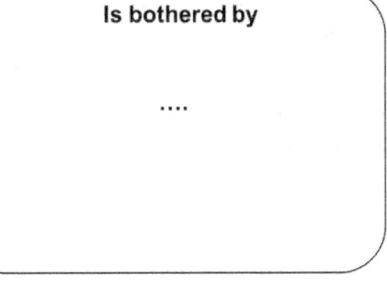

Figure 18: Example for the use of the Persona method

4.3 Description of customer needs

When describing the customer need/problem one should pay attention to a recognizable pattern and answer why this is so and why the potential customer/user has this problem, this behavior, these feelings, these needs. The Customer Journey method, which was discussed in detail in chapter 3.4.7, is very helpful in this context. The customer need/problem should lead to a concrete task for which ideas and solution concepts are sought and developed in the following steps.

In a very condensed form, the information about the target group and their needs / problems can be focused on one sentence with a so-called **user story** (Cohn (2004)):

> **How can we offer our customers**
> NAME OF THE PERSONA
> **help/support/ bring to it**
> HIS PROBLEM/NEED
> **to solve/satisfy?**

The aim should be to formulate this sentence with 140 or 280 characters (in short message format à la Twitter). This central sentence should be clearly visible to all participants of the Design Thinking process in a prominent place in the common premises. All other information should also be made visible (photos, graphics, interviews). So-called moodboards (see below), which are collages of text/photo material and/or objects intended to capture the moods of situations, are ideal for this purpose. Special findings during the customer observation are to be emphasized, e.g. what surprised, astonished, frightened or also made thoughtful one.

Moodboards (or image boards)

Moodboards (also called image boards) are collages of text/photo material and/or objects intended to capture the moods of situations.

How to do it:

Pictorial material, smaller objects and, if necessary, striking texts such as newspaper articles/headlines on the subject, the place of service or product use, the persona with the customer's needs and/or the Customer Journey are first collected and attached as a large collage on a metaplanar wall/whiteboard. They should be permanently in the field of vision of the idea/product developers. Over time, the images can also be "clustered" thematically (see chapter 6.3 on visualization techniques) and supplemented with (photo) materials from product development. These topic clusters can be positioned on different walls (e.g. wall with information about customers, about needs / problems of the customer, about first solutions). This serves as inspiration. Digital moodboards can be easily created and shared with Pinterest.

4.3.1 Jobs-to-be-done

„People don't want to buy a quarter-inch drill. They want a quarter-inch hole." – Theodore Levitt (1986), Harvard Business School

The Jobs-to-be-done concept, which was essentially developed by Christensen/Raynor (2003) and Ulwick (2005), focuses on the tasks/activities – the so-called jobs – of or for customers in order to solve a specific problem for the customer, satisfy needs and/or realise wishes. In general Christensen et al. (2016) understands a job as a task that has to be completed in a certain situation or context in order to achieve progress from the customer's point of view. The task is not so much the result ("event") as the process. This job must always take the specific situation or context into account. This means that jobs are always dependent on a specific situation, which may have limitations, specifics, etc. This can be a particular stage in the customer's life, family status, financial or personal situation, local environment or other situational factors. Christensen (2003, 2016) speaks of customers not simply buying products and services, but "hiring" them to do certain jobs (tasks/activities). This concentration on the task and less on the product is also expressed in the above quote from Levitt (1986). Ultimately, customers do not want products, they want solutions for their tasks (problems, needs, wishes).

Jobs can be further differentiated according to Christensen/Raynor (2003) and Ulwick (2005):

➢ **Functional Jobs:**

Certain functions / characteristics / activities / process steps must / should (from the customer's point of view) be available / executed / completed.

➢ **Social Jobs:**

With the completion of the task/activity the attainment of prestige, power/influence, status or a certain (desirable) image for the customer is achieved. This means that the question is answered how the customer wants to be perceived by others (family members, friends, acquaintances, other organizations).

➢ **Personal Jobs:**

The customer enjoys it, finds it interesting, exciting, stimulating, entertaining, "cool", aesthetically pleasing, feels secure or then feels pride or personal satisfaction that the job has been done. This means that the question of how the customer wants to feel after the job is done is answered.

The social and personal jobs (= **emotional jobs**) thus represent a psychological benefit for the customer. With this differentiation it is possible to analyse why customers want certain tasks (jobs) done. The information and answers to the questions mentioned above and below (see following description of the procedure) can again be obtained using various methods. In connection with the development of innovations, personal surveys, observations of customers and workshops with certain customers are to be mentioned here. Tips for the systematic observation of customers can be found in chapter 3. Information on conducting customer interviews can be found in chapter 7.2.

4 How to define the problem

In the following, a concrete procedure for the application of the Jobs-to-be-done concept will be explained.

How to do it:
Based on Osterwalder et al. (2014) (modified and extended)

❶ Identify customer segment

First create or select a persona (see chapter 4.2) and add an empathy map (see chapter 3.4.3). As already mentioned with Persona, different Persona can be used to work out differences and peculiarities of customer problems or customer needs and wishes. Of course, customers can not only be individuals, but also organizations (companies).

> **Tip:**
> It is advisable to consciously also take current non-customers (Christensen (2016): 65) and analyse them according to the jobs-to-be-done concept. This will generate interesting new search fields for innovations. Instead of customers, each stakeholder can also be taken in the broadest sense and analysed in this way.

❷ Identify jobs

A possible method for identifying potentially interesting jobs is the so-called **job mapping** by Bettencourt/Ulrick (2008). Job mapping does not analyse what a customer is actually doing or how he interacts with a product/service, but what and why he wants to achieve something in a certain situation/situation. This is also the main difference to the concept of the Customer Journey, which focuses on the activities actually carried out and is explained in chapter 3.4.7. The jobs should therefore be as detached as possible from certain products and services. They are not characteristics, functions or process steps of products and services.

According to Bettencourt/Ulrick (2008), job mapping consists of the following eight steps:

① **Define**
What aspects does the customer need to clarify/what steps does the customer need to take before completing the task/activity? This can include the following: What are the customer's objectives for the task/activity? How does he plan to perform these tasks? How does the customer rate the resources he needs to complete the tasks and how does he select these resources?

② **Search:**
Which necessary resources or aids must the customer look for in order to complete the task? These can be material (tools, materials) or immaterial (information, knowledge) resources. How difficult is it for customers to locate these resources?

③ **Preparing:**
How must the customer prepare/organize the resources and resources or the situation so that the task can be completed?

④ **Confirm:**
What does the customer have to check before the concrete task so that he can actually start with it? Does the customer have to confirm the functionality of the resources and tools?

⑤ **Execute:**
What must the customer do to ensure that the task is completed successfully?

⑥ **Monitor:**
How does the customer check the success after completion of the task?

⑦ **Adaption:**
What does the customer need to adjust if the task is to be completed successfully?

⑧ **Closing:**
What must the customer do to complete the task? What are the steps that follow or must be completed after this task?

These steps of job mapping must always be analysed against the background of the specific situation. One challenge is to identify the jobs at the right level of abstraction. It must not be too abstract, as this will result in the loss of important detailed information. It must also not be too small, in order not to limit the search space too much for the later generation of ideas. The evaluation of the jobs below can provide information on the correct level of abstraction.

In addition to job mapping, the following checklist should be used to identify (relevant) jobs.

4 How to define the problem

Table 11: Job Identification
Source: According to Osterwalder et al. (2014) and Christensen et al. (2016)

Checklist for identifying jobs
• With which tasks do the customers want to achieve their goals?
• Why do the customers want to do these tasks/activities?
• In which situation/context do the customers want to have the tasks done? Where are the customers when they want to complete the task/activities? When should the task/activity be solved? What have the customers done before? What will the customers do after the doing the job?
• What are the framework conditions for the completion of the job with which the customer is confronted? What limitations are there in doing the job? Do the customers have the skills to solve the tasks themselves?
• Have certain characteristics of the customer and his experience from the past an influence on the perception of the job?
• Which social, cultural or political influences effect the perception of the job?
• How, by whom and with what are the customer's tasks/activities currently being performed?
• With what else could the customer realize the task? What are the alternatives at the moment? Alternatives can also be: Nothing to do, move, do something else or partial solutions or indirect solutions.
• What results (outcomes) do customers want to achieve with these tasks? What progress do customers want to make in a particular situation?
• Is the task/activity important for the customers? (see also below evaluating jobs)
• Are there any differences between customers and non-customers with regard to the tasks/activities?

❸ **Identify customer problems**
As already explained with the methods Persona (see chapter 4.2) and Empathy Map (see chapter 3.4.3), this step is about identifying the problems, frustrations and "pains" of the customers with the desired completion of the job. A detailed analysis is possible using the checklist below.

Table 12: Customer problems
Source: According to Osterwalder et al. (2014)

Checklist for identifying customer problems
▪ In what tasks/activities must the customer (physically, intellectually) to make an effort? Which tasks/activities are inconvenient for the customer?
▪ Which tasks/activities generate costs for the customer?
▪ What tasks/activities does the customer have to wait for? Which tasks/activities take (too) long?
▪ For which tasks/activities are the customer responsible? Where occurs frustration/nuisance/annoyance/problems? What tasks/activities feels the customer as too complex?
▪ Which tasks/activities does the customer perform inefficiently (with the current solutions) or not ideal? What are the typical mistakes made by the customer when does he or she carry out tasks/activities himself?
▪ What are the biggest difficulties for the customer?
▪ Which tasks/activities result in the customer not being 100% satisfied?
▪ Does the customer understand how his tasks/activities are performed?
▪ Does the customer hesitate to perform the tasks/activities himself or by others?
▪ What risks are involved in fulfilling the tasks/activities from the customer's point of view?
▪ Does the customer expect negative social or emotional disadvantages, if the task/activity is not completed?
▪ What barriers prevent the customer from obtaining external help or aids for his or her tasks/activities procured? Does the effort (in the form of time or money) prevent the customers to use external help or aids for their tasks/activities.
▪ What are the barriers to the customer solving the task in a different way, such as so far? How could these barriers be overcome?
▪ Which tasks/activities are barriers for non-customers?

❹ **Identify customer needs / wishes**

As with the methods Persona (see chapter 4.2) and Empathy Map (see chapter 3.4.3), this step is about identifying the needs and wishes of the customer ("Gains") in the form of the completion of a job. A detailed analysis is possible using the checklist below.

4 How to define the problem

Table 13: Customer needs/wishes
Source: According to Osterwalder et al. (2014)

Checklist for the identification of costumer needs/wishes
• Which tasks would the customer be happy about?
• Does the customer expect a personal advantage from the task?
• Does the completion of the task trigger emotional feelings in the customer? If so, which ones?
• Does the customer expect social recognition from the completion of the task?
• What cost savings would the customer make in carrying out his tasks/activities?
• How much time would be saved in carrying out his tasks/activities?
• What quality is expected or expected in the performance of his tasks/activities?
• What would make the tasks/activities of the customer easier? Which service would the customer wishes for his tasks/activities?
• How does the customer assess the quality or deficiencies in the performance of his tasks/activities?
• When would the customer use help or aids for his tasks/activities? What he expects (higher quality, lower costs/investments, convenience, lower risk)?
• What does the customer want if problems arise during the completion of the task?
• Which additional tasks would the customer be happy about?

❺ **Describe jobs**

The result of these previous steps should lead to descriptions of the jobs that can be formulated with the following format:

Job description:

The (name of the customer/persona) _____ wishes to (solve problem/ satisfy need/realize) _____ with the following result _____ in/at the following situation _____ or under the following restriction _____.

In addition to the concept of Jobs-to-be-done, Ulrick (2005) defines not only the job itself, but also the desired outcome from the customer's point of view. According to Ulrick (2005), this outcome can also be specified as follows:

- Definition of the direction of improvement (faster, more convenient, longer, shorter, minimize, maximize, less expensive)
- Definition of the measurement unit (number, time, frequency, probability)
- Definition of the desired result state

However, the result should not be linked to a specific solution that is only openly sought in the idea generation phase.

The comparison with the current alternatives can not only provide indications of unfulfilled results (underserved outcome), but can also show overfulfilled results (overserved outcome) through the alternatives (see below). This means that the current alternatives complete the task with the desired result, but are equipped with too many functions and features ("**overengineering**" or "**gold plating**"). This can be an indication that there is waste in the alternative, that it is too expensive or too complex. Disruptive innovations take advantage of this situation to achieve competitive advantages through simplicity, convenience, ease of use, accessibility and a competitive price for the customer.

❻ Evaluate jobs

Ideally, the customer should evaluate the jobs himself. As already mentioned above, personal surveys of the customer are possible, as explained in detail in chapters 6.2 and 7.2. A possible evaluation procedure from the customer's point of view is the so-called opportunity algorithm according to Ulwick (2005) (see box below). The Kano model (see chapter 7.4) can also be used to differentiate between basic requirements, satisfier and delighters from the customer's point of view.

In addition to the evaluation from the customer's point of view, an evaluation from the company's point of view (is the task economically significant?) and from the competitive point of view (can a competitive advantage be achieved by (better) completing the task?) must also be carried out.

4 How to define the problem

Opportunity Algorithmus/Customer-Scorecard:

The calculation of the so-called Opportunity Algorithm or Customer Scorecard according to Ulwrick (2005) makes it possible to determine the most attractive customer needs (jobs) that are most important but at the same time least satisfied by existing solutions.

(Potential) customers are asked two questions:

- What importance do you attach to the task (Jobs) XY?
  Rating with 1= not important; 5 = very important
- How would you rate the current solution (product/service) for doing this job?
  Rating with 1 = not satisfied at all; 5= very satisfied

The results in percent are transferred to a 10-point scale and the following formula is used to calculate the chance of the respective customer need (job):

$$\text{Chance (Opportunity)} = \text{Importance} + (\max (\text{Importance} - \text{Satisfaction}, 0))$$

The result can range from 0 to 20 according to this formula. From 15 and more the opportunity is very attractive from the customer's point of view (unfulfilled results). At 10 and less, the opportunity is not very attractive from the customer's point of view. According to the formula, the intermediate value in brackets does not assume a negative number for a higher satisfaction than significance, but in this case the intermediate value is set to zero. This is not only to measure the discrepancy between importance and satisfaction, but the level of significance becomes more apparent and important jobs are not excluded from further consideration.

In the mentioned case "Satisfaction with the current solution is greater than the importance" can be interpreted as drawing for an overfulfilled result (overserved outcome). This in turn can be an indication of disruptive innovation characterised by simplicity, convenience, ease of use, accessibility and a low price for the customer.

Table 14: Checklist for Evaluation of jobs

Checklist for Evaluation of jobs
• Is the task important?
• Can you quantify the customer's problems in the form of a unit of time and money?
• Can customers see the benefits associated with doing the job? (In terms of time and costs)
• How large (on a scale from unimportant to very important) is the need/desire?
• Are there alternatives? How good (on a scale from bad to perfect) are they?
• Is the customer willing to pay for the job? How much? Are there many customers who have these problems or needs?
• What does the context mean? (Situation, general conditions, environment)
• What functional, social and emotional importance does the task have for the customer?

Table 15: Tips for using the Jobs-to-be-done concept

1	Not only functional jobs have to be analysed, but also emotional (personal) and social jobs have to be considered.
2	Jobs must never be seen detached from the specific situation.
3	One should never try to unite different customers with different tasks or in different contexts in one customer segment.
4	The description of the tasks should not be too vague. The above-mentioned job mapping gives hints on how to do this.
5	The above-mentioned format for job descriptions should be used consistently. The jobs should be expressed as verbs describing a process rather than as adjectives or adverbs describing a state.
6	The Jobs-to-be-done concept is relevant for all phases of the innovation process, especially for innovation marketing in market introduction.
7	The jobs of customers change dynamically and are exposed to various external influences. In this respect, the concept should be used regularly.

With the help of this Jobs-to-be-done concept, solutions/offers in the form of product, process, service or business model innovations can be developed to handle these jobs (better than the alternatives). This approach is also recommended in a late innovation phase for market segmentation, e.g. to plan and execute targeted activities in innovation marketing.

4.3.2 Means-end approach

With the means-end approach it is possible to differentiate the above-mentioned functional, social and personal jobs more precisely and to analyse them more in-depth with a suitable interview technique (the so-called laddering; see below). The means-end approach provides explanations of why customers prefer certain product features and what they (unconsciously) actually hope to achieve from these features. This implicates that the basic motives of buying behavior are the focus here. These findings about the – often unconscious – personal desired goals of customers are helpful both in an early innovation phase in the development of ideas and in a late phase in the design of marketing.

The means-end approach is based on the concept that customers understand product/service innovation as a means to achieve a personal wish or goal (ends). The mental connection between the product attributes and the value attitudes takes place via hierarchically arranged cognitive levels with the customer.

As the following figure shows, this can be represented in the form of cognitive steps of a ladder (following Reynolds/Gutmann (1984)). Product features (means) (= chemical-physical-technical product characteristics) initially achieve a functional benefit for the customer, which can also generate a psychological benefit for the customer. This psychological benefit can be emotional (the customer perceives the product as aesthetically pleasing) and/or social (the customer can share the benefits of the innovation with friends). These functional and psychological benefit components can in turn influence short and long-term value retention. The short-term so-called **instrumental values** represent desirable forms of behaviour for the customer, e.g. that the customer wants to be helpful, performance-oriented or imaginative. The long-term so-called **terminal values** are ultimately desirable goals in life, such as fun, vitality, wisdom, freedom, equality, security, social recognition or self-realisation. Altogether it is to be considered that also several values can determine several use components, which determine again several product attributes and vice versa.

However, the benefit components and values cannot be seen independently of external influences. The benefit components depend on the one hand on the situation in which the customer is currently using the innovation or on social effectsto which he is exposed (e.g. expectations of the social environment). These social effects also determine the values generated.

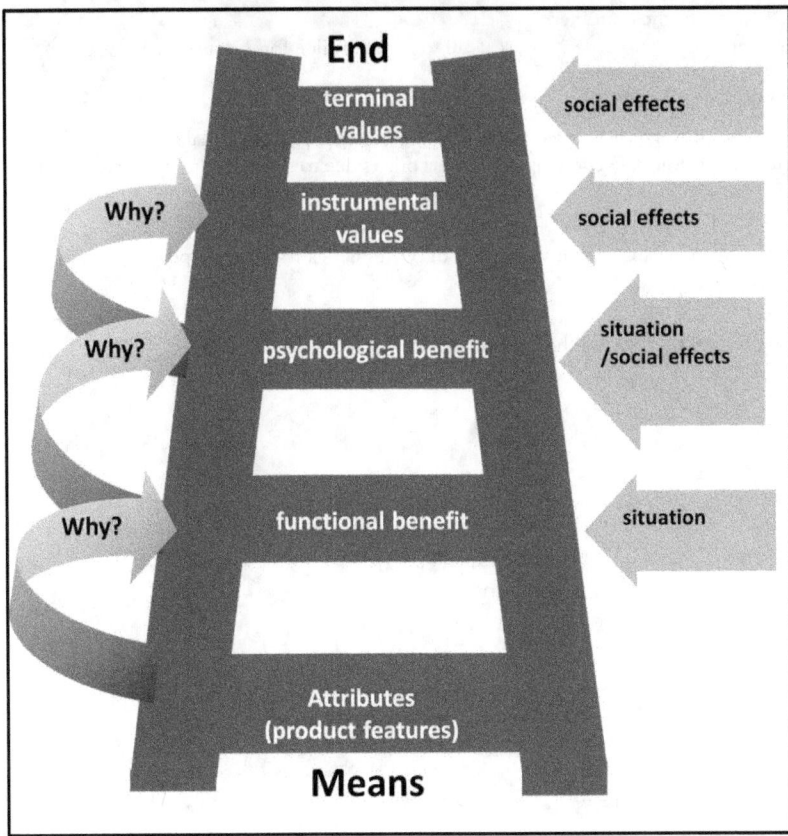

Figure 19: Cognitive Ladder of the means-end approach

On the basis of this means-end approach, the so-called **laddering technique** is used to gradually analyse these steps – like the steps on a ladder – from the concrete product features to the more abstract values (see Reynolds/Gutman (1988) for details). With the so-called **vertical laddering**, the recurring question: "Why is this important for you?" is gradually pushed forward from the product features via the benefit components to the values. In addition, the **horizontal laddering** is used to determine whether the features determined correspond to the real product properties from the customer's point of view.

Another variant is the so-called **laddering top-down technique**. Starting from the values, the reverse order is used via "How"-questions. Here the customer is asked how he wants to achieve a certain goal or value retention through which (product) benefit component or features (e.g.: "How would you like to achieve XXX?"). The product features can be named as an example of a selection decision for the customer in the interview.

The laddering technique can ultimately be used to answer the following questions, which are important for developing ideas in the Design Thinking process:

Functional benefits:

- What is really valuable for the customer?

- What is a benefit for the customer?
- Which characteristics, properties, services lead to benefit/value for the customer?

Psychological benefits:

- How would the customer like to feel after using the innovation? (emotional benefit)
- How would the customer like to be perceived by others due to the innovation? (social benefit)

Instrumental value:

- What short-term goal can the innovation that the customer can achieve help?

Terminal value:

- Which long-term (life) goal can the innovation help the customer achieve?

5
How to find and select ideas

5 How to find and select ideas

5.1	Ideate phase	79
5.2	The creative process and creative principles	79
5.3	Creativity techniques	84
5.3.1	Intuitive Creative Techniques	85
5.3.2	Systematic Analytical Techniques	96
5.3.3	TRIZ	107
5.3.4	Systematic Inventive Thinking (SIT)	128
5.4	Evaluation of ideas	132
5.4.1	Checklists / Pro-Cons lists	133
5.4.2	PPCO method	135
5.4.3	SWOT Analysis	135
5.4.4	Pair comparison method	136
5.4.5	Scoring model	137

5 How to find and select ideas

"Creativity is a journey, not a magic event." – Goller/Bessant (2017): 319

After a brief introduction to the topic of creative thinking, especially regarding the creative process and its principles, some creativity techniques are explained in chapter 5.3. In chapter 5.4 evaluation methods are presented that allow a decision to be made when selecting the ideas generated.

5.1 Ideate Phase

It is only in this phase of the Design Thinking process that initial ideas for problem solving are developed. The methods mentioned in chapter 5.3 are suitable for this. Ideally, different techniques should be combined in order to get new impulses for the generation of ideas.

Especially in this phase it is important to generate as many ideas as possible and to select them in a second step. Here you should always pay attention to the rule "Stay focused! As already explained in chapter 1.1, it is desirable to limit the search space ("necessity makes inventive"), e.g. by demanding the ability to fit the company vision/strategy, by time/cost targets or by limited available resources. Furthermore, one should always keep an eye on alternative ideas and not commit oneself too early to a single idea.

As with all creative phases, the basic creativity technique is of course brainstorming, for which extensive tips and variants can be found in chapter 5.3.1.1.

5.2 The creative process and creative principles

Creativity means thinking something new, whereas innovation means implementing something new. In this respect, creativity is an integral part of every innovation project, regardless of whether it is aimed at a new product, service, process, social/organisational change or business model.

Creativity is not an event, but can rather be understood as a process. The following figure describes a general creative process according to Graham (1926), which has lost nothing of its general validity. In order to develop an idea, an initial phase requires recognition and intensive examination of the problem or opportunity (preparation). Alternatively, the entrepreneurial opportunity can also be created on one's own. Only when one moves away from the situation again (incubation) can ideas be developed spontaneously in the form of a flash of inspiration (illumination) or systematically (ideation). This (solution) idea must then be further developed, tested and communicated (verification). In practice, these phases are not run through sequentially – as the following illustration suggests. Rather, there are numerous and varied feedback and reflection loops in this process. The Design Thinking approach takes up this creative process.

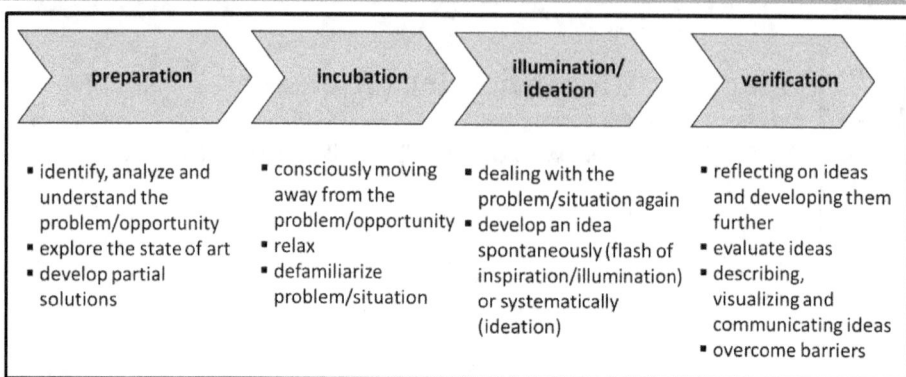

Figure 20: The creative process
Source: According to Wallas (1926)

In order to identify problems or business opportunities in general as a starting point for the preparation phase or alternatively to create new opportunities, one should become aware of the potential sources of problems/opportunities and systematically search for them using the following internal and external sources of information:

Internal sources of information on business opportunities:

- Survey (if necessary, observation) of own employees at various hierarchical levels in innovation management or in research, development, production, marketing, sales, accounting/controlling as well as in the legal/patent department
- Evaluation of internal documents from the above-mentioned areas

External sources of information on business opportunities:

- Observation of new trends (trend scouting) (see chapter 2.4.1)
- Observation of developments outside the industry (so-called cross-industry analyses)
- Competition analyses
- requirement analyses
- Customer survey/observation (see chapters 3 and 7.2 and 7. 3)
- Supplier survey/observation and cooperation
- Use of trade fairs and conferences
- Evaluation of publications, e.g. specialist articles, patents/databases
- Survey and cooperation with cooperation partners from science (experts)

With the help of these information sources, the problem or opportunity can be analysed more precisely (see chapter 2.4). After a phase of incubation (see above), a creative solution can be developed on this basis (illumination or ideation phase).

5 How to find and select ideas

Creative principles

Some general (heuristic) basic principles can be determined for this solution step of the illumination or ideation phase, which, however, cannot be classified without overlapping in individual cases and which partly occur in combination in the creativity techniques explained in chapter 5.3:

- **Principle of Decomposition:**
  The problem, the task, the process steps or the product/service to be redesigned is broken down into its components and then these components are varied/combined anew. The creativity techniques of morphological boxes, attribute listing, SIT methodology (see chapter 5.3.2, 5.3.4) and some techniques of the TRIZ methodology (see chapter 5.3.3) function according to this principle.

- **Principle of Association:**
  By association one understands the linking of ideas, information, perceptions and emotions. In the sense of a free association, brainstorming or brainwriting are to be mentioned here (see chapter 5.3.1.1 or 5.3.1.2). The Walt Disney method (see chapter 5.3.1.8) and the 6-thinking-hats-Technique can be understood as structured associations (see chapter 5.3.1.9).

- **Principle of Analogy and Confrontation:**
  Analogy and confrontation are targeted changes of perspective and are based on the confrontation with a different area (also called bisociation). Thus, relationships are formed that did not exist before. In the analogy, this area is compared with the problem/task in order to obtain suggestions for new ideas from the identified similarities or differences. When analogies are applied, numerous positive effects can be achieved, such as high originality, reduced risk, shorter development times and low development costs. Synetics or bionics are typical representatives of the analogy principle (see chapter 5.3.2.4 or 5.3.2.5).

  During the confrontation, the selected area deliberately contrasts with the initial problem/question. The random word method (see chapter 5.3.1.3), the forced relationship (see chapter 5.3.1.6) and TRIZ innovation principles (see chapter 5.3.3) are techniques which take up this principle. The confrontations can exist in different ways: It can be an inversion, i.e. the problem is viewed from the opposite perspective. This principle is followed e.g. by the brainstorming variant of the headstand technique (see chapter 5.3.1.1). But one can also create by a conscious provocation in order to stimulate the flow of ideas (see chapter 5.3.1.7).

- **Principle of Abstraction and Imagination:**
  In the basic principle of abstraction and imagination, the problem is solved on a higher or illusionary level. The aim here is to consciously gain as wide a distance as possible from the problem in order to better understand the actual problem from a "helicopter perspective" or to find suggestions for solutions.

  From a higher perspective, it is also possible to search for typical success patterns of innovations (evolution principle of the TRIZ methodology (see chapter 5.3.3).

  In the case of imagination, the most promising approach is thinking in images, in which one tries to see the problem or question as it were. The visualization of one's own thoughts or metaphorical thinking support this principle.

5 How to find and select ideas

In addition to these basic principles, the following further success factors for the creative process exist:

- **Challenge common wisdom and industry conventions!**

  Nothing is to be accepted as "given". Ask questions why this is so, why this is not so, why this should be so or not be so and why this can also be different. Everything can be changed. Take other paths, both actually and figuratively. Conventions and assumptions are to be questioned and to break with them consciously.

- **Start where others (or yourself) left off!**

  Edison has said: "Most of my ideas originally belonged to people who didn't take the trouble to develop them further." Or as the American non-fiction writer Brian Tracy said: "No one lives long enough to learn everything by starting". Innovations don't emerge in a vacuum, but are based on the experiences, insights, knowledge and solutions of others. Nothing is perfect and could be done, used or combined differently. Modify the existing, deliberately falsify it or use it for completely different applications. Your first ideas should also never be seen as the final solution (see also chapter 6.2). Perseverance and tenacity are the hallmarks of successful inventors in this context.

- **Do mental exercise!**

  Demand a minimum number of new ideas from yourself. Put yourself under pressure and try to develop new ideas for one or more problems per day/week. This is to force the coincidence quasi. At the beginning the idea generation will run still hesitantly, so that one should not give up simply fast. The ideas don't have to be of high quality either. It's about stimulating a flow of ideas.

  Furthermore you should interrupt the reading of books and articles again and again between through and ask yourself how the story or article could go on. Imagine the continuation of novels or think about what the solution might look like with advice articles.

- **Observe everything and everyone in different situations!**

  From systematic but also coincidental observations of everyday or unusual situations, a variety of suggestions for new ideas can be gained. One should not hesitate to analyze even trivial situations. This also includes observing one's own habits and business processes. Curiosity and attention are prerequisite for successful observation. Chapter 3 dealt in detail with observation techniques. According to Michalko (2006), a good exercise for training for observation is to observe an object or a situation in peace for ten minutes and to take a close look at every detail without digressing. Then try to recall as many details as possible and describe them in your own words.

- **Change your habits! Do something completely different!**

  Changing habits and conventions is a success factor especially for radical innovations. Habits and conventions are sometimes pursued unconsciously and represent a blockade of thinking that is difficult to change. Ask yourself the question: "When was the last time you did something for the first time? In order to solve mental blockades through routine and habits, you should start with yourself and change your habits. This starts on a small scale (Michalko (2006)): Take another way to work, use your left hand as a right-handed person and vice versa, completely change your eating habits and eat at different times, read novels and science fiction instead of reference books, bathe instead of showering, read other newspapers, listen to another radio station, change your working hours, date and discuss with other people ("Hang out with more people who don't do what you do.", Austin Kleon, American author/artist) etc.

- **Do experiment!**

  The trial-and-error approach has already given rise to countless innovative ideas. Not only in the field of research and development for technical product and process innovations is this approach goal-oriented, but for all kinds of innovations (service, social and business model innovations) and for all ideas in the context of the innovation process thinking in experiments is helpful. Experiments also help to select from several – possibly even competing – possibilities/alternatives. Creative ideas in the sense of implementable and desired innovations can only be developed or selected from the desk to a limited extent through purely logical thinking. An experimental approach, which checks one's own ideas and assumptions, delivers a "reality check" and new ideas. The Lean Sstartup method (see chapter 6.2) is one of the most prominent examples of this approach. For experimentation, the necessary freedom must also be created and mistakes tolerated.

➢ **Do Networking!**

Search or promote the exchange with others, i.e. people from other disciplines, cultures, business areas, departments or external partners (customers, suppliers, business partners). Work in workshop formats in diverse teams (see chapter 1.3). Confront other people with your (solution) idea. From the interaction new suggestions can be won by complementary authority and other points of view.

➢ **Overcome the barriers to creativity!**

One of the essential success factors for the creative process is overcoming the numerous and varied creative blockades. Examples of creative blockades are the following:

- Creativity disturbing environment
- Stress
- Lack of recognition /no reward for creative work
- Too rigid or strict institutional controls
- Bureaucracy, formalism
- Not-Invented-Here-Syndrom)
- Fear of change, risk aversion
- Perfectionism, search for the absolutely right thing
- Pure logical thinking
- Self-satisfaction with what has been achieved so far

5.3 Creativity techniques

The following table lists creativity techniques, divided into intuitive-creative methods and systematic-analytical methods. The intuitive-creative techniques try – mostly in a group – to stimulate spontaneous ideas, associations and analogies in order to overcome blockades of thought in a rather free design. The above-mentioned principles of decomposition and abstraction are increasingly applied to the systematic-analytical techniques. It should be noted that not every creativity technique is suitable for every question and for every team. Creativity is ultimately very individual: everyone has their own experiences, habits, preferences as well as strengths and weaknesses. In this respect one should experiment with these creativity techniques.

Table 16: Creativity techniques

Intuitive Creative Techniques	Systematic-analytical techniques
• Brainstorming	• Osborn Checklist (SCAMPER)
• Brainwriting	• Mind Mapping
• Random word technique	• Synectics
• Semantic Intuition/The perfect prefix	• Bionics
• Forced Relationship	• Morpholoical box/ Sequential morphologys / Attribute Listing
• Provocation technique	• HIT
• Walt-Disney method	• Lotus Blossom
• Six thinking hats	• TRIZ
• Delphi method	• SIT

5.3.1 Intuitive Creative Techniques

5.3.1.1 Brainstorming

Brainstorming is, so to speak, the mother of all creativity techniques (linguistically from: "using the brain to storm the problem"). Ideas about a question or a solution to a problem should be expressed spontaneously in a group.

Rules of brainstorming

- **No criticism**
  Each criticism or rating is postponed to a subsequent phase. The so-called killer phrases must be strictly prohibited. In this way it should be prevented that the flow of ideas is interrupted or participants are blocked. Comments are also forbidden.

- **No copyright**
  The ideas of others can and should be taken up, changed and further developed.

- **Free expression of ideas**
  The participants should give free rein to their imagination so that new and original ideas can be found. Even the craziest ideas are welcome.

- **Quantity over quality**
  As many ideas as possible should be produced in a short time. This rule ensures the spontaneity of the ideas presented.

These rules should be written on a flipchart and visible to everyone during the brainstorming session. Yellow cards may also be shown if one of them breaks these rules.

Tips for how to brainstorm

- Take sufficient time to clearly define the problem or question in advance.
- The question/problem should be challenging to motivate.
- The question should be focused and not too abstract (but not too specific or even imply a solution).
- In addition, it should be a customer-oriented question that is actively formulated.
- The question can also be communicated in advance with the invitation, and it is asked to already think about possible solution ideas as a kind of "homework".
- The group size should lie between 2 and all at most 12 persons (ideally 5 to 8).
- In the case of a heterogeneous group of participants or participants who do not yet know each other well, you should insert a warm up phase beforehand.
- After a productive first phase, the flow of ideas often ebbs quickly. In order to give new suggestions, so-called trigger questions (see below) and the Osborn checklist (see chapter 5.3.2.1) are suitable.
- Always structure a creativity workshop with fixed time phases. This means that the brainstorming sessions must be limited in time.
- Use "Yes, and..." instead of "Yes, but..." in the introduction.

5 How to find and select ideas

- Number the ideas.
- Build on ideas of others and jump from idea to idea.
- Only one speaks.
- Always encourage the active participation of all participants.
- The participants should be informed at a fixed time what has become of their idea.

After the brainstorming session, the ideas should be structured together in terms of content. For this the Card Sorting (see chapter 6.3) or – very similarly – the so-called KJ method with an affinity diagram (see also chapter 6.3) can be used. With the KJ method of the Japanese anthropologist Jiro Kawakita similar ideas are put together, "clustered". An affinity diagram (see chapter 6.3) can be used for this purpose, in which cards or Post-Its are grouped together with the ideas and labelled with a heading. With the KJ method it is recommended that the participants do not talk to each other during these groupings. However, it can be interesting to allow group discussions and to get further inspiration from the exchange. The more dissimilar the ideas (groups) are, the further away they are from each other. The individual groups can be linked together with arrows, e.g. the symbol →shows a cause-effect relationship, the symbol ↔ shows an independence relationship, the symbol – links groups together and the symbol ∦ shows a contradiction or a conflict relationship. Alternatively one can arrange the ideas in a tree structure hierarchically or with a workflow diagram temporally chronologically.

Finally a few tips on how to guarantee you "destroy" a brainstorming session:

- The boss talks first and sets the goal and the requirements.
- The contributions should be given in sequence.
- Only experts are allowed to submit ideas.
- No silly ideas are allowed.
- Everything is written down.

Trigger-questions for Brainstorming

A brainstorming session can be initiated with the following techniques: (see grey box below).

How-might-we…?-Technique:

This is a similar questioning technique to the user story (see chapter 4.3):
How could we (how-might-we...)_____ (product service offer)
for (PERSONA)_____
develop/offer/create under the following conditions_____ (problems, legal regulations, environmental conditions, changes).

Yes, and-Technique:

It must not be started to comment with "Yes, but..." but only with "Yes, and...". This should support the ideas put forward by others in the sense of a constructive feedback and further develop them.

What-if-Technique:

With the question, "What if we..." (What-if) is to be put into another person/company (What if we were Coesus/Apple?) when finding a solution.

Why-How-Laddering-Approach:

In the sense of the means-end approach (chapter 4.3.2) the questions Why? and How? are asked alternately. With Why questions the reasons for the problem should be summarized (again) and recapitulated with the subsequent How question. With "How" you get detailed answers.

In order to maintain the flow of ideas or to enrich the ideas, so-called trigger questions (excitation or tuning questions) can be asked. In addition to the Osborn checklist (see chapter 5.3.2.1), the following questions, based on van Aeerssen/Buchholz (2018): 813, are helpful:

- What can be added to or exaggerated about the idea? Frequency, use, duration?
- How could the idea be made flexibly scalable?
- How could the solution be automated?
- How could the idea be fun for the customer?
- How could the idea be turned into an adventure?
- How would the idea become a big secret?
- How would a child solve the problem?
- How would a robot solve the problem?
- How could the idea be packaged differently?
- How can you bring a repeating pattern into the idea?
- What would happen if some elements of the idea were removed?
- What would happen if you used the idea the other way around or turned it upside down? Can you make the idea backwards instead of forwards?
- What would the idea say if it could speak?
- What does the idea change for the customer?
- How could you earn money by giving the idea away?
- What would the advertising message look like if you were to conceal the most important thing?
- What would happen if you double the price of the idea?
- What would the idea look like in 2050?
- What do the customers do shortly before or shortly after they have used the ideas?
- What happens within 10 meters of the idea?
- What is the idea not supposed to be right now?
- Can ideas/products be combined? Can ideas be combined? Integrate into a larger whole?
- Is it possible to offer an (additional) service in addition to the product idea?
- What can be replaced by the idea? Could something be left out to make it cheaper, more convenient, faster, more environmentally friendly?
- What can be exchanged or converted? A new order?
- Assuming you had 10 million euros at your disposal: What would the solution be?
- Assuming you had only 1000 euros at your disposal: What would the solution look like?

Another helpful suggestion is the question of how a certain company or person would develop a solution. The analogy is used to develop or enrich an idea.

- "How would **IKEA** solve the prolem?" (e.g. principle of self-service)
- "How would **Wal-Mart** solve the problem?" (Principle of reduction to the bare essentials)
- "How would **Rolls-Royce** solve the problem?" (Principle that money doesn't matter)
- "How would **Apple** solve the problem?" (Principle of attractive and user-friendly design)
- "How would **Google** solve the problem?" (e.g. principle of analysis of immense amounts of information)
- "How would **Walt-Disney** solve the problem?" (e.g. principle of storytelling, see chapter 6.3)
- "How would **Lego** solve the problem?" (e.g. principle of modular (product) architecture)
- "How would **NASA** solve the problem?"

- "How would **LinkedIn** solve the problem?" (principle of networking people)
- "How would **Airbnnb** solve the problem?" (principle of common sharing)?

This analogy can also be expressed in other ways, such as Lego for XY, where XY can represent the initial problem, the topic or the most important customer benefit.

Alternatively, living or deceased personalities from the business world (Steve Jobs, Bill Gates, Mark Zuckerberg, Thomas Edison etc.), sports (football, tennis, Formula 1), art/culture (Goethe, Picasso, van Gogh), entertainment (TV, radio, newspapers/magazines), society etc. can be used for inspiration.

Variants of Brainstorming

Step-by-step Brainstorming
After a first brainstorming session, the most interesting idea is used as a starting point for another brainstorming session. This allows you to find ideas from a general solution to a special one. For very large groups, small groups can also be formed, which either deal with a different aspect of the problem or solve the same problem in competition.

Anonymous Brainstorming/-writing
The ideas are written by the participants in block letters on cards/post-its (so-called "Braincards"). A moderator reads the anonymous ideas aloud and on this basis they are brainstormed further or the ideas are clustered and evaluated.

Visual Brainstorming/Brainpainting
The ideas are recorded graphically with paper and pencil (or digitally). This creates sketch-like images in the form of spontaneous scribbles, which do not have to be perfect. According to Michalko (2006) these can be abstract, symbolic and/or realistic.

Blindstorming
The brainstorming takes place using face masks or in complete darkness so that the participants are not distracted by visual stimuli or gestures/mimics of other participants.

Brainwalking
The spontaneous ideas of the participants are written on whiteboards or posters distributed throughout the room. The movement of the participants in the room should trigger "movement" in the head. In accordance with the brainstorming rules, the ideas can also be supplemented or changed on site. Also a small talk about the idea at the poster/whiteboard is desired. Can be combined with the brainstation version below.

Speedstorming
The participants exchange questions in pairs for a few minutes and then change chairs in order to talk to another person.

Stop-and-Go Brainstorming
The brainstorming session is deliberately interrupted at fixed times and filled with pauses or other techniques in the meantime. Alternatively, phases of idea generation can be alternated with phases of evaluation.

Bodystorming/Rolestorming
During the brainstorming session the participants should take on a certain role and associate/formulate their contributions/ideas from this point of view. The roles can be specific customers/users who have been characterized, for example, by the Persona technique (see chapter 4.2). Roles can also be direct competitors or a famous personality from a completely different field (politician, sportsman, artist, historical person). This variant has a similar approach as the Walt Disney or the 6-thinking-hats methods described below. By using first prototypes for problem solving (the so-called Minimum Viable Products, see chapter 6.2) bodystorming can also be used for the test phase (see chapter 7).

Brainshaping
The ideas are presented in the form of kneading models.

Object Brainstorming
The participants are confronted with objects that seem to have nothing to do with the problem/question at first and come from very different areas (sports, household appliances, tools, toys, containers, office/computer objects). From the visual and haptic confrontation, ideas will be developed as to how these objects can contribute a solution to the problem.

Brainstation
Groups of participants work on different questions at different stations (rooms without separate work areas) using brainstorming. The participants change stations after fixed periods of time.

E-Brainstorming
Ideas are communicated electronically via chat/instant messaging systems so that people can participate at different locations.

Imaginary Brainstorming
The actual question/problem is strongly alienated and is thus located in a completely different imaginary (non-industry) area. The imaginary area should show certain similarities to the original problem, but should be completely different (possibly even absurd). To this imaginary problem first ideas are looked for, which are then transferred back to the problem of origin in the second step. The participants may initially be completely unaware of the problem of origin.

Instructional brainstorming (also called Little technique)
The participants are informed only very roughly in a rather abstract way about the subject area in the form of a general question. Only the moderator knows the concrete problem/question. Step by step, when the flow of ideas decreases, the participants get more information about the concrete problem. This makes it possible not to restrict the search field for ideas too much right from the start.

Question storming
No answers are sought, but questions are thought up about the problem.

Big Brainstorming
The brainstorming session will be held with a larger number of people. The participants can be separated into sub-groups that compete against each other for the largest number of ideas or for the best ideas.

5 How to find and select ideas

Reverse Brainstorming

There is also talk of reverse brainstorming when only negative aspects are sought. Here different aspects of the question/problem can be considered: What is currently bad about the situation? Why can't the problem be solved? What could go wrong? All in all, this approach of reverse brainstorming is also suitable for letting off "steam" first. However, this rather destructive phase should be continued quickly with a constructive approach.

Headstand method

If the question is completely reversed, one also speaks of the "headstand method" (de Bono (1972)): How can we make X worse? Make it as complicated as possible? Increase in price? To discourage customers as much as possible? In the next step, all ideas can be turned back into positives.

Premortem method

A similar approach is the Premortem method (Klein (2007)), which looks into the future with a crystal ball and asks why the solution developed failed so disastrously. Here all possible reasons for the failure of a problem solution not yet developed are to be found.

5.3.1.2 Brainwriting

Brainwriting can be conducted in the following way: 6 participants each write down 3 ideas in periods of 5 minutes each. Ideally, method 635 is completed after 30 minutes and has produced 108 ideas.

How to do it:

The procedure is explained in the following figure. A pattern for the form is shown in figure 22.

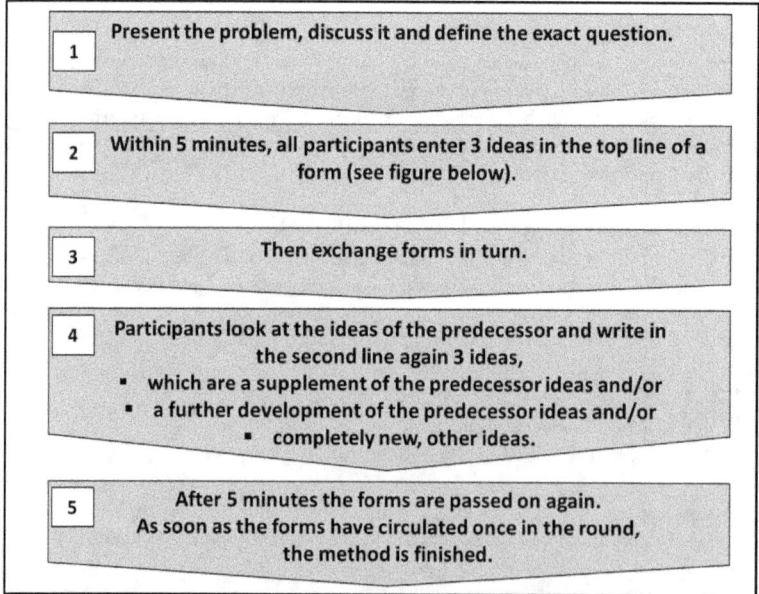

Figure 21: Procedure of Brainwriting

problem: _____		
participants: _____		
date: _____		
A1 1. Idea from person A	A2 2. Idea from person A	A3 3. Idea from person A
B1 Further development of idea A1	B2 New idea from person B	B3 New idea from person B
C1 New idea from person C	C2 Further development of idea A2	C3 Further development of idea B3
D1 ...	D2 ...	D3 ...
E1 ...	E2 ...	E3 ...
F1 ...	F2 ...	F3 ...

Figure 22: Template for Method 635 (Brainwriting)

One variant of this brainwriting method is the collective notebook method, in which participants are asked to briefly describe their ideas in a notebook over a longer period of several weeks. Anyone can create a notebook for themselves or as a group. You can specify that this should be done as in a diary, i.e. once a day you should deal with the problem/question. After a certain time, the notebooks are exchanged between the participants (randomly or according to a predetermined principle), and – as with the method 635 – the ideas from the notebook are supplemented or further developed or new ideas are described. Basically, this can also be done in the form of a virtual notebook. Finally, the participants can discuss, further develop, evaluate and/or evaluate the ideas in a joint workshop.

5.3.1.3 Random word technique

A randomly chosen word should be confronted with the question/problem in order to get completely new suggestions.

How to do it:

After defining the question/problem, a (concrete) word is randomly selected from a dictionary. As an alternative to a dictionary, (technical) lexicons, newspapers, magazines, catalogues, brochures, books on specific topics, etc. can be used. A moderator may also have already prepared suitable stimulus word lists. Even if the word seems completely inappropriate, one should not discard it too fast. First each participant considers (and notes if necessary) itself, which comes to him to the stimulus word still everything. This random word should then be related to the question/problem.

The following questions, for example, can serve this purpose:

- What are the properties/characteristics of the random word?
- How does the random word work?
- Where and by whom is the random word used?
- What feelings/emotions does the random word trigger?
- What do they associate with the random word?
- What are the similarities between the random word and the question/problem?
- What are the differences?
- Can the random word be used to solve the problem?

In addition to stimulus words, randomly selected photos, drawings, pieces of music or objects can also be taken.

5.3.1.4 Semantic intuition / The perfect prefix

In semantic intuition, words from different areas are combined with each other and placed in relation to the question/problem.

How to do it:

A list of words is created as nouns that have something to do with the question/problem. Then (all) terms from the list are combined in any order. These combinations should be visualized. The combination of terms is then transferred to the initial problem/question, and possible solutions are searched for on the basis of the combination of terms.

The perfect prefix method by Vullings/Heleven (2017) works in a similar way. Here certain prefixes, which are of a technical, economic, social and/or personal nature, are to be associated with the initial problem in order to obtain suggestions for new ideas. Such inspirations are particularly helpful for the development of cross-industry innovations. In detail, Vullings/Heleven (2017) propose the following prefixes:

Table 17: List of Prefixes
Source: Vullings/Heleven (2017), S. 171ff. with own supplements

mixed	dual	hybrid	functional	smart	personal	convenience
retro	emotional	artificial	3D	colored	mood	visual
guerrilla	underground	free	easy	self	transparent	invisible
perfect	safe	all-inclusive	zero	direct	micro	multi
mini	nano	pocket	minimal	low	flexible	foldable
soft	light	sustainable	local	urban	eco	slow
fair	solar	economical	diverse	second-hand	healthy	service-oriented

5.3.1.5 Forced Relationship

The principle of Forced Relationship is that elements that do not belong together are thoughtfully combined. Each element is brought into relation with each other. The combination with foreign terms should lead to new traces.

How to do it:

1) A generic term for the problem to be solved is searched for.
2) Collection of nouns that have nothing to do with the problem to be solved.
3) The nouns found are linked to the generic term, from which ideas can in turn be developed.

The method is most effective when as many combinations of terms as possible are played through.

5.3.1.6 Provocation technique

The ideas/problem solutions are formulated as provocative statements, e.g. in order to get new suggestions through exaggeration, contradictions or wishful thinking.

How to do it:

In the style of brainstorming, statements are deliberately formulated provocatively for the brainstorming of ideas/problem solving. The type of provocation can be different:
- Wishful thinking: Money and time play no role, everything is technically possible.
- Over- or understatement: faster/slower, bigger/smaller, expensive/free, etc.
- Reverse: The exact opposite of what you are striving for is formulated.
- Naturals are negated or assumptions or conventions are completely abolished.
- Comparison with another product/service that is completely absurd.

The word "PO" can be used to introduce the provocative statement (according to de Bono (1972) this stands for provocative operation), e.g. "PO, if we had as much money as Bill Gates, we would...". On the one hand, this is supposed to make the provocation recognizable, and on the other hand, it lowers the inhibition threshold to formulate really absurd statements.

5.3.1.7 Walt-Disney method

The Walt Disney method is a creativity method based on a role-playing game in which one or more people view and discuss a problem from three angles.

The method goes back to Robert B. Dills, who wrote about the famous film producer and cartoon pioneer Walt Disney: "...there were actually different Walts: the dreamer, the realist, and the spoiler" (Source: Robert B. Dilts quoted from Martin et al. (2000)). This method is very similar to the 6-thinking-hats method described below.

How to do it:

The three perspectives of the dreamer, the realist and the critic are accepted one after the other. The separation of these three roles is symbolized by three different chairs. For example, if you sit in the dreamer's chair, you have to argue from this perspective. As "dreamers", the participants should remember a beautiful situation in life. As "realists" they remember a situation that they have practically solved. As a "critic", a situation should be recalled in which they have analysed something critically. For the actual problem, the questions on the three roles are to be used in turn as assistance, as they are schematically outlined in the following illustration.

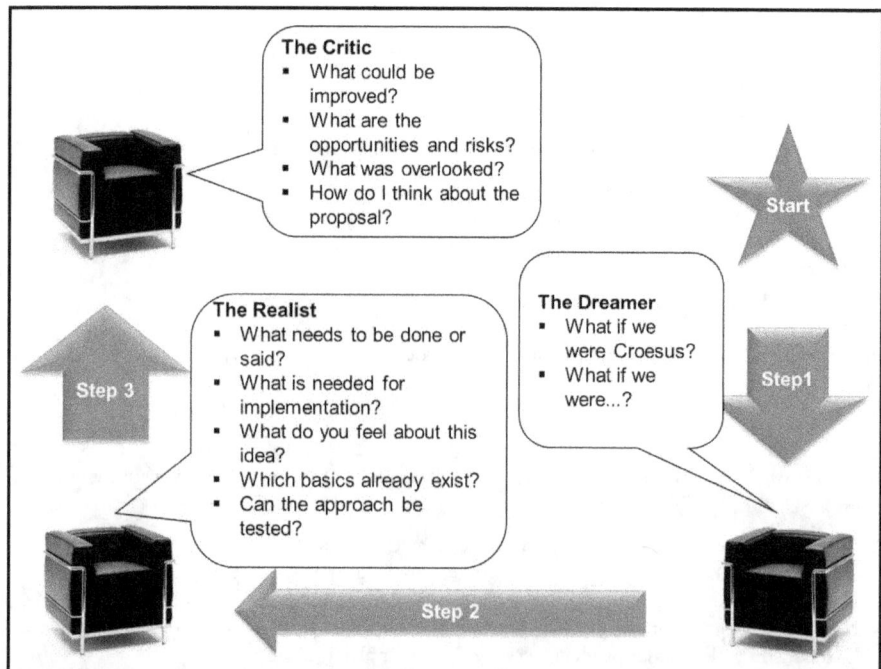

Figure 23: The Walt-Disney method

5.3.1.8 Six Thinking Hats

The Six Thinking Hats (de Bono (2016)) is intended to encourage people to adopt different perspectives when looking at problems or coming up with ideas. In a workshop the participants will put on hats with different colors. A total of six colors stand for different ways of thinking such as objective, emotional, negative/positive criticising, creative and moderating.

How to do it:

If the participants want to examine and solve a problem, they can put on all six hats one after the other and write down their thoughts and evaluate them afterwards. It is a good idea to start with the white hat. The hats have the following meaning in detail:

Table 18: Six Thinking Hats

Hat color (perspective)	Description
white hat (the neutral and objective thinker)	<ul><li>Try to solve the problem objectively and neutrally.</li><li>Bring in numbers, dates and facts and present statistics in the form of illustrations.</li><li>Think about what important information is missing and how this information is obtained</li><li>Never judge!!</li></ul>
red Hat (the emotional thinker)	<ul><li>Express your feelings and emotions when you evaluate the problem/idea.</li><li>Describe what you think is great about the challenge/idea.</li><li>Express what you find threatening at the challenge/idea.</li><li>Formulate your hopes but also your fears with the idea/problem.</li></ul>
black Hat (the negative-critical thinker)	<ul><li>Analyze the problem/idea critically.</li><li>Argue why the problem/idea is not solvable/not feasible in your view.</li><li>Make it clear which errors/dangers the problem/idea has and why.</li></ul>
yellow Hat (the positive-critical thinker)	<ul><li>Argue why the problem/idea from your point of view chances or advantages possesses.</li><li>Point out the opportunities from an objective point of view, which has the problem/the idea.</li><li>Always be logical and rational.</li></ul>
green Hat (the creative thinker)	<ul><li>Which spontaneous ideas on the problem do you think of?</li><li>Use the Osborn checklist to do this (see chapter 5.3.2).</li><li>What else can I add?</li><li>Never be critical!</li></ul>
blue Hat (the facilitator)	<ul><li>Evaluate the contributions of the another thinkers.</li><li>Remind them to follow the rules.</li><li>Summarize the results.</li><li>Moderate without contributing your own ideas.</li></ul>

5.3.1.9 Delphi Method

Chapter 2.4.4 already described the process of this multi-stage expert survey.

5.3.2 Systematic Analytical Techniques

5.3.2.1 Osborn Checklist

Numerous different creativity techniques use a catalogue of questions, which should stimulate the analysis of the problem as well as the development of new solution ideas. A very common method is the Osborn checklist, which shows ways of thinking for the search of problem solutions. Often, the acronym SCAMPER is used for this method, which is composed of the words of the various possible ways of thinking: **SCAMPER**: **S**ubstitute, **C**ombine, **A**dapt, **M**odify, **P**ut other uses, **E**liminate and **R**earrange.

How to do it:

During the problem solving phase, questions are asked which are intended to provide suggestions for new possible solutions. The central question is: Can I solve my problem by using or adapting something differently or changing or replacing or enlarging or reducing or rearranging or transforming or reversing or combining? There are further sub-questions for each of these possible ways of thinking (see Osborn checklists below).

Table 19: Osborn-Checkliste (I)

Use differently:
▪ Can this idea, thing or matter also be used and applied differently?
▪ Are there other ways of using it?
▪ How and where can the idea also be used?
Adapt:
▪ What is similar to this idea, thing or matter?
▪ What parallels can be drawn? Are there parallels from the past?
▪ Do they refer to another idea or thing.
▪ Can the thing / idea be assigned to a class, a system or a structure?
▪ What could be imitated?
Change:
▪ What can be redesigned or changed? Color? Size? Meaning? Odour? Shape? Sound? Movement? Material etc.?

Table 20: Osborn Checklist (II)

Replace:
▪ What can be replaced by the idea/thing?
▪ Is there any other material, accessories, persons, parts, components, a different process, new conditions, new positions?
▪ What or who can join them? Elements from other countries or times, from e.g. the Middle Ages?
Magnify:
▪ What can be enlarged or added? Duplicate, multiply, exaggerate, etc.? Frequency, strength, height, length, value, distance, mission, duration?
▪ Can something be exaggerated, led to the extreme?
Reduce:
▪ Can something be reduced? Or can it be omitted?
▪ Smaller? Deeper? Shorter? Thinner? Lighter? Lighter? Split? As a miniature? More compact?
Convert:
▪ What can be exchanged or converted? Parts or passages of the item/idea? Other structures? A new order? Replace cause and effect?
Transform:
▪ Can it be disguised?
▪ Perforated?
▪ Stretched?
▪ Hardened?
▪ Fluid?
▪ Upholstery?
▪ Make transparent?
▪ Make stiff?
▪ Extend?
Reverse:
▪ Backwards instead of forwards? Do the opposite? Mirroring? Negative instead of positive? Slow instead of fast? Small instead of big? Role reversal? Above instead of below? Inside instead of outside? Turn the thing / idea around.
▪ Is there an opposite possibility of use?
▪ What can be exchanged?
▪ Would a different order be possible?
▪ Can a new order, structure be created?
Combine:
▪ Can units, functions, parts, components, services or process steps be combined?
▪ Can intentions be combined? Mixing? Networking? Into a larger whole integrate? Fusion?
▪ Can products and services be linked together?

5.3.2.2 Mind Mapping

Mind Maps (developed in the 1970's by Buzan (2013)) are graphical representations of the problem and its various solution facets. The problem or question is written in the center of a large sheet of paper (or blackboard or screen) and the solutions spread over the entire sheet surface.

How to do it:

The focus is on the topic (see example below). It is written in the middle of the paper and enclosed by a circle. From this circle branches fork out, which divide and fan out the topic into its individual areas. Keywords are written on the branches. Topics represent the main branches. Details are written to the branches. Color and pictures or symbols can make a mind map even more meaningful. After creating a mind map, branches can be combined again or branches that were previously not connected can be connected with each other. In addition, you can search for missing branches in order to identify gaps for problem solving/idea acquisition. Mind mapping can also be understood as a continuous process in which you start with a mind map on a more abstract level and become more and more detailed over time through additions but also deletions. There are also software programs for mind mapping.

Rules for Mind Mapping

- ◐ Use nouns only.
- ◐ Use block letters.
- ◐ Corrections are allowed.
- ◐ Symbols (arrows, emojis, figures etc.) and pictures help.
- ◐ For reasons of legibility, the labels must be written horizontally.
- ◐ Use colors for differentiation.
- ◐ Use question words as structural tools (Who? What? Where? How? When? Why?)

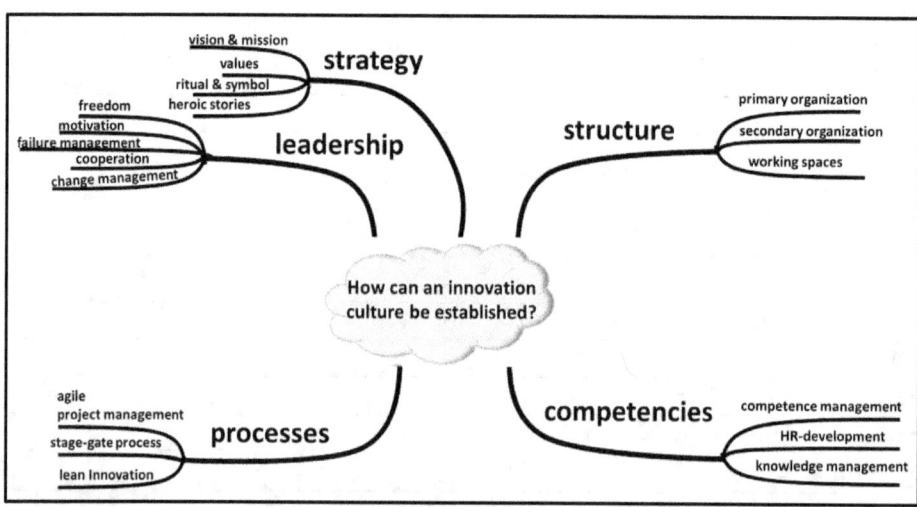

Figure 24: Mind Map on the topic of innovation culture

5.3.2.3 Synectics

Synectics is a method of analogy which, in several alienation steps, first looks at the question from completely different perspectives and searches for suitable analogies. The basic principle is to make the familiar foreign and the foreign familiar. By comparing the analogy with regard to similarities and differences, ideas or problem solutions are attempted to be transferred to the initial problem. Significant innovations are often created by re-combining existing solutions (analogy formation).

How to do it:

In a moderated session of several hours with five to seven participants from as many different disciplines as possible, a problem is first analysed, alienated in several steps and then a connection is established between alienation and the initial problem in order to find a new solution for the problem. In detail, a synectic session according to Gordon (1961) is divided into the following steps:

1. **Problem definition:**

   In accordance with the recommendations in chapter 2, the problem must be analysed from different angles and, if necessary, redefined.

2. **Spontaneous solutions:**

   With the help of a brainstorming session (see chapter 5.3.1.1 for recommendations), first ideas are spontaneously "unloaded".

3. **Reformulation:**

   The spontaneous solutions in the previous step are used to reformulate the problem in terms of an objective or to look at it from different perspectives. The recommendations in chapter 2.5 are helpful here.

4. **Direct analogies:**

   Within the framework of the first alienation step, a completely different subject area (nature, social area, foreign sector) is sought, from which analogies for the problem or possible solutions are formed. For example, the bionic approach (see chapter 5.3.2.5.) can be used here (Where can a similar problem be found in nature? Where and how has nature solved a similar problem? Our problem A is like X from nature).

5. **Personal analogies:**

   Personal analogies are formed in order to achieve a stronger empathy of the participants with the problem. How does it feel to be an X (example from step 4)? How would I react/behave if I were X? What would I do in place of X? For this, the participants have to write keywords on cards that are discussed and selected in the group.

6. **Symbolic analogies (contradictions):**

   Symbolic, unusual, paradoxical, contradictory analogies are formed from the example of step 4. Like e.g: What would be the opposite of X (example from step 4)? This is mainly about alienating the idea.

7. **Direct analogies:**

   Direct analogies to the found symbolic analogies are sought, this time from a different area than in step 4. What is similar to Y (example from step 6)? The answer should be formulated in the same way as for a book title consisting only of a noun and an adjective.

8. **Analogy analysis:**

   In the analysis of the direct analogies from the last step, this analogy should be described in very simple words (i.e. whether one would have to explain the analogy to a four-year-old child). Participants present their descriptions in the group.

9. **"Force-Fit"**:

    The last analogies are associated with the original problem as with the method Forced Relationship (see chapter 5.3.1.6). This means, what meaning do the essential principles, the special functions or the most important features have on the actual problem found in step 7 or 8.

10. **Development of (concrete) solution approaches**

    The last step can already include the development of first concrete solutions.

The individual steps can be more systematically alienated using questions of stimulation as presented in chapter 5.3.1.1 and the Osborn checklist (see chapter 5.3.2.1). Also the methods random word technique (see chapter 5.3.1.3) as well as the Semantic Intuition/The Perfect Prefix (see chapter 5.3.1.4) can be helpful to find analogies.

5.3.2.4 Bionics

Bionics (or biomimicry) is also an analogy method in which "inventions from nature" are transferred and adapted to technical problems. The model can refer to a product characteristic/function, to a process or to an entire system (Baumeister (2014):. 12). The context factors/conditions under which biological systems are optimized must always be taken into account, such as light irradiation, temperature (heat/cold), water, gravity, wind, air conditions, etc., some of which change dynamically.

The central question is therefore: How does nature solve our problem under which conditions? Examples from bionics are the lotus effect, Velcro fastener, bird flight observations of the Wright brothers as well as winglets in airplanes, ventilation systems such as in termite constructions, swarm intelligence from the animal kingdom, etc.

How to do it:

Natural systems are particularly characterised by their iterative character and incremental steps. The bionic approach should therefore also be iterative and incremental in the sense of the model of nature, as required, for example, by agile project management (see chapter 8.5). Therefore, the following phases are listed in a sequential order only for reasons of presentation.

Basically, two different approaches can be differentiated for the procedure: With the **top-down approach** (also called **abstraction approach**), a technical/economic problem is defined more precisely and possible solutions are sought in nature. In the **bottom-up approach** (also called the **analogy approach**), a biological phenomenon is characterized from basic biological research and a technical/economic application is sought via abstraction. The bottom-up approach in particular promises to produce radical innovations.

In the following procedure according to Baumeister (2014): 86, both approaches are integrated through minor changes and additions by the author: It promotes creativity to combine both approaches.

① **Analysis phase:**

  A) **Definition of the technical/economic problem (top-down approach):**
    In terms of the Design Thinking approach, the definition of the technical/economic problem is an important first task. Various methods can be used for this, such as company/environment analysis, persona method (see chapter 4.2), empathy map (see chapter 3.4.3), jobs-to-be-done (see chapter 4.3.1), etc.

    When defining the problem, the context in which the problem occurs must also be determined (e.g. physical/chemical conditions, situation, constraints, resource availability at the time/space of the problem). Here the following further questions are to be specified:

- What exactly must the solutions be in principle under these conditions?
- How are solutions influenced by changes in these conditions?
- What risks and opportunities arise from these changes?
- How can changes be measured?

It is helpful to further concretize the fundamental solution possibilities with Why-questions: Why should the product/process have this possible solution?

B) **Characterisation of the biological phenomenon (bottom-up approach):**
Find interesting phenomena from the animate and inanimate nature, which you do not know yet or not so from a technical system, by articles in technical journals, technical books, expert discussions or also by own observations. In particular, search for interesting phenomena and patterns that repeat themselves, such as structures, forms, processes, properties/characteristics or functions. Observe and study potentially interesting biological phenomena over time and/or under changing conditions. Note changes in the environment and biological system over time.

Literally put yourself in the biological system and ask yourself: What do I consist of? What does my survival depend on? What role do I play in the entire ecosystem? What is the role in my niche? What characteristics have I used to adapt optimally to the niche?

When characterizing the natural system, it is helpful to search specifically for a multi-functional design (see below). That is, identify a function and observe which function this characteristic still assumes, namely how and why.

Observe the principles of nature mentioned below in step 3. Which of them is particularly fascinating? Which of these principles of nature are necessary for the application in any case and should include the goal of application? Also ask yourself the opposite question, why one of the mentioned below principles should not be used.

② **Discovery phase:**

Based on the results of the analysis phase, the question is asked how nature would realize these functions/properties/steps under consideration of the defined conditions. Realization can be understood in the literal sense, but also in the metaphorical sense.

In order to identify a suitable natural system/object that has similar biological functions and runs under similar conditions in the top-down sense, the following questions can be raised – possibly in cooperation with experts from biology, specialist books, databases/internet sources (e. g. asknature.org):

- Who or what in nature lives from realizing these functions/properties/step?
- Who and what in nature will be particularly affected by the problem/conditions?
- Who and what in nature lives under extreme conditions?
- Who and what lives in nature only if the defined conditions do not prevail?

Both for the top-down approach and for the bottom-up approach, the model of nature must be abstracted: In other words, how does the mechanism of the biological phenomenon function or how is the function achieved? Describe the functions and the situation without using biological terms. Describe the biological resources, functions, properties, processes with appropriate terms from technology and/or the business world. Translate what you perceive from the biological system into an abstract, technical drawing.

③ **Creative phase:**

For the transfer of solutions from nature into technology (top-down) as well as for the search for applications in technology and economy for solutions from nature one can use further creativity techniques presented in this section. Brainstorming (see chapter 5.3.1.1) is particularly popular for this purpose.

5 How to find and select ideas

For both approaches, the comparison of forms, characteristics, processes and/or functions between the natural system and the (current) technical/economic system is helpful. In addition, it is advisable for this creative phase to bear in mind the fundamental principles of nature. According to Baumeister (2014): 33ff., the following principles of nature can be identified:

- **Principle of evolution:**
  - Can successful functions, characteristics and processes be (re)repeated?
  - Can errors be consciously incorporated that lead to new properties, functions or processes?
  - Can information be exchanged/changed for new solution options?

- **Principle of adaptation to dynamic changes:**
  - Create diversity by integrating/offering several (easily) different forms, processes or systems.
  - Can parts, functions or processes be renewed by the supply of material and/or energy?
  - Double features, functions or processes at different decentralized locations of the product/process, so that a redundant system is introduced.

- **Principle of local adaptation:**
  - Use cyclic processes of the environment in which the product or process is used.
  - Use materials and energy that are readily available on site in abundance.
  - Use feedback loops to quickly adapt to local needs.
  - Establish relationships with local partners that enable a win-win situation.

- **Principle of balance between development and growth:**
  - Promote the self-organisation of the actors during implementation by establishing a few clear rules to achieve a jointly formulated goal.
  - Build up the product/process bottom-up from individual components/steps piece by piece/step with high complexity of the task.
  - Use modular and nested components/steps that build on each other piece by piece.

- **Principle of resource efficiency:**
  - Avoid waste in the form of too much material, equipment, tools, energy, time, personnel and information, whereby effectiveness (achievement of objectives) always takes precedence over efficiency.
  - Use low energy processes, because no temperature or pressure changes are necessary.
  - When using energy, consider the optimal time for this.
  - Use energy sources from the environment (sun, heat, water, fermentation).
  - Search for a multi-functional design so that one solution can satisfy several needs.
  - Recycle the materials in a closed loop system.
  - Adapt the form to the function, so that ideally the form (structure) of a product becomes a function.

- **Principle of the use of eco-friendly chemistry:**
  - Search for chemicals that can be broken down into harmless components during degradation.
  - Use as few composite materials/mixtures as possible.
  - Use water instead of chemicals as solvent.

④ **Evaluation phase:**

The ideas that emerged from the creative phase should be subjected to a (first) evaluation. In this early phase, feasibility and desirability from the point of view of a potential customer should be in the foreground. Viability, scalability and sustainability are to be considered in the next phase in more detail (general assessment procedures).

⑤ **Transformation/development phase**:

In order to transform the solution of nature into a technical/economic solution or to develop a solution of nature for a concrete application, an innovation project should be set up.

5.3.2.5 Morphological box

In the morphological box, a product/procedure/service/business model is first broken down into its components/functions/process steps. For each component / function / process step, different forms (variants) are then searched for. These forms (solution variants) are combined so that new products/procedures/services/business models can be created.

How to do it:

In the following figure the procedure of the morphological box is sketched.

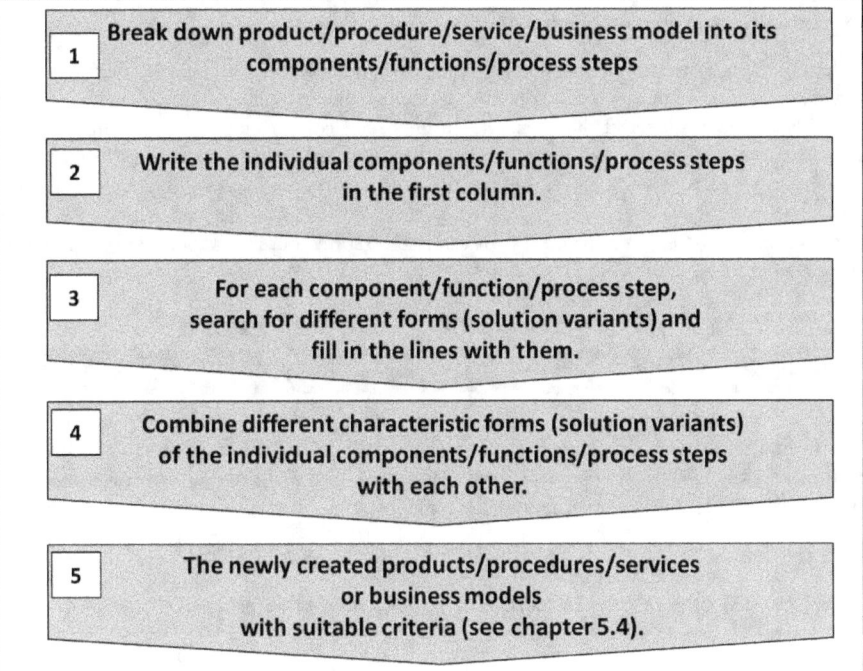

Figure 25: Procedure for the morphological box

The table below gives an example of the development of ideas for a new alarm clock using a morphological box.

5 How to find and select ideas

Table 21: Morphological box for an alarm clock

functions	forms							
wake up by	ring the bell	music		voice message	jiggle		light	temperature change
stop the alarm signal	pass through photocell	on call		switch	weight alleviation		weight load	typical first activity
reminder	none		phone rings	other signal	repeat louder	hurt	search run	waterjet
wake-up time entry	dial setting		keypad	voice entry	written entry		search run	
time entry	clock face		LCD / LED	acoustic message	mechanical counter			
alarm time display	dial setting		acoustic message	LCD / LED on demand	LCD / LED permanent		printout	hand-write
energy source	manually		vibration	ray energy	power supply		battery	
energy storage	weight		spring	bimetal	pressure tank		magnetic storage	none

Tips for how to use the morphological box:

When selecting components/functions/process steps, care should be taken to ensure that they are as independent as possible from each other (this is the only way they can be freely varied and combined). In addition, you should not select more than seven important components/functions/process steps, otherwise the approach becomes too complex. Other creativity techniques such as the 635 method or brainstorming can also be used in the search for the various forms of expression (solution variants). Not only the best solution is interesting, you can also further develop sub-optimal solutions. Known or established components/functions/process steps can also be sorted out in advance or marked in color in the morphological box.

The sequential morphology presented below is a variant of the morphological box.

Sequential Morphology

In the so-called sequential morphology according to Schlicksupp (2004), the morphological box is combined with an evaluation procedure in order to narrow down the selection of suitable ideas and thus focus on interesting creative approaches at an early stage. The evaluation is similar to the scoring model (see chapter 5.4.5). The selective approach is multi-level:

How to do it:

1. Analysis and definition of the problem as well as derivation of all parameters (see above) from which potential solution variants (see above) can be developed.

2. Derivation of the criteria according to which the quality of the derived parameters can be evaluated. Recommendations for this can be found in chapter 5.4.5.

3. Weighting of these evaluation criteria in a priority order (e.g. highest priority is evaluated with 1.0 and everything else is weighted less).

4. Evaluation of the parameters on the basis of the respective evaluation criteria and multiplication by the respective weighting factor. These values are then added together for each parameter so that each parameter receives an overall rating.
5. According to the ranking order, only the two most important parameters can be sorted into a morphological box. As with the morphological box above, different forms of expression (solution variants) are collected for these important parameters (see above).
6. On the basis of the selected two most important parameters, two/three optimal combinations of the forms of expression are sought. These in turn can be assessed with the evaluation criteria and their weightings. The best combination is the core solution.
7. Step by step (sequential), the other (less weighted) parameters are now taken into account, forms of expression are formed for these again and then the best form of expression is combined with the core solution. Very low weighted parameters are not considered any further.

5.3.2.6 Attribute Listing

Attribute listing is a simplified form of the morphological box by searching for possible variations of properties/components/functions/process steps from the current solution.

How to do it:
1) Dismantling a product, process, service, etc. into its individual parts.
2) Description of the current designs of all characteristics (atual state);
3) Systematic search for possible variations in the design of each characteristic;
4) Selection and realisation of interesting variations.

5.3.2.7 HIT-Matrix

The so-called Heuristic Ideation Technique (HIT) by Edward E. Tauber (see Silverstein/Samuel/DeCarlo (2012)) makes it possible to get new ideas by comparing them with a competing approach. Product characteristics (but also characteristics/process steps of services) of two completely different products (services) are to be related and, if necessary, combined. After selecting the products to be compared, which should be very different, the individual product features/functionalities/materialities are listed and selected. In a matrix, each selected characteristic of product A is written to the top row next to each other and each selected characteristic of product B is written to the first column below each other. In each cell, a comparison of two characteristics of product A and B takes place. For each comparison pair, the system decides whether and how they are similar or whether a combination or exchange of characteristics is of interest. Completely unsuitable comparison pairs are not considered with one another.

5.3.2.8 Lotus Blossom

The Lotus Blossom technique according to Yasuo Matsumura makes it possible to derive further ideas for a solution from a core problem or idea by creating different perspectives (Michalko (2006)). This technique is particularly suitable for further developments.

How to do it:

The core problem or the core idea is written on a card or better on a Post-It and this/these is stapled/glued in the middle of the middle box (see following illustration), which consists of 3x3 fields. A box is supposed to symbolize a lotus blossom. Further ideas, derived from the core problem or the core idea, can be positioned in the fields (the lotus petals) around it (A to E). In this case there are eight further outer fields, which can also be reduced to six fields. A copy of each of these ideas (A to E) is made and this card or post-it is stapled/glued in the middle of a new box. From this respective idea ideas are derived again and placed in the fields 1 to 8. Theoretically 72 ideas were created in the end. If there are several participants, first all of them can be involved in filling in the central box and then each group can be responsible for one box (= lotus blossom).

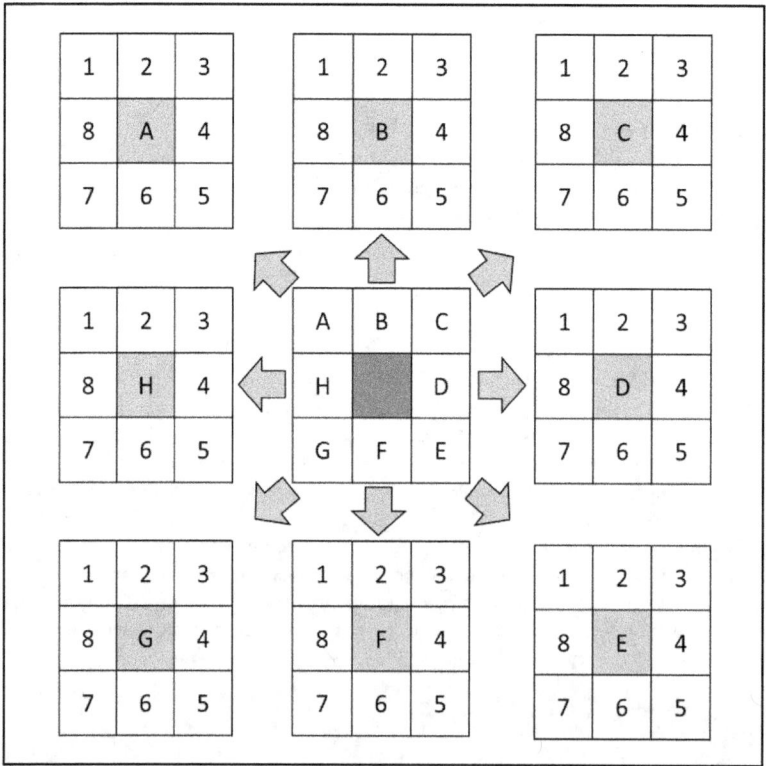

Figure 26: Lottus Blossom

5.3.3 TRIZ

The approach of the "Theory of Inventive Problem Solving" (TRIZ from Russian: "Teorija reschenija isobretatatelskich Zadach") originates from the Russian scholar Genrich Saulowitsch Altschuler (1994), whose various methods, which are summarized under the word TRIZ, have attracted worldwide attention and which enjoy great popularity especially in the technical sciences. The approach is essentially based on the following consideration: "Someone has somehow, somewhere, somehow already solved your problem". From the analysis of hundreds of thousands of patents, he has derived various principles and methods that can be applied very effectively to different technical questions (but also to the service sector). TRIZ consists of a whole set of methods, whose most effective methods are presented in the following with concrete recommendations for action.

5.3.3.1 Principles of evolution

Many inventions (also of different sciences) are based on few general solution principles. Due to insufficient exchange of knowledge between different sciences, existing solution principles are often not known. Therefore, solutions from other scientific fields can be found by analysis and abstraction of the problem. When analysing inventions/patents, Altschuler discovered that certain patterns of development occur in every (technical) system. These patterns consist of laws, trends and lines of development, which follow the path of a product/process or even a service to an "ideal" state.

The following general evolutionary principles of products, processes or services can be observed:

1. Gradual development
2. Increasing the degree of ideality
3. Inconsistent development of system parts
4. Increasing the dynamics of the control system
5. From complexity to simplicity
6. Evolution with suitable and specifically unsuitable components
7. Trend towards miniaturisation and increased use of fields
8. Decreasing human interaction and increase in automation

In the following, these principles and further trends and lines of development are explained, which can give various suggestions for your own development work:

❶ Gradual development

A general model scheme of evolution of products/procedures/services is the subsequent step-by-step development:

- First, a useful function or an advantageous process step is achieved. What is the solution to the problem?
- Then this useful function is improved in its performance.
  How can the performance of the function of the process step be improved?
- Possible harmful/disadvantageous effects in connection with the use of the function are reduced or eliminated.

What harmful/negative effects are there when using the product/process/service? How can these be eliminated or reduced?
- Subsequently, the efficiency in the use or production of this function is improved (faster, more resource-saving, etc.).
  How can the product/procedure/service be produced or used faster, with less resource consumption, etc.?
- At the same time, attempts are made to improve the reliability of this function so that fewer errors occur during use and/or manufacture (quality management task, e.g. via Six Sigma).
  How can the product/procedure/service be faultlessly produced/provided or used?
- Finally, an attempt is made to further reduce costs for all tasks related to this function.
  How can the effort for all tasks/process steps in production, marketing and/or use or disposal be reduced?

The unambiguous sequence is not important here, especially since many steps can be carried out in parallel. Rather, this pattern scheme can be used everywhere. If one is aware of this pattern, the next development step or the medium/long-term goal can be better described and understood.

❷ Increasing the degree of ideality

For the development of new products, processes or services, it is helpful to consider what the ideal solution might look like.

In general, an ideal solution can be described by the following formula:

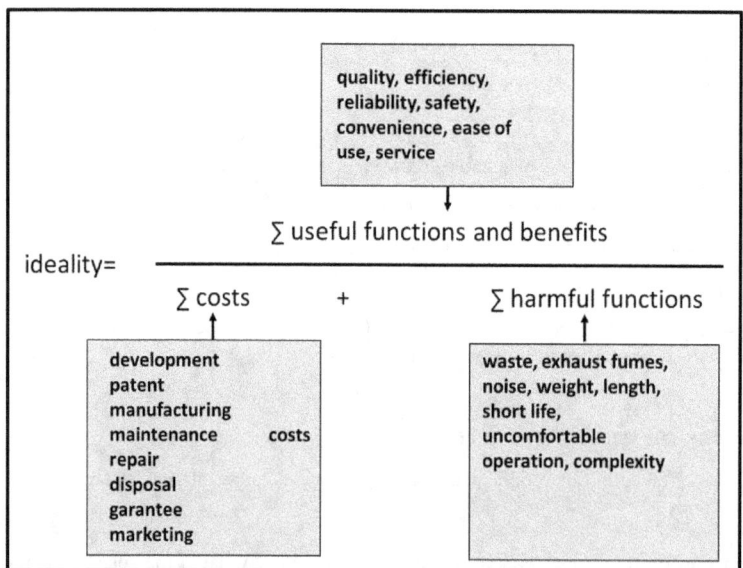

Figure 27: Ideality formula

From this it can be seen that one must start with the useful functions, with the harmful functions and/or with the costs.

The ideal product/procedure/service can be described, for example, by the following features (source: Koltze/Souchkov (2017)):
- Anytime, anywhere, unlimited, accurate, reliable, robust, intuitive, convenient, ergonomic, simple, predictable, easy to use, no time required, compact, complete/all in all, multifunctional, automatic/automatic
- No damage, no optical/technical defect, no waste/exhaust gases
- Without financial expenditure, free of charge.

Table 22: Ideality
    Source: Gadd (2011)

Checklist ideality
• What does the ideal solution look like?
• What is the best way to achieve this?
• Where should the developments go in the next step in order to achieve the ideal?
• What would the solution be if there were no physical limits?
• What would the solution look like if time didn't matter?
• What would the solution look like if costs didn't matter?
• What would the solution look like if there were no legal regulations/standards/technical standards?
• What are the useful/desired functions? Can these functions be maximized?
• What are the harmful and unwanted functions? (Environmental Harmfulness, Costs and effort for the customer) Can the damage/expense be reduced?

In order to come closer to ideality, the following approaches can provide possible suggestions (cf. Gadd (2011)):

1) **Eliminate supporting (auxiliary) functions:**
   Try to eliminate all functions that have little or no direct benefit. The following questions can be asked:
   - What is the main function, what are the secondary functions?
   - How can I remove the secondary function without affecting the main function?

2) **Eliminate a component / function / task / process step:**
   (also referred to as trimming by TRIZ)
   For almost every product or service there are components or process steps that can be reduced or eliminated on closer analysis or whose tasks/functions can be taken over by other components.

   The following questions can be asked:
   - Is the component/function, task/process step required at all?
     - Can functions / tasks of several components / process steps be combined in one component / process step?

3) **Recognize potential for self-sufficiency and self-service:**
The useful main functions/process steps can often take over additional secondary functions/process steps, so that the system becomes more versatile and/or more efficient without additional components/process steps. In addition, there can be feedback options in the product/process/service itself, so that complex controls can be eliminated.
The following question can be asked:
- Can functions be taken over by other components/process steps or by the component/process step itself?

4) **Replace components, process steps or the entire system:**
The following questions can be asked:
- Replace individual components or the entire system
- Replace expensive components with inexpensive, short-lived copies
- Replace the entire system with a low-cost disposable part
- Can unwanted functions be replaced by other functions?

5) **Change the operating principle:**
For example, use electrical or electromagnetic systems instead of mechanical functions.

6) **Components can be replaced by existing resources:**
The following questions can be asked:
- Which resources are available in the system? Can these existing (environmental) resources (e.g. water/steam, air, ice, earth, gases, oxygen, nitrogen, carbon dioxide, wood, rock) be used directly?
- Can existing (environmental) resources be used after modification?
- Can the functions/tasks of components/process steps be transferred to generally available or already existing resources (e.g. air, waste etc.)?

These approaches do not have to be worked through completely, but should only serve as a stimulus to come up with new ideas/solutions.

Overall, the evolutionary principle of ideality provides rather abstract solutions that can be applied to concrete real problems. In addition, only the mental examination of an ideal product, process or service can break through or overcome possible mental blocks.

❸ Inconsistent development of system parts

Products/processes/services often do not evolve as a whole. Rather, individual components/functions/tasks/process steps will have different development speeds. Therefore one should always start at the level of these components/functions/tasks/process steps for further development.

Tips:
- Identify components that are of central importance and have high potential for further development.
- Prioritize all other components according to importance and development potential
- Analyse development bottlenecks quickly and thoroughly
- Parallel development processes and set clear, measurable milestones in development

❹ Increased dynamics and controllability

Dynamic modification can affect objects, substances, or even fields:

Increase the dynamics of objects:

- Rigid products are becoming more and more dynamic.
- The individual components are connected more and more flexibly/elastically/movably until the whole product is flexible.
- The individual components become smaller and smaller and thus also increase flexibility.

Increasing the dynamics of substances:

- The development goes from the use of a solid substance, to a fragmented substance, to powders, gels or liquids over aerosols / gases up to fields.

Increasing the dynamics of fields:

- Fields are first permanent, then pulsating/oscillating, phase-changing, use of refractions/deflections up to the use of gradients.

In addition, there is an increase in controllability along the following development lines:

Increasing degree of control of objects:

- At first a product/procedure/service as a whole is only conditionally controllable.
- The product/procedure/service then becomes controllable step by step for various possible uses.
- Individual components/functions/tasks/process steps become directly controllable.
- Finally, the product/procedure/service controls itself partially or completely by itself.

Increasing degree of control of fields:

- The control of the product/procedure is usually first carried out via mechanical fields.
- The following control mechanisms are then possible: acoustic, thermal, chemical, electrical, magnetic or via biological mechanisms.

For the controllability on the one hand a suitable sensor technology and on the other hand the transparency of the function mode are necessary, with which one can frequently observe the following development lines:

Increasing use of different types of sensors:

- During the control a sense (to see) and a corresponding sensor is used first.
- The control is then extended to several senses (seeing and hearing and/or smelling and/or tasting and/or tasting at the same time) or several correspondingly different sensors.

Increased transparency:

- The way it works is initially rather opaque.
- Transparency regarding the functioning of a product/procedure/service is becoming increasingly higher.

❺ From complexity to simplicity

Firstly, the development of new products, processes or services tends to become more complex as more and more functions are integrated. However, this ultimately leads to very complex systems that are no longer manageable for the customer and are very susceptible to faults and require intensive maintenance. Subsequently, there is often the opposite trend that products, processes and services are becoming simpler, more user-friendly and more intuitive to use. This can also be seen in the concept of disruptive innovations (Christensen (1997)), since cheaper, simpler product innovations can displace established products from the market.

<u>Tips</u>:
- Summarize components or process steps that have similar functions or take over tasks.
- Reduce unnecessary auxiliary functions that do not represent substantial added value.

❻ Development with suitable and specifically unsuitable components

The targeted installation of unsuitable components of a product/process/service can exclude undesirable, disadvantageous functions or fulfil contradictory requirements.

❼ Trend towards miniaturisation and increased use of fields

The trend towards miniaturization is due on the one hand to the merging of functions and process steps:

- ➲ A product/procedure/service often consists of a large number of components or process steps with different tasks/functions.
- ➲ Step by step, individual components/process steps take over the tasks/functions from other components/process steps. This reduces the number of components/process steps.
- ➲ This is often associated with increasing miniaturization or increasing process speed.

On the other hand, miniaturization also takes place through the transition to the micro level:
- ➲ First, an object is used as a whole.
- ➲ It is then segmented into individual components, which are then used again.
- ➲ In the case of technical products/processes, development can take place via the use of powdery, liquid and ultimately gaseous objects.
- ➲ Finally, the use of fields is transferred.

❽ Decreasing Human Interaction and Increase in automation

The decreasing human interaction or increase in automation is often reflected in the following steps:
- ➲ First of all, a product/procedure/service is often little automated.
- ➲ Automation initially increases step by step along individual functions/tasks/process steps.
- ➲ The automation can then be individually adapted (adaptive automation).
- ➲ Finally, automation is developed by the system itself.

Further principles/trends/development steps are presented in the following section, some of which are closely related to the above-mentioned evolution principles (cf. Gadd (2011)):

Trend towards the development of shape

- The shapes of the components of products or the shape of products to other products and their environment are initially not well coordinated.
- These are then rigidly matched and next flexibly/individually/dynamically matched.
- Finally, the form and shape of products or their components are intelligently/automatically and at the same time flexibly/individually/dynamically adjusted to the requirements.

Evolution of geometry

- The development of geometric shapes is becoming more and more multidimensional..
- A completely symmetrical product (or part of a product) becomes a completely asymmetrical product and vice versa.

Coordination and Evolution of Rhythmics

Coordination of frequency:

- If there are vibration frequencies for products/procedures or usage intervals for products/procedures/services, these are initially not coordinated.
- Subsequently, they are coordinated or deliberately not coordinated.
- Finally, the natural frequency is used for technical products/procedures.

Coordination of different functions/tasks/process steps:

- If the product/process/service has different functions/tasks/process steps, these are initially not coordinated.
- Subsequently, more and more different functions/tasks/process steps are coordinated with each other or deliberately not coordinated.
- Any breaks in coordination are reduced or used elsewhere.
- After all, the product/procedure/service is completely synchronized.

Increasing the use of energy

- Increasing the efficiency of energy use
- A non-energy-optimised system often uses different types of energy/fields for the different functions/tasks/process steps, so that their number should be reduced and if possible only one energy work is used for the entire system.
- In addition, the length of the power lines should be reduced.
- Ideally, the energy should be supplied free of charge from the waste of other products or from the environment.

Transition to the upper system

- First, a product/procedure/service is considered and used separately.
- Increasingly, functions/tasks/components/process steps of products/processes and services are combined with identical/similar/similar products/process/services.
- Products/processes/services are linked with completely different products/services.
- Products/processes/services are completely merged with completely different products/processes/services.
- The number of combined and even merged products/processes/services is increasing.

5.3.3.2 Innovation checklist

The following innovation checklist is suitable as an entry method for the other TRIZ methods. In particular, the focus here is on describing the problem situation. The following questions in the checklist (cf. Gadd (2011)) should be answered in as simple a language as possible, consistently avoiding technical terms, in order to gain a somewhat broader view of the problem situation.

Table 23 Innovation checklist (I)
Source: Gadd (2011)

System description:
• How does the product/procedure/service work?
• What is the most important function/task of the product/procedure/service?
• What are the components / tasks / functions / process steps of the product / process / service?
List of available resources:
• What are the resources used for the product/procedure/service?
• What resources are still (freely) available in the environment?
Description of the problem:
• What is the problem with the product/procedure/service? What does not occur as problem?
• When and where does the problem occur? When does the problem not occur? Where is there no problem (although it might occur)?
• What is the extent of the problem? How strong is not the extent of the problem?
• What requirements are currently not met?
• What harmful, adverse effects does the product/process/service have? Where is time, cost, material and/or energy wasted?
History of the Problem:
• How and when did the problem first occur?
• Was there a triggering event when it occurred?
• Is the situation before the problem recoverable?
• Why have the previous attempts at a solution failed?
• Where are there products/procedures/services that have a similar problem? Have there already been successful solutions for other products/procedures/services? Solution attempts? If so, can these be transferred? If not, why not?
Cause of the problem:
• What are the causes of the problem? Which causes can be excluded?
• What are the conflicting requirements for the product/procedure/service? is there? Which conflicts need to be solved?
• What do you not know about the problem, but would like to know?
• Which of the assumptions made could be questioned?

Table 24: Innovation Checklist (II)
Source: Gadd (2011)

Improvement of the system:
▪ What could be improved?
▪ In which direction could it be improved?
▪ What is the actual state, what would be the target state of the product/procedure/ service?
▪ What does the ideal solution look like? What prevents this ideal solution from being achieved?
System environment:
▪ What could be changed in the environment to solve a problem?
▪ Which technical, economic, ecological, political, societal factors could be changed?
▪ Which limits or limit values must the problem solution not exceed?

5.3.3.3 Operator Time-Size-Cost

In this method, extreme situations are considered mentally, in terms of size (S), time (T) and costs (C).

The following hypothetical questions are asked when solving a problem for a product/procedure/service:
- What if the problem solution were very large/very small, very long/very short, very much/very little, etc.?
- What if parts or the whole process of using the product/procedure/service were very fast/slow, very little/very frequent, always/never? What if time would not play a role in the product/procedure/service?
- What if the product/process/service would be very expensive/service free? What if costs did not play a role/if there was no money available?

5.3.3.4 Resource analysis

In resource analysis, checklists (see below) are used to examine the extent to which certain resources can contribute to problem solving. Resources are to be understood in the broadest sense (cf. Gadd (2011)):

Material resources:

Materials in the form of solids, crystals, granulates, suspensions, liquids, gases, gels, foams, nanoparticles, vacuum or chemical substances.

Field-shaped resources::

- Mechanical fields (gravitational field, buoyancy forces, friction, stresses, torques, centrifugal forces, oscillations, pressure waves, capillary pressure, diffusion, absorption, osmosis, van der Waals forces)
- Thermal fields (heat, cold, temperature gradients, heat radiation)
- Electric/electromagnetic fields (electric charges/voltages, electromagnetic fields, radio/microwaves, light/infrared, X-rays, radioactive radiation)
- Chemical fields (chemical reactions, odour fields, aroma)
- Biological fields (photosynthesis, fermentation, muscle strength)

Spatial resources::

Geometric shapes and objects such as machines, plants, assemblies, etc.

Time resources::

Specific times, durations, time intervals required for the use of products/procedures/services.

Information resources::

Specific data, information or knowledge necessary for the use of products/procedures/services.

Functional resources:

Existing functions/tasks/process steps used for the product/process/service or occurring in the environment.

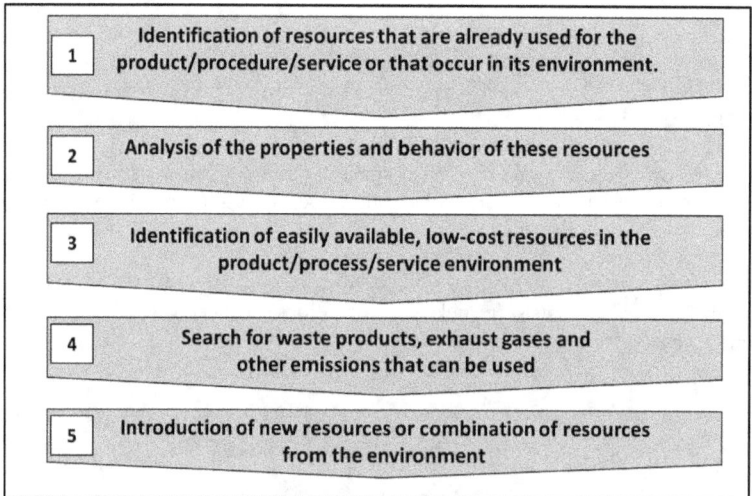

Figure 28: Procedure for Resource Analysis

Table 25: Resource checklist (I)
  Source: Gadd (2011)

General:
• Which resources are already used in the product or process? Which resources are in the immediate vicinity?
• Which problem can be solved by using which resources and how?
• Can this resource be used to solve a problem?
• How can I use the resource's property to solve a problem?
• What resources are still (freely) available in the environment?
• How can I use the behavior of the resource to solve a problem?
• **Can** harmful effects be reduced by using the resource? Can useful effects be increased by using the resource?
• Can this resource be used to solve problems?
• Where can the resources be obtained from?
• When are the necessary resources available?
History of the problem:
• How and when did the problem first occur? Was there the problem always has?
• Was there a triggering event when it occurred?
• Is the situation before the problem recoverable?
• Why have the previous attempts at a solution failed?
• Where are there products/procedures/services that have a similar problem? Have there already been successful solutions for other products/procedures/services? Solution attempts? If so, can these be transferred? If not, why not?

Table 26: Resource checklist (II)
Source: Gadd (2011)

Cause of problem:
• What are the causes of the problem? Which causes can be excluded?
• What are the conflicting requirements for the product/procedure/service? Which conflicts need to be solved?
• What do you not know about the problem, but would like to know?
• Which of the assumptions made could be questioned?
Material resources:
• Combine all or part of material resources with an empty space in the product.
• Modify existing material resources by combining them with other material resources.
• Identify change processes in the material resources and prevent, reduce or eliminate them or reinforce them.
Field resources
• Can field-shaped resources be used in the product/process or in the environment?
• Can field-shaped resources be combined in the product/process or in the environment with material resources?
• Identify change processes in material resources and prevent, reduce or eliminate material resources or reinforce them.
Spatial resources
• Can the spatial resources be used at different levels?
• Can the spatial resources be used in different directions?
• Can the spatial resources be used with or in empty spaces?
• Can different pages be used externally or internally by the spatial resources? will be?
• Can the spatial resources be nested into each other?
Time resources:
• Is it possible to gain, extend, shorten or postpone periods of time before, while and/or after the use of a product/procedure/service?
• Can different tasks/functions/process steps be performed simultaneously or overlapping?
• Can breaks, empty/waiting times be shortened or used for other purposes?
• Does it make sense not to use the product/procedure/service continuously but only in to use intervals?
• Should the use of the product/procedure/service be divided into different intervals?

Table 27: Resourcen list (III)
Source: Gadd (2011)

Information resources::
• Is there any information/data that may be required for the use of a product/procedure/ services are generated that have not yet been used?
• When does information/data arise during the use of products/procedures/services?
• What information/data is generated about the state/properties of material or field resources and how could they still be used?
• What information/data is collected about spatial or temporal resourcesand how could it be used?
• What changes/losses/interruptions are there in the flow of information/data? before/during/after use?
Functional resources:
• Which useful main and secondary functions/tasks/process steps are available for the product/procedure or service?
• How can the main functions/tasks/process steps be improved/strengthened/ be extended?
• Can the secondary functions/tasks/process steps be dispensed with or reduced?
• What harmful functions/process steps are created when using the Products/procedures/services and how can they be eliminated or reduced?
• Should the main functions/tasks/process steps before, during, and after the auxiliary functions/tasks/process steps be be spatially or temporally separated after use?
• Can functions from the environment be used?

5.3.3.5 Separation principles

If there are conflicting requirements, i.e. if the improvement of one objective results in the deterioration of another objective, one solution may be to use the following separation principles (cf. Gadd (2011)):

Principle of separation in space

Spatial separation of requirements on different levels (layers, steps, layers), in different directions (axial, radial, tangential), by using two/three-dimensional structures (chessboard, spiral), by using different inner or outer sides, by positioning in different places in the environment, by nesting or by movement forces.

Principle of separation in time

Separation of fulfilment of requirements at different times/periods, fulfilment of one requirement before or after the other requirement, use of intervals, creation of pauses/waiting or regeneration periods, partial fulfilment of requirements at specific times/periods.

5 How to find and select ideas

Principle of separation in the structure

Dividing the product/process/service into different variants/components/process steps, which execute the different requirements separately.

Separation by Condition Change

The conditions for the use of a product/procedure/service will be changed in such a way that only useful and no harmful functions/process steps can be performed. For example, other (aggregate) states such as phase transitions (from solid to liquid) can be used.

5.3.3.6 Innovation principles

A central TRIZ method are the following 40 innovation principles, which can help to find suggestions for simple solutions, especially in the case of technical contradictions (cf. Gadd (2011)).

Table 28: Innovation principles

1. Principle of Decomposition and Segmentation
- Disassembly/segmentation of the product/service/method into independent components/functions/tasks/process steps that are completely separate or still interconnected.
- Disassembly/segmentation so that it is easy to reassemble.
- Increase the number of individual components/functions in a product or the number of tasks/process steps in a service or process.

2. Principle of Separation
- Separate disruptive, undesirable components/functions / tasks / process steps from a product / service.
- Separate the only necessary components/functions/tasks/process steps from a product/service/procedure and only use them.

3. Principle of Local Optimization
- Optimally and individually adapt the product/service/process in its properties to the local conditions – either by increasing a positive effect or by avoiding/reducing a negative effect.
- Change an otherwise homogeneous product/service/process so that individual components/functions/tasks/process steps are optimally adapted to the local conditions.
- If the local situation requires a different function/task, divide/segment the product/service/procedure into different tasks/functions.

4. Principle of Asymmetry
- Replace a symmetrical shape/property of a product with an asymmetrical shape/property.
- Change the shape to fit asymmetries in the environment.
- Increase the degree of asymmetry of a product.

5. Principle of Combination

- Combine identical or similar components/functions/tasks/process steps of a product/service/procedure.
- Combine identical or similar components/functions/tasks/process steps of a product/service/procedure.
- Group identical or similar components/functions/tasks/process steps of a product/service/procedure together.

6. Principle of Multifunctionality

- Combine different components/functions/tasks/processes of a product/service/procedure so that it can be used multifunctionally.
- Use different standardized components together.
- Eliminate unnecessary functions/tasks.

7. Principle of Integration

- Nest products/services (Matryoshka principle): one component is inside another, which is also inside another.
- Increase the number of nested components/tasks/functions/process steps.
- Use the cavity (or component) of a product.
- Integrate a new task/process step within another existing task/process step.
- Make tasks/functions/process steps appear in time only as long as they are needed.

8. Principle of Weight Compensation

- Compensate the weight/force/energy by coupling or interacting with another object.
- If a weight/force interferes with a useful function, compensate it with an opposite weight/force.
- If the weight causes problems, use aerodynamic or hydrodynamic or magnetic forces to compensate.

9. Principle of Early Counter-Action

- Load or claim the product or a component in the opposite direction to an undesirable or permissible effect prior to use.
- If the product is exposed to a harmful effect during use, expose it to the opposite effect prior to use.

5 How to find and select ideas

10. Principle of Early Action

- Perform the action — partially or completely – before the actual use.
- Position the product so that it can start from the most appropriate location without wasting time.
- If the product is subject to harmful environmental effects during use, change the conditions of use so that these harmful effects are eliminated/minimized.
- If the product is to be changed during use and this is difficult to do, make these changes – if necessary at a different location – before use.

11. Principle of Prevention

- Provide resources or measures to prevent or mitigate damage before using/using a product/procedure/service.
- Compensate for poor reliability by taking counter-measures beforehand.
- Create conditions in advance that do not appear/reduce/prevent the damage.

12. Principle of Constant Potential

- Use products/processes without changing the energy potential – e.g. no lifting or lowering of the product is necessary.
- Reduce the need for movement by changing the environment.
- Integrate a new component / function / task / process step that reduces or eliminates the need for movement.
- Eliminate components/functions/process steps that require motion or replace them.

13. Principle of Inversion

- Perform the opposite function/task/process step to achieve a positive effect.
- The product/component/process step must be reversed or reversed.
- Make moving parts immobile or moving parts immobile.
- Exchange components/tasks/functions/process with their opposite.

14. Principle of Bending

- Use bended, spherical contours instead of straight surfaces.
- Use rollers, balls or spirals.
- Use rotating/rotating motions/flows instead of linear motion.
- Go from linear movements to rotary movements. Use centrifugal force.

15. Principle of Dynamisation

- Make an immovable part movable, adjustable or interchangeable.
- Dismantle the product/service/process into its components/functions/tasks/process steps that can be flexibly rearranged.
- Dynamically change the product/service/process or its environment so that it is optimally adapted to its conditions.
- If the product is movable/the service/process is already dynamically changeable, increase the degree of movement/changeability.

16. Principle of Partial or Exaggerated Solution

- If it is difficult to achieve 100% of a function, use a little less or a little more to achieve the goal.
- If an exact amount of material is difficult to use, use more material and eliminate the excess.
- If an exact amount of energy is difficult to achieve, use more energy and compensate for the surpluses for other functions.

17. Principle of the Higher Dimension

- Move/place a product on a surface or in space instead of on a line.
- Move/place a product in several layers instead of in one layer, multi-layer instead of single-layer, multi-layer instead of single-layer.
- Place the product tilted or inclined, use another side.
- Use light/projections that fall onto the surroundings/sides of the product.

18. Principle of Vibrations

- The product or its components must be made to vibrate or, if it is already vibrating, its frequency or amplitude must be changed. Use ultrasound.
- Use the natural frequency.
- Use piezoelectric vibrations instead of mechanical vibrations. Connect ultrasonic vibrations to electromagnetic fields.

19. Principle of the Periodic Function

- The continuous use of the product/service/system shall be replaced by a periodical use.
- If the use is already periodic, increase the frequency of this periodic use.
- Pauses between the periods of use of a product/service/system shall be used elsewhere (e.g. by performing other – additional – functions/tasks/process steps in these pauses).
- The periodicity of the function must be coordinated with the natural frequency of the product: either this should match or not match.

20. Principle of Continuity

- Perform the function/task/process steps continuously.
- Avoid interruptions, waiting times, or idling.
- Fill interruptions, wait times or idle times with other (useful) functions/tasks/process steps.
- Replace linear with rotating motion.

21. Principle of Speed

- Perform unwanted, harmful or dangerous functions/tasks/process steps very quickly.
- Increase the speed of execution of functions/tasks/process steps abruptly step by step in multiple steps.

22. Principle of Conversion from harmful to useful

- Use harmful or negative factors to achieve beneficial effects.
- Combine harmful factors or superimpose several harmful factors to achieve something positive.
- Increase the harmful factor until it stops being harmful.
- Increase acceptance of harmful factors.

23. Principle of Feedback

- Implement feedback to improve a process.
- If feedback is already included, increase/modify or reverse it.
- Use feedback to directly reduce or compensate for negative effects.
- Automate feedback.

24. Principle of the Intermediary

- Use a temporary component of a product/procedure/service that transmits (or performs itself) effects as an intermediary.
- The temporary component of a product/procedure/service should be easy to remove when no longer needed.
- Check whether existing resources or components of a product/process/service can be used as intermediaries.

25. Principle of Self-Supply and Self-Service

- The product/service/procedure is self-sufficient and carries out auxiliary, coordination and repair work itself.
- Use waste or loss energy.
- Use the (freely) available resources from the environment for self-sufficiency/servicing.

26. Principle of Copy

- Use a cheap, simple copy instead of a complex, expensive, fragile or poorly manageable component of a product/procedure/service.
- Replace a component of a product/procedure/service with an optical or virtual copy. If necessary, enlarge or reduce the copy.
- Use a simplified model instead of an expensive, complex product/process/service.

27. Principle of Short-Term Durability

- Replace an expensive, complex product/process/service with simple, cheap products/process/services that dispense with expensive, costly quality features.
- Use disposable products.
- Replace an expensive long-life or durable product/process/service with one or more short-term products/process/services.
- Use environmental resources or waste products to produce a short-lived product.

28. Principle of Substitution of Mechanical Processes

- Replace mechanical processes/mechanisms with optical, acoustic, magnetic, electromagnetic, electrical, thermal, chemical or odor-based processes.
- Replace immobile by mobile, constant by variable, and unstructured by structured fields.

29. Principle of the Replacement of solid, rigid Media

- Replace solid, heavy parts with gaseous or liquid parts. Use water or air.
- Use negative pressure or vacuum.

30. Principle of Use of flexible Sleeves and Films

- Use flexible/flexible sleeves, foils or membranes.
- Isolate a component of a product or process step in a process by using sheaths, films or membranes.
- Use sheaths, films or membranes as coatings to perform functions. Use piezoelectric films.

31. Principle of Use of Porous materials

- Use porous materials.
- If a product is already porous, then fill the pores with a beneficial substance (solid, liquid or gas) / useful function.
- Use capillary forces in the pores.

32. Principle of Color Change

- Change the color of the product or its components.
- Change the degree of transparency of components/products relative to other components or their environment.
- Use colored, self-illuminating or fluorescent additives to improve detection or visualize changes in products/processes.

33. Principle of Homogeneity

- Use the same(-like) material(s) in the manufacture of products.
- Use materials/materials that are similar to their environment.

34. Principle of Discarding and Regenerating

- If components/functions/tasks/process steps in products/procedures/services are only required temporarily, introduce them only during use and/or remove them after use.
- Used parts are regenerated immediately.
- If a used part causes a harmful effect, remove or modify it immediately.

35. Principle of Change in physical/chemical Properties

- Change the aggregate state of substances/materials.
- Change the concentration of substances/materials.
- Change the density of substances/materials.
- Change the volume of substances/materials.
- Change the temperature of substances/materials.
- Change the pH of substances/materials.
- Change the degree of flexibility/elasticity of fabrics/materials.
- Change the pressure.
- Change the outer medium or adjacent objects.
- Change other properties / parameters.
- Use physical or chemical effects.

36. Principle of Phase Transitions

- Take advantage of the effects during the phase transition of a substance: Volume/form change, heat development or absorption.
- Take advantage of the phase transitions of the second kind: Shape memory in metals and plastics, demagnetization of ferromagnetic materials after heating above the Curie temperature, etc.

37. Principle of Thermal Expansion

- Take advantage of thermal expansion or contraction (change in length or volume) of materials.
- Use materials with different coefficients of thermal expansion.

38. Principle of Media Responsiveness

- Use oxygen enriched air.
- Use strong oxidizing agents.
- Use or increase ozone.
- Create an environment enriched with certain substances.

39. Principle of Use of chemically inert Media

- Use inert media/gases.
- Use inert coatings.
- Use a vacuum environment.
- Introduce a neutral substance or additive.
- Isolate the product/process from the environment.
- Use foam.

40. Principle of composite Materials

- Use composite materials.
- Use composite structures in the form of layered structures, fiber composites, granules, cell structures, etc.
- Use materials with different aggregate states.
- Create products/services whose components/functions/tasks/process steps have different or opposite characteristics.

www.triz4engineers.com

www.triz.it

www.triz-journal.com

Gadd, Karen (2011): TRIZ for Engineers: Enabling Inventive Problem Solving, John Wiley & Son, Chichester/UK.

Orloff, Michael (2010): Inventive Thinking through TRIZ: A Practical Guide, 2nd edition, Springer, Berlin/Germany.

5.3.4 Systematic Inventive Thinking (SIT)

The Systematic Inventive Thinking (SIT) method (Boyd/Goldenberg (2013)) is a simplified and user-friendly further development of the TRIZ method(s). The basic principle is the use of the so-called "closed world": In principle, only resources (materials, tools, machines, personnel) should be used in the innovative process that are either already used for the products, processes or services or are (freely) available in the environment. Thus, no additional resources are to be introduced into the system, but only resources within the sphere of influence or reach of the developer are to be used. Boyd/Goldenberg (2013) therefore aptly speak of "Thinking Inside the Box" to counteract the "mainstream" approach of "Thinking Out of the Box".

For the systematic use of the "Closed World", the following five methods are proposed (according to Boyd/Goldenberg (2013)):

❶ Method of Subtraction

Simply omit an essential component/task/function/process step for products/processes or services. Essential does not necessarily mean that it is the most important component, but also not unimportant components. The meaning should rather lie in the middle. The component/task/function/process step that is removed should have a useful effect (removing harmful/unusable functions is often only an incremental innovation). In addition, the rest of the product/process/service should remain intact even without this component/task/function/process step.

❷ Method of Division

Divide products/procedures or services into individual components/tasks/functions/process steps and take one out ("divide it out") and use it in another place – even where one would supposedly achieve no useful effect. A different place can mean a different place and/or a different time.

❸ Method of Multiplication

Duplicate individual components/tasks/functions/process steps in products/processes or services and then change their properties/characteristics – change it in such a way that one would (initially) not recognize any useful effect from it. The duplication should include not only one but several (modified) copies.

❹ Method of Unifying Functions (Task Unification)

Merge different components/tasks/functions/process steps that initially appear incoherent with each other. Merging can also take place for products with external components from the environment or for services with external activities outside the actual process.

5 How to find and select ideas

❺ Method of Dependency between Variables (Attribute Dependency)

Link together individual variable functions or process steps in products, processes or services that were originally not linked to each other, so that they now influence each other anew. This means that if a function changes (by the user or by environmental influences), then another function/process step also changes. Functions/process steps can thus be understood as variable variables that influence each other. Alternative: Disconnect individual functions or process steps from each other that were previously closely linked.

Table 29: Identification of new dependencies
Source: According to Boyd/Goldenberg (2013)

variable variable → ↓	function/process step A	function/process step B	function/process step C	function/process step D	external factor 1	external factor 2
function/process step A	-					
function/process step B	0 (no dependency possible)	-				
function/process step C	1 (dependency possible)	0	-			
function/process step D	1	1	0	-		
external factor 1	0	1	1	0	-	
external factor 2	1	1	0	1	-	-

These five methods are similar in their application (according to Boyd/Goldenberg (2013)):

Step 1:

Dismantle a product/procedure/service into its components/tasks/functions/process steps and list them individually. This breakdown can be systematic or random. The decomposition can also take place on different levels (zoom in or out) – from the level of the overall system, via individual objects, via their components down to the substance/atom level (for services: from the level of the overall process, via individual process steps up to individual activities).

Step 2:

A) Subtraction:

Select an essential component / task / function / process step and remove or reduce it completely or partially. The selection can be systematic or random.

B) Division:

Select an essential component / task / function / process step and place it spatially and/or temporally elsewhere. The selection or rearrangement can be done systematically or randomly.

C) Multiplication:

Select an essential or also a harmful component / task / function / process step, reproduce and change (as simplified as possible) these in the product / process / service. Selection and modification can be systematic or random.

D) Unifying:

Select an essential component/task/function/process step and merge it with another internal or external component/task/function/process step that previously appeared (completely) incoherent. Selection or merging can be systematic or random.

E) Dependency between Variables:

Select two or more essential variable functions/process steps that were not originally linked, and now link them together so that they influence each other. If no dependency is possible, change the function or process step.

Step 3:

Describe the new characteristics of this new product/process/service.

Step 4:

Identify the benefits of potential (new) customers for this new product/process/service.

Step 5:

Check whether the concept is feasible, producible, feasible and marketable. If not, can it be changed, can it still be simplified?

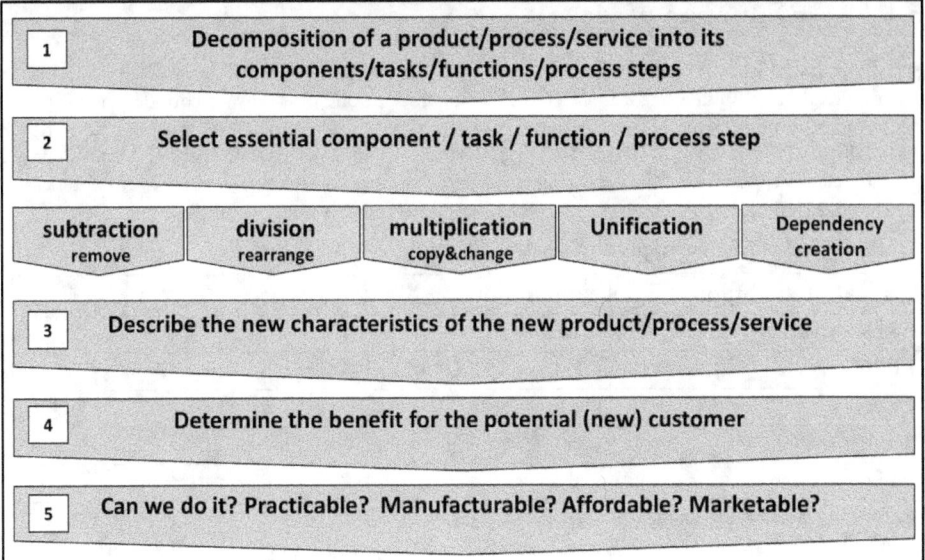

Figure 29: Procedure for the SIT Method

5.4 Evaluation of ideas

Strictly separated from this idea generation phase, it is then a matter of selecting promising ideas. Here again there are a multitude of idea evaluation techniques, but one must always consider the very early phase of the development. The uncertainty about the ideas, their feasibility, their profitability or their desirability is still very high. In this respect, one must select suitable evaluation methods that also have a strong qualitative character. The following table lists a number of techniques, each with references to the chapters or literature in which the method descriptions can be found.

Table 30: Evaluation techniques for Design Thinking

evaluation techniques	explanation
SWOT-Analyse	s. chapter 5.4.3
PPCO method	s. chapter 5.4.2
Checklist	s. chapter 5.4.1
Scoring model	s. chapter 5.4.5
Pair comparison	s. chapter 5.4.4
6-thinking hats/Walt-Disney method	s. chapter 5.3.1.7/5.3.18
Dot Voting (Dotcrazation)	Voting with adhesive dots, which each participant receives in a certain number and may distribute freely.
COCD-Box	Ideas are sorted into three fields based on the two dimensions of originality and difficulty of implementation: Now: Ideas that can be implemented immediately. Wow: Ideas that are very original and can be implemented. How: Ideas that are very original, but difficult to implement. With different coloured dots each participant can classify the ideas.
Card Sorting	Cards with suggestions will be ranked (see chapter 8.2.1).
Cherry picking	Each participant chooses his favourite and gives a brief explanation.
Pros-cons balance sheet	Arguments for and against are juxtaposed in tabular format.
I like, I wish, what if	Each evaluator should write what he likes about the selected ideas, how he would like this idea to be a solution, and how, in his opinion, the solution could be if anything were possible.
Opus method	The statements below on the developed ideas are written on cards and the evaluators sort these cards into boxes that say "I agree", "I partially agree", "I disagree", "I have no opinion". Statements about the ideas can be, for example: "Customers will buy the ideas because...", "The use of the idea is...", "The idea is superior to the competition because...", "The implementation of the idea will work, like...", "The financing of the idea will work because..." (according to Michalko (2006)).
Advocatus Diaboli vs. Advocatus Angeli	One person each slips into the role of critic (Advocatus Diaboli) and/or defender (Advocatus Angeli) of the idea.

5.4.1 Checklists / Pro-Cons lists

With the checklist you check binary different possibilities for each given idea. For each idea or alternative, a matrix is used to check whether the opportunity or risk exists (yes), whether the opportunity or risk does not exist (no), or whether a number is given that quantifies the opportunities or risks.

One lists the different possible chances and the different possible risks. Knock-out questions ("show stoppers") can also be formulated, which must always be answered with "yes". On the basis of these checklists, Pro-Cons lists can be derived which summarise the advantages and disadvantages of the idea.

In the checklist and review of ideas, e.g., the following questions are checked (based on Day (2007)):

Is the idea desirable/useful from the customer's point of view? "(**"Desirability"**/ **"Utility"**)

- Are customers identifiable?
- Is it possible to create a customer benefit with the idea? Does it satisfy (undiscovered) customer wishes?
- Does the idea fit into the innovation strategy and can it make a significant contribution to the strategy? Is the idea desired by top management?
- Is the idea accepted in the company? Does it fit in with the culture?
- Are there synergies to other products or competences of the company?
- Can learning effects be achieved for the company?
- Is the idea ethically desirable?

Is the idea feasible? "(**"Feasibility"**)

- Is the invention/idea new?
- Is the idea clear/understandable/traceable?
- Is the invention patentable? Easy to imitate?
- Are licenses/know-how from others necessary for the implementation?
- Is it technically feasible?
- Is it technically (easily) producible?
- Are high investments necessary for development, production and/or market introduction/distribution?
- Does the company have the necessary resources/competencies for implementation? If not, are these easily/quickly obtainable?
- Are partnerships with others (companies/research institutions) necessary or possible? Are they quick to implement?
- Are there high barriers to market entry?

Depending on the product, further criteria may be added e.g.:

- Is the product safe and reliable?
- Does the product have an attractive design?
- Are the required materials easily/quickly/cost-effectively procurable?
- Are the materials used robust, durable and of high quality, e.g. in their feel?
- Is the product easy to operate?
- Is the product easy/cost effective to maintain?
- Is the product (individually) adaptable/flexible to the wishes of the customer?
- Can the product or its production process be standardised?

Is the idea economical? "(**"Business Viability"**)

- Is there great purchasing power and willingness among customers?

5 How to find and select ideas

- Is the market attractive and growing (dynamic and long-term)?
- Is the expected return attractive?
- Are the risks determinable/quantifiable/acceptable?

Is the idea long-term or sustainable? "(**Sustainability/Scalability**")

- Are there advantages over existing (or possible new) competitor products?
- Are potential customers willing to pay for them in the long term?
- Is the idea scalable?
- Does the idea have ecological/social advantages?

Is the idea suitable for the dynamic environment? "(**Adaptability**")

- Is the idea adaptable or adaptable to the dynamically changing environmental situation?
- Is the idea adaptable to the political, social, economic, legal/regulatory framework conditions?
- Can further products for changing situations arise from it?
- Is the time of market launch ideal?

In addition, the following basic questions can be asked (see also the figure below):
- What is technically feasible? "**Feasibility**"
- What use is the idea ("**utility**") to people, how user-friendly (simple, intuitive to use) is the idea ("**usability**"), how emotionally appealing ("**emotionality**") is the idea or what do customers/users really desire/need? "**Desirability**"
- How economically viable or scalable is the idea? "**Viability**" or "**Scalability**"
- How sustainable is the idea? "**Sustainability**"
- How adaptable is the idea to the dynamically changing environment? "**Adaptability**"

"Feasibility", "Desirability" (with the components "Utility", "Usability" and "Emotionality") and "Viability" or "Scalability") describe the internal perspective of the assessment. Due to the volatility, uncertainty, complexity and ambiguity of the environment, the so-called VUCA-World, an external evaluation perspective with "adaptability" and "sustainability" is also required. These assessment areas are shown in the figure below.

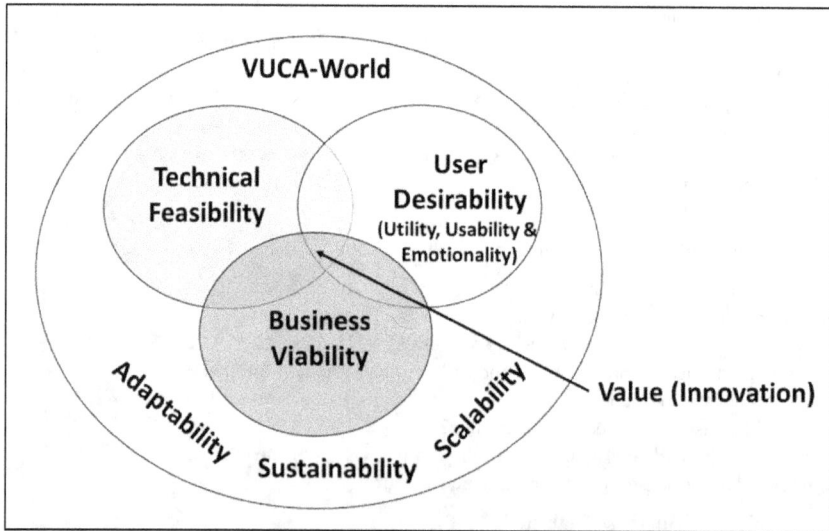

Figure 30: Assessment Areas of Innovations

5.4.2 PPCO method

The acronym PPCO stands for "Pluses" (positives of the idea), "Potentials" (potentials of the idea), "Concerns" and "Overcome Concerns". It was originally developed by Foucar-Szocki/Shepard/Firestein and further expanded by Lunken. With these four aspects the advantages and potentials or concerns as well as ideas for coping with these ideas are to be summarized briefly and clearly.

How to do it:
(according to Puccio et al. (2011))

Along the dimensions Pluses, Potentials, Concerns and Overcome Concerns, ideas are to be developed in the group for this purpose and represented in key words in the following matrix.

Pluses	Potentials
What do you like about the idea? What is unique/good about the idea? - Keyword A - Keyword B - Stichwort C - ...	What possibilities/opportunities do you see in the future with the idea? What are possible future gains from the idea? - Keyword A - Keyword B - Keyword C - ...
Concerns	**Overcome Concerns**
What concerns do you associate with the idea? - Keyword A - Keyword B - Keyword C - ...	How could these concerns be overcome? - Keyword A - Keyword B - Keyword C - ...

Figure 31: PPCO scheme
Source: According to Puccio et al. (2011)

5.4.3 SWOT Analysis

In principle, SWOT analysis can be used at the level of ideas to analyse the strengths ("strengths"), weaknesses ("opportunities") and risks ("threats") of one or more ideas.

How to do it:

The questions in the matrix below should be answered in keywords. Then the questions should be addressed on how to build on strengths, reduce weaknesses, seize opportunities and avoid risks. Suitable measures should be developed for this, which can be found, if necessary, by means of the creativity techniques listed in chapter 5.3.

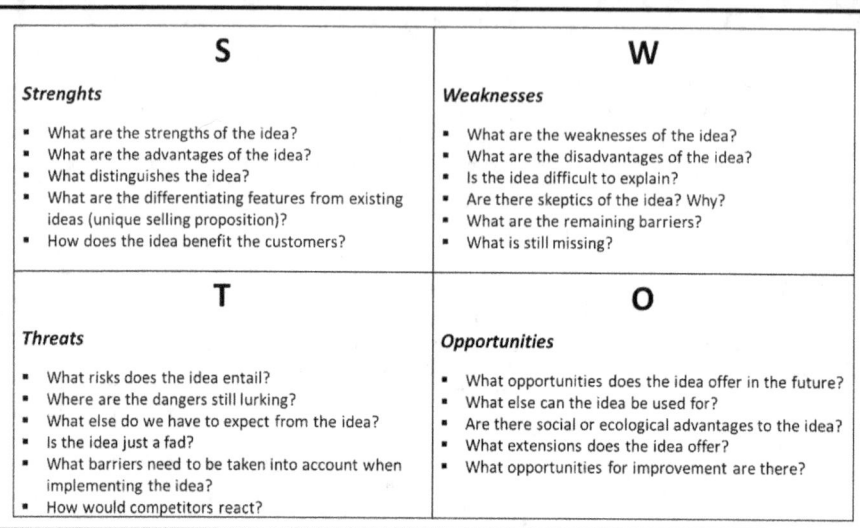

Figure 32: SWOT analysis for ideas

As already mentioned above, one should not concentrate on one idea, but also continue to pursue alternative ideas that initially appear sub-optimal (which one archives in a "memory of ideas").

5.4.4 Pair comparison method

If many ideas exist, it is recommended to first select ideas using the pair comparison method in a preference matrix (see figure below). All ideas are compared in pairs, i.e. each idea is compared with each other. The better idea is entered in the respective field with "1", equivalent ideas with "0" and worse ideas with "-1". The sum can be used to determine a ranking of the ideas. This method can also be used within the scoring procedure (see chapter 5.4.5) to determine the weighting factors of the individual evaluation criteria.

	idea 1	idea 2	idea 3	idea 4	idea 5	sum	rank
idea 1		-1	0	0	-1	-2	4.
idea 2	1		1	-1	1	2	2.
idea 3	0	-1		-1	-1	-3	5.
idea 4	0	1	1		1	3	1.
idea 5	1	-1	1	-1		0	3.

1 = better than
0 = equivalent
-1 = worse than

results logically from the information in the white fields

Figure 33: Preference matrix (pair comparison matrix)

5.4.5 Scoring Model

The scoring model is also referred to as the so-called Pugh matrix. In the scoring process, several project alternatives are compared using multidimensional evaluation criteria. Measurable, objective but also not directly measurable, subjective criteria can be considered. This form of analysis is used in particular when monetary quantifiable evaluation criteria are missing or difficult to formulate.

A scoring procedure is carried out in the following five steps:

- Definition of evaluation criteria
- Determination of weighting factors
- Evaluation of alternatives
- Determination of utility value and
- Determination of ranking order and selection

When defining the evaluation criteria, a matrix is created with the (most important) criteria that you want to evaluate. In the first column the criteria are written and in the first line the alternatives. In the second column, the weighting factor of each criterion is added.

According to Cooper (2011), the following evaluation criteria can be used, for example:

➢ **Strategic importance and fit**
- Strategic importance of the idea for the company
- Degree to which the idea harmonizes with the corporate strategy
- Influence on the business modell

➢ **Product attractiveness and competitiveness:**
- Perceptible benefit for the customer (value proposition)
- Significance for the customer
- Conformity with customer trends
- Novelty degree
- Differentiation advantages over competitors
- Sustainability of the competitive advantage
- Entry barrier for competitors
- Protection against imitation/patent situation

➢ **Market attractiveness**
- Market size and market growth rate (decreasing/constant/increasing (strong))
- Competitive situation
  (price competition/differentiation possible (easy/difficult)/monopoly position)
- Market entry barriers (high/medium/low/none)

➢ **Feasibility**
- Probability of technical application (low/medium/high)
- Development duration and development costs
- Technical complexity
- Technical Uncertainty
- Technological competence (if necessary in partnership) for development

Depending on the product, further criteria may be added, e.g.

- Product safety/reliability
- Product design
- Material availability/quality
- Product usability
- Maintenance friendliness
- Product adaptability
- Product standardizability

> **Synergy effects**
> - Learning effects: strengthens/deepens own technical know-how, specialist knowledge
> - Improves the production possibilities
> - Increases your company's marketing, sales and sales competence/resources
> - Strengthens the high-tech image
> - Possible follow-up projects/products

> **Return vs. risks**
> - High net present value
> - Attractive internal rate of return
> - Short payback period
> - Competitor development activities
> - Length of market phase
> - Familiarity with the market
> - Certainty over financial estimates

The selected criteria are to be standardised on a uniform scale (e.g. rating scale with 0 to 6 point system).

The weighting factors can either be determined by experts or derived from customer surveys. These assessments/surveys can be evaluated methodically to determine the weighting factors by simple point evaluations (or percentages) or by means of pair comparisons (see chapter 5.4.4), regression analyses or conjoint analyses. The weighting factors must ultimately be converted into a scale, e.g. with 0 ("irrelevant") to 5 ("very high significance").

The values are calculated using the following formula, where N_{sum} represents the total value, N_i the respective partial values and g_i the weighting factor of the respective evaluation criterion.

$$N_{sum} = \sum_{i=1}^{n} N_i \times g_i$$

Finally, the ranking of the different alternatives is established and a selection is made on this basis. The alternative with the highest overall benefit is called the most advantageous alternative and thus the "winner" among the various alternatives. An example of a scoring procedure with the corresponding evaluation matrix can be found in the table below.

Table 31: Evaluation matrix of the scoring modell

	valuation from 0 - 6	Weighting factors	idea 1		idea 2		idea 3	
			evaluation	partial value	evaluation	partial value	evaluation	partial value
evaluation criteria	Strategic importance and fit	0,2	5	1	2	0,4	5	1
	Product attractiveness and competitiveness	0,25	4	1	4	1	4	1
	Market attractiveness	0,15	4	0,6	3	0,45	3	0,45
	Feasibility	0,2	3	0,6	2	0,4	3	0,6
	Synergy effects	0,05	4	0,2	4	0,2	3	0,15
	Return vs. risks	0,15	4	0,6	3	0,45	3	0,45
	total value			4		2,9		3,65
	Ranking:		1.		3.		2.	

6

How to prototype

6 How to protoype

6.1	Prototype phase	143
6.2	Lean Startup Method for Prototype Development	144
6.2.1	Principles and benefits	144
6.2.2	How to lean startup	145
6.3	Visualization and presentation techniques	160

6 How to protoype

"People don't know what they want until you show it to them." – Steve Jobs

"Prototyping is the shorthand of innovation." – Kelley/Littman (2001): 101

After an introduction to the prototype phase (chapter 6.1), the lean startup method with its principles and procedures will be explained (chapter 6.2). Subsequently, further methods for the visualization and presentation of a prototype or a business idea are presented (see chapter 6.3) in order to systematically obtain customer feedback.

6.1 Prototype Phase

In this phase, the idea selected as the best is expanded into a design concept. In particular, it has to be clarified how the idea can be visualized and in particular made tangible in order to test it at and with the customer. If time and cost allow, further ideas are to be developed as alternatives in this sense. Ideally, several alternatives should be tested simultaneously and comparably. Strikingly Schrage (2014) speaks of the 5 x 5 x 5 x 5 x 5-formula: Five teams of five people each do five tests in five weeks for a maximum of five thousand dollars each.

The interaction with the potential customer/user is a decisive phase in the Design Thinking process. This can also lead to feedback on the previous phases (iterations) if the feedback from the customer results in the need for changes to the problem/need description or to the solution idea developed to date.

According to the rules **"Be visual and make it tangible!"** and **"Fail early and often!"**, the idea concepts are to be visualized as quickly and easily as possible or made tangible and comprehensible in order to test the effect on the customer and to learn from positive or, in particular, negative feedback. A variety of visualization and prototype techniques are available here, which are presented in more detail in chapter 6.3.

On the basis of the idea concept, it has to be clarified which visualization and prototype techniques should best be used. As a first step, it must be clear which goal is to be pursued, i.e. which aspects of the idea concept one would like feedback on from the customer:

- What do you want to learn from customers/users with the help of surveys, interviews, observations, surveys, prototype tests, pilot applications?
- How uncertain are the results?
- What can you not experience?

The time and cost budget is also a factor to consider when selecting visualization and prototyping techniques. In addition, the degree of maturity of the idea determines the choice of the appropriate visualization and prototype technology. The more immature the idea is, the simpler the prototype will be. In the following section, the lean startup method is used to introduce an approach based on early customer feedback on a minimally designed prototype.

6.2 Lean Startup Method for Prototype Development

6.2.1 Principles and benefits

The Lean-Startup™ method ("Lean Startup is a trademark and service by Eric Ries") by Eric Ries (2014) is a concept to get customer feedback early and quickly by means of experiments in product/service and business model development and to change one's own business idea if necessary. It is quasi an experimental approach, since (measurable) hypotheses are formed based on the business assumptions, which are then tested for their validity. This concept is particularly suitable for products that have short product development cycles, but ideas for more complex products and services can also be tested at an early stage. In the highly regulated area (pharmaceutical development), however, this approach can only be used to a limited extent.

The lean concept is based on the following principles, among others:

- **Plan less, experiment more:**
  No long range planning, but fast **"learning-by-doing"** through early customer feedback by means of experiments. Blank (2014) speaks here of **"Get out of the building"**, because there are no facts in one's own office.

- **Minimize the effort:**
  A Minimum Viable Product (MVP) should be created for customer feedback. A minimum functional prototype of the product or service should be created, which allows to get a measurable customer feedback about one or a few (new) features (according to the motto: "Try it, make it, fix it").

- **Fix early:**
  Customer feedback always requires price corrections and regular minor changes (iterations) or, if necessary, larger changes, the so-called **pivots**. The term pivot comes from basketball, where you change your direction with the ball while keeping one foot on the ground. When changing direction, you don't just throw away your knowledge, you base the whole thing on your wealth of experience. In an early phase of innovation such pivots are quite common and frequent. In a later phase they should occur less and less.

- **Tolerate, no, even expect failures:**
  Failure is an integral part of this approach and should be tolerated, accepted and even expected by all parties involved.

Benefits of the Lean Startup:

- Overcomes the misconception that you already know everything the customer wants. This can only be proven in experiments with facts.
- The basis for business decisions is therefore less subjective estimates and (corporate) political reasons, but rather fact-based market feedback.
- Overcomes the so-called "conformation bias", which is based on the false assumption that one pays more attention to information that confirms what one expects or knows anyway.
- Helps to overcome risk aversion, fear that one's own assumptions are not correct.
- Systematic "stress test" to eliminate customer/market uncertainties.
- Answers the crucial questions for a lucrative business model: Have you found a problem/need that many people want you to solve/satisfy? Does your product/service solve the problem in a convincing way? And are customers willing to pay for it?

- Leads to founding a successful company or a new business area with as few investments as possible in advance.

Basically, the concept is not only suitable for start-ups, but it is also – with adaptations – useful for established large companies.

According to the above mentioned principles, the own (business) statements and beliefs should be transformed into hypotheses and then verified (validated) in experiments together with the customer. The requirement here is always to carry out experiments that can be carried out quickly and with little effort (what market feedback do we need for our assumption?).

6.2.2 How to lean startup

Following and supplementing Olsen (2015), the following procedure is proposed:

1. Select a suitable customer segment that has a common problem/need, for which you want to offer a solution.
2. Identify the assumptions about the customers, their problems/needs, their product or service range and the business model components and form measurable hypotheses from them ("hypothesize"). Always ask yourself step by step which insights you need to gain in order to continue.
3. Create a test design, e.g. in the form of a Minimum Viable Product (MVP) ("Design").
4. Test this hypothesis in an experiment, by observe/question ("test").
5. Measure the result and learn from it ("learn") by
   A) If confirmed, test the next hypothesis
   B) In the case of ambiguous results, go back to previous hypotheses (e.g. Who is actually the customer? What problem does he really have?) or
   C) If the hypothesis is not confirmed, a pivot (substantive change of direction).

Steps 2-5 are to be carried out in the form of a feedback loop for each of the following topics: customers, product/service offering and business model.

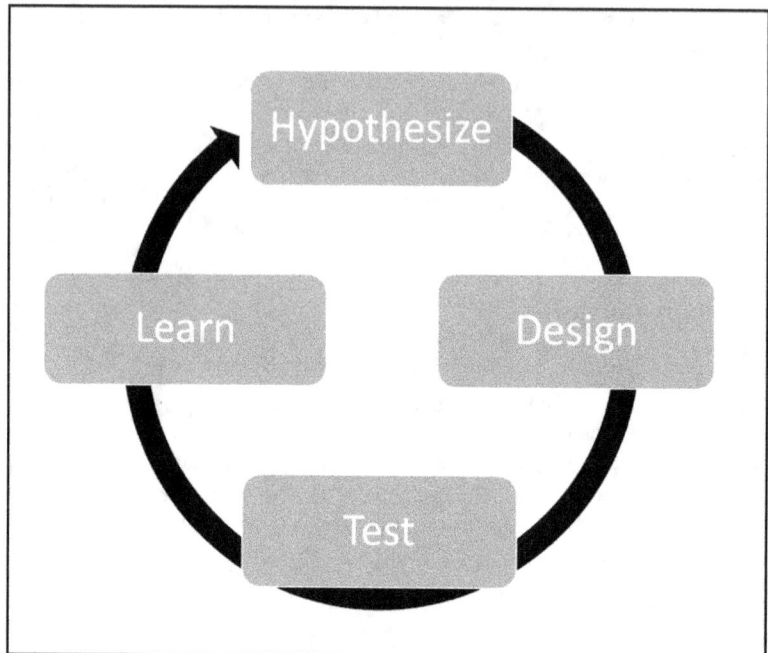

Figure 34: Hypthesize-Design-Test-Learn-cycle
Source: According to Olsen (2015), S. 169

In the following, the above steps are explained in detail and tips for their implementation are given.

Selection of customer segments

The usual marketing approach for segmenting end customers according to geographical or demographic criteria (e.g. place of residence, age, gender, married/disabled, income, educational level) or corporate customers according to size, industry, market positioning, etc. is (initially) not very helpful for highly innovative business ideas. Likewise, purely socio-psychological criteria (attitudes, opinions, values, interests, etc.) or (purchasing) behaviour-related criteria (price sensitivity, type of buying, etc.) are only of limited use.

It is more effective to segment customers in a problem- or need-oriented way. This means that customers with the same/similar problem or need are categorized as one segment. A specific solution (product/service) should also be developed for this problem/need. Following Christensen (1997), Ulwick (2005) speaks of "Jobs-to-be-done", i.e. what should be done to solve a specific problem or satisfy the customer's need (see chapter 4.3.1 for details). This customer task-oriented approach can be further differentiated into functional (certain functions/characteristics/activities in products/services), social (prestige, status) and emotional (e.g. "cool" to have/do something) "jobs-to-be-done".

In this sense, both questions are therefore posed simultaneously for segmentation purposes:

> ➤ **What is the concrete problem/need ("jobs-to-be-done") and**
> ➤ **who has this problem/need?**

These two questions are often inseparable.

If a larger group of people has the problem/need, it makes sense both for the lean startup method and for the later market launch phase to focus on a sub-segment first. For pragmatic reasons, it makes sense to initially concentrate on an easily accessible customer sub-segment (easily accessible via media, existing distribution channels) and/or on a customer sub-segment with particularly high purchasing power.

For the hypothesis-driven approach that follows, it is also advisable to look for a particular group of (potential) customers: The so-called Innovators/Early Adopters (Steve Blank (2014) speaks of "early evangelists"). This group has often been the first to recognize the problem/need or feel it is serious. In addition, these customers are already actively looking for solutions and may already have developed their own initial solutions. They often have purchasing power and accept even the not yet perfect solution. The latter is particularly helpful when MVPs (see below) have to be tested.

The selected customer segment (ideally the "early evangelists" mentioned above) with the same problem/need should then be further characterized. For this, it is advisable to first create three to four personas (the method is explained in chapter 4.2). The above-mentioned geographical, demographic, socio-psychological and behavioural criteria can now also be included, provided they are relevant.

In this context, the question of who influences the persona in purchasing decisions should also be asked. Are influencers e.g. partners, family members, friends, acquaintances, certain media, bloggers, reference customers, experts/opinion leaders etc.? In the B2B business, end users, influencers, internal/external recommendations, buyers, decision makers and even saboteurs (who oppose any innovation) can be differentiated. It can also be helpful to create personas for these people and to include them in the subsequent hypothesis formation and testing in order to gain a better understanding.

Through this further characterization, it can also become obvious that the personas have the same problem/need, but they differ in other business model-relevant characteristics. For example, other communication and sales channels are required, the customer relationship is different (online vs. personal advice) or customer loyalty must be different. Therefore, the following hypotheses should be made and evaluated specifically for the respective persona.

Another interesting approach is to create an anti-customer segment with persona (Cooper/Vlaskovits (2014)), in which one asks oneself what are the reasons why these customers would not buy the product/service.

For further analysis, the Empathy Map method (see chapter 3.4.3) and a Customer Journey (see chapter 3.4.7) can also be used.

How to Hypthesize

Theoretically, a hypothesis is a statement that can clearly be proven to be false (falsifiable). Hypotheses often take the form of statements like "if ..., then ...." or "the more ..., the less / more ...". In connection with the Lean Startup Method, hypotheses can be formulated as follows:

> **IF** – statement e.g. about customer segment, customer problem or product/service offering, business model component -,
>
> **THEN** – statement about (qualitative/quantitative) customer/market feedback or change of a certain key figure.

In other words, the hypothesis is that an observation or a specifically repeatable activity, which is understood as an independent variable, leads to an expected measurable outcome at the customer/market, which is mathematically understood as a dependent variable. In practice, of course, numerous other factors (disturbance variables) often have an influence on the result.

The hypotheses should be as specific and focused as possible. Specific means, among other things, that the hypotheses are tailored to a persona. The more focused the hypothesis is, the faster one can learn from it. In addition, the broader and more general the statement, the more ambiguous the answers become. It is better to be wrong with a concrete statement than to express something too vaguely. The motto is: "Fail fast to succeed sooner". If the hypothesis is too extensive, it should be broken down into subhypotheses.

Hypotheses can be derived either from intuitive (inputs) estimates (abductive), from already known observations / results (inductive) or from theoretical considerations (deductive). It is recommended to use all three variants if possible and not just one (Furr/Dyer (2014)).

The following topic complexes should be tested step by step by hypotheses in order to learn from the results:

Customers:
- Hypotheses on the customer segment (Who are the customers?)
- Hypotheses on the customer problem/need (What problems/needs do they have?)

Product/service offering:
- Hypotheses on product positioning strategy (In which respect is the offer different/superior? What are the competitive advantages?)

Business model:
- Hypotheses on pricing (What price do customers accept?)
- Hypotheses on the sales channel
- (Which sales channel should be used how?)
- Hypotheses on customer acquisition (How can customers be won?)
- Customer retention hypotheses (How can customers be retained?)
- Sales growth hypotheses (How to increase sales?))

The hypotheses are to be written down and best documented in the form of a hypothesis list with their results.

Hypotheses regarding the customer

The hypotheses on the customer (segment) must answer the questions: Who does what, how much, when and why.

Table 32: Hypothesis list customers

IF Statement	THEN measuring criterion (How can the statement be verified?)
The customers ("early evangelists") can be characterized by A)_____, B)_____, C)_____ etc. (your assumptions)	
Customers are influenced at X (e.g. purchase decision, product usage) by _____ (your assumptions)	
The influence is shown by the fact that _____ (your assumptions).	
The customer uses the product/service X _____ hours per day (your assumptions).	operating time
The customer is online _____ hours per day (your assumption).	online time
The customer is _____ hours a day (your assumption) in location X.	
The customer uses the device X _____ (your assumption) per week.	
The customer visits _____ (your assumption) place Y per week.	

Hypotheses regarding the customer problem/needs

The examination of the hypotheses regarding the customer's problem/need is exclusively concerned with the customer's current situation. Speculative questions (what would you like to know?) should be avoided or only addressed briefly at the end (see chapter 7.2.). One should also concentrate on the problem/need and not on a possible solution.

The problem/need can be present at the customer in the following form (one should consider this with the questions and with the evaluation):

- **Latent problem/need:** Customers have it, but don't know it/are not aware of it.
- **Passive problem/need:** The customers know the problem/need, but are not motivated/willing to change anything.
- **Active (urgent) problem/need:** The customers know the problem/need and are already looking for a solution/a suitable offer.

In addition, the above-mentioned innovators ("early evangelists") among the customers often already have an idea of how the problem/need could be solved/satisfied and would be willing to pay for its implementation.

Before and/or after testing the following hypotheses or questions to the customer, it is highly recommended to conduct a customer journey (see chapter 3.4.7). The problems ("pain points") and emotions of the customer can be analyzed step by step. In order to analyse the deeper causes of customer problems, it is particularly useful to obtain greater clarity by asking the customer why. Likewise afterwards an effect and cause analysis (see chapter 2.4.5) is very helpful.

Table 33: Hypothesis list Customer problem/need

IF Statement	THEN measuring criterion (How can the statement be verified?)
The customers are the most bothered / annoyed / frustrated by A)_____, B)_____, C) _____ etc. (your assumptions).	Frequency of mentioning in interviews
The customer has the following problem _____ (your assumption).	Frequency of mentioning
The customer must overcome the following restrictions/obstacles when selecting / using X _____ (your assumption).	Frequency of mentioning
The problem causes _____ at the customer (cost and/or time expenditure; administrative/organizational expenditure) (your assumptions).	Indication of cost/time expenditure or organisational expenditure
The problem occurs _____ per week for the customer.	Frequency
The customer is currently investing _____ minutes/hours (your assumption) to solve the problem.	average time expenditure
The customer is currently using _____ (alternative) to solve the problem.	Frequency of mentioning
The reason why the own and alternative solution are unsatisfactory for the customer is _____ (your assumption).	Frequency of mentioning
From the customer's point of view, the cause of the problem is _____ (your assumption).	Frequency of mentioning
The customer does not perceive the problem because_____ (your assumption).	Frequency of mentioning
The customer is most enthusiastic/motivated forA)_____, B)_____, C) _____ etc. (your assumptions).	Frequency of mentioning

Further general and in-depth questions on the customer problem/need:

Please explain to me how you use X during the day. Can you please describe the (process) steps to perform X? What do you do before/after? Is there anything you would use but can't do? What would they want to do better?
[Note: To prepare and structure this question, use the Customer Journey method, see chapter 3.4.4].

- When and for how long did you last use X? Was this possible without any problems? If not, why not?
- Other interview partners have told me the following_____. Have they had similar experiences/impressions? If not, why not?
- Please describe the environment in which you used X? Have you used/needed to use special tools/devices/methods/tricks?
- Who is involved in the decision to use/purchase X from you (in the company/at home)? Please describe the decision-making process? Were there any delays/questions, if so, why?
- How much time/money would they (be able to) spend on solving your problem?
- Is the problem related to another problem?
- Do you know the current possibilities to solve the problem?
- Have you ever actively searched for a solution (e.g. via Google) and with what result?
- If they had a magic wand, what would they want to do better? What would inspire them? Think also about functions / tasks / activities that do not seem feasible today.
- Do you know people who have similar problems/needs as you?
- Are there any other aspects I haven't asked that are relevant to you?
- Could you please name other people I could also contact in the matter.
- Would they be available for further interviews/product testing at a later stage of development?

In order to summarize the results of the previous investigations briefly and concisely, the use of so-called user stories (see chapter 4.3) is helpful. User stories are a method that originates from agile project management (see chapter 8.5).

User stories are short sentences in the following form:

As a _____ (customer type – here are the results about the characteristic features of the customer (see above) to insert)

I would like to _____, (to be empowered to something / to get a problem solved – here are the main results to add to the customer problem / need)

so that I _____ (desired result from customer view – insert results see above).

Bill Wake (2003) has set the following requirements for writing good user stories, which he summarizes with the acronym INVEST:

- **I(ndependent):** User stories should be independent of each other.
- **N(egotiable):** How to fulfill the customer's wish should be discussed in discussion with the customer (be negotiable with the customer).
- **V(aluable):** A good user story has a high value for the customer.
- **E(stimable):** The scope of the user story can be estimated.
- **S(mall):** User stories should not be too extensive, or their insecurity will increase.
- **T(estable):** The result of a user story should be clearly measurable (testable).

Hypotheses regarding the product/service offering

Based on the customer problems/needs examined, these should be listed and compared with the current or planned offers (see table below).

Table 34: Comparison of current solution with planned offer

Problem/need	Current solution	Planned offer
1. problem/need A		
2. problem/need B		
3. problem/need C		

In the previous step, customers should already have evaluated the correctness and order of these problems.

With the hypotheses on the planned product/service offering, it is not advisable to ask speculative and/or abstract questions as to whether customers would like/find/buy something good etc. that they themselves have not yet seen or tried out.

Rather, the techniques described below should be used to create a **Minimum Viable Product (MVP)**, asking the customer/user for concrete evaluations or activities related to the new features/functions/subscription elements. In doing so, you should always concentrate on one new characteristic/property/function/offer element for each test.

Table 35: Hypothesis list for product/service offer

IF Statement	THEN measuring criterion (How can the statement be verified?)
The following features/functions/offer elements are what customers like best (or worst) among competitors _____.	Frequency of mentioning in interviews
From the customer's point of view, the new feature/property/function/offer element is better than the current possibilities (possibly competitor products/services) for the following reasons _____ (your assumptions).	Frequency of mentioning in interviews
The satisfaction/enthusiasm for the new feature/property/function/offer element in our business idea is reflected in _____ (feedback/activity of the customer) (your assumptions).	Criterion depends on selected MVP (see below)
The new characteristic/feature/function/offer element enables customers to do the following _____ (your assumptions).	Observation or frequency of mentioning in interviews
The new characteristic/feature/function/offer element changes the following for the customer _____ (your assumptions).	Observation or frequency of mentioning in interviews
The new characteristic/feature/function/offer element allows customers to save time and/or money by _____ (hours/US$).	Money or time amount (US$/h)

The planned product/service offering (benefit promise) should be condensed into one simple sentence. This brings the Unique Selling Proposition (USP) to the point. Moore (2014) has developed a scheme for this as follows:

For _____ (customer target group) **who need** _____ (product/service offer).
_____ (product/service name) **is a** _____ (product/service category) **that provides** _____ (important advantage), **unlike** _____ (main competitor) **with** _____ (product name of competitor) (most important differentiation).

Net Promoter Score (NPS)

The Net Promotor Score (NPS) was developed by Reichheld (2003) and allows a simple question from the customer's point of view to evaluate either the product/service offering or even the entire company. The question that customers should answer is as follows:

How likely is it that you would recommend our product/service offering (or our company) to a friend or colleague?

From 10: extremely likely to 0: not likely at all

Three groups are formed according to the response behaviour:

"Promotors" answer with 9 to 10, "Passives" with 7 to 8 and "Detractors" with 0 to 6.

To calculate the NPS, the percentage of "Detractors" is subtracted from the percentage of "Promotors" (see following figure), with an NPS of +50. This NPS can also be tracked as an indicator over time.

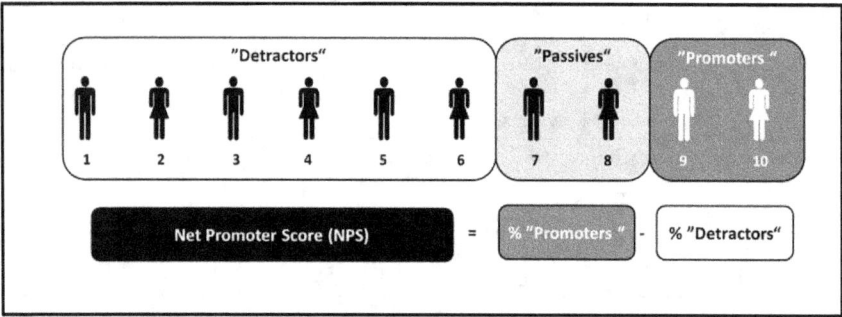

Figure 35: Calculation of the Net Promoter Score
Source: Accordingt to Furr/Dyer (2014), p. 133

Sean-Ellis-Test:

The Sean Ellis test is an equally simple way to have customers evaluate the potential of a product/service offering in a condensed form (Maurya (2013): 158). The following question is put to the customers:

How would you feel if this product/service no longer existed?

- Very disappointed
- Somewhat disappointed
- Not disappointed
- No specification/I do not use it

The goal is that more than 40% give the answer "very disappointed".

Viral coefficient:

Whether the product/service offering has the potential to spread virally can be assessed with the viral coefficient, which can be calculated as follows:

(1) The number of users multiplied by the average number of recommendations of these users
(2) Determine the average conversion rate of these recommended users (i.e. how many users in percent were activated to do something): For example, buying something, registering on a website, "downloading" something, etc.)
(3) Number of activated users = How much are X % (2) of the (1)
(4) Number of activated users/old users = coefficient

A coefficient below (1) means stagnation.

Design of the prototype test

When selecting the appropriate prototype test methods for the hypotheses, one should always ask which is the simplest test to perform in order to arrive at a certain conclusion. Use the above hypotheses to think about what you want to find out at all. Then it has to be clarified by which answers of the customer a hypothesis could be (unambiguously) validated at all. Finally, it must be clarified how this information can be obtained most quickly and easily.

In addition, you should always set yourself a clear time and cost budget for the implementation. The tests should never last longer than two to three months.

As test methods the classical test methods or MVPs briefly described in the following come into question. Also a combination of the test methods to the same hypothesis complex could be goal-prominent.

Classical test methods

Contextual Interview/Inquiry of customer
If the environment is important or if you want to observe the customer/user in a particular activity, surveys or observations on site are very useful (tips on observations can be found in chapter 3 and on oral or written surveys in chapter 7.2 or 7.3). It is also possible to analyse activities carried out by several people at the same time. However, these test methods are time-consuming, costly and difficult to coordinate. In the case of end consumers, problems with privacy can then arise or customers can change their behaviour as a result of observation or questioning on the spot (uncertainty relation).

Interviews on neutral location
These interviews can be conducted undisturbed and without distraction. However, this is also time-consuming and costly or even more difficult to coordinate.

Phone interviews
A simple method of choice are phone interviews. This makes it easy to reach busy people or people in distant places. A larger number of interviews can be conducted efficiently. Notes can also be taken undisturbed. However, no gestures or facial expressions can be observed – this can be a serious disadvantage with certain product/service offers. In addition, no physical MVP (see below) can be shown to the customer.

Video Chats
Video chats can (partially) compensate for this disadvantage. However, this method is more recommended for customers with an affinity for technology. In addition, additional information can be exchanged electronically.

Instant Messaging
Instant messaging can be used for customers who are afraid of verbal communication or do not want any image transmission. However, misinterpretations of the statements are often possible – despite the use of so-called emoticons.

E-mails
E-mails can be used to exchange questions and answers electronically with a time delay. Especially when interviewing customers in distant places and in other time zones, e-mails can be a way. Customers can also answer questions at a time that suits them.

Online survey
A rather impersonal possibility to get customer feedback about concrete hypotheses is the use of online surveys with a questionnaire. The response rates here are often rather low. However, in order to reach a large number of people or to achieve quantifiable statements quickly, online surveys can still be effective. For support there are also some software solutions (surveymonkey, wufo, survey.io).

Focus groups/customer clinics/Usability-Tests/Live Testing
In a moderated group discussion, products are evaluated by (potential) customers/users. The individual participants should come into contact with each other and share their opinions and assessments of the product/service. The number of participants should be limited between 5 and a maximum of 12 and should have a balanced mix (in terms of age, gender, educational background, concern with the topic, hobbies, character traits, etc.). It is best that participants do not know each other beforehand.

These test methods are suitable in a late development phase or shortly before market launch. However, an existing product/service offering is already expected by the customers, only in this way can meaningful results be drawn from this type of customer feedback. Group dynamic effects can also falsify the results.

The usability of (quasi) finished products under known and constant conditions can be tested by usability tests, for which customers are invited and with or into a moderator the product in use is tested and observed (possibly even filmed) and/or questioned. A systematic evaluation of the discussions and interviews, e.g. via a qualitative content analysis, is recommended.

Eye-Tracking System: With Eye-Tracking System it is possible to evaluate what people look at in turn when they see a product, environment, website, etc. Heatmaps can also be used to analyze the eye behavior through the colors yellow, orange and red in detail, whereby the more saturated the color is, the more often the eyes are focused on individual regions.

MVPs as test methods

The creation of a Minimum Viable Product (MVP) is a very good way to get meaningful information from potential customers, especially for innovation projects. Instead of "products" it is better to talk about "prototypes", because it is not about saleable offers. Although MVPs are particularly suitable for (physical) product developments, service offerings can also be tested prototypically with some of the approaches mentioned below. When creating an MVP – as already mentioned above – the simplest method should be chosen in order to arrive at a certain conclusion. It is not a question of testing a quasi-finished (perfect) product, but quite the opposite: Individual functions / characteristics of the product / service offer are to be checked by the customer. Each additional function is to be regarded as a waste. If, in hypothesis testing, the customer wants to have more functions, then these should be integrated in the next MVP.

When creating an MVP, one wants to avoid high investments for the product development, therefore one should always carry out these tests either with very low costs or at least with a high proportion of variable costs. This means that for the MVPs one should borrow, lease, use freely available resources (e.g. software) or use external solutions or service providers. Another factor that speaks for a simple MVP is the time factor. You want to get customer feedback as quickly as possible to reduce uncertainty during development. The maxim when creating or selecting the MVP is: As simple as possible, as meaningful as necessary.

Consequently, in the protype test this means that one always tests with only one function or a change of function. A prototype should always answer only one hypothesis/question.

The benefit of MVPs is to save costs, quickly generate customer knowledge and learn from it. Either the hypothesis tested with an MVP is confirmed or the hypothesis is refuted and a change of direction must be made (a so-called "pivot").

When selecting one of the following MVPs, one should not only ask which information is required for the hypothesis to be examined, but also clarify which person, with which background knowledge and ideas will interact with the MVP. Clarify in advance what you actually want to test and what you expect from the customer, how he should react to the prototype.

Drawings or design of models

Drawings and photo collages of product/service offerings on paper, whiteboard or electronic devices (laptop, smartphone, tablet) are the easiest and fastest way to create an MVP. Product design, but also sketches for the visualization of the customer's problem/need or for functions/features of the planned product/service are possible.

It is also possible to evaluate future marketing material (flyers, brochures, product information, website, etc.) or images of competitors by the customer. For example, potential customers can be shown the material for five seconds and then asked what they can remember and how it worked. Simple models made of paper/cardboard/modelling clay/styrofoam/foam etc. can symbolize or imitate certain functions/features/properties. The use of 3D printers allows very impressive MVPs with little effort. Disadvantages are the often even more abstract representations and the difficulty to use such simple MVPs for service offers or technically complex product developments. At least for the internal purposes of product development they are indispensable.

Storytelling/Comics/Lego Serious Games

The narration of a fictitious or real story, e.g. about a prototypical customer (persona), his daily routine and his problems or needs, can be given to customers with a request for feedback (Is this also the case with them?). Is it different? If so, how? What would they add/remove in the story?). For the storytelling see in detail chapter 6.3. This enables the customer to put himself in a situation better and compare it with his situation. In addition to the narrative form, the whole thing can also be presented as a comic. For this purpose, there are some tools on the internet to create comics for such purposes yourself (www.wittycomics.com; bitstrips.com; stripcreator.com).

Lego has published the Lego Serious Games series to recreate situations in the business world with Lego characters. Also service offers can be presented with the sequence of single Lego scenes. All this serves as an illustration to approach the subject from a different (more abstract) perspective and, if necessary, to avoid blindness to the company.

Wireframe

So-called wireframes can be used to display the first visual representations of control elements/buttons ("user interfaces") that will later be used on a website, on displays, on electronic devices or on other projection surfaces. The control elements/buttons/websites are only schematically displayed and are intended to show the position and size of symbols or, if necessary, to use text in the form of placeholders. For the latter one could use "lorem ipsum" texts, but this is not recommended, as these would only confuse the customer and short correct texts do not represent a substantial additional expenditure. These wireframes can be drawn by hand, made from paper/cardboard or digitally created with appropriate software tools. These control elements/symbols can also be changed in position and size by the customer himself. Wireframes can also be "clickable", i.e. certain buttons/symbols can be clicked to call up another page or function. To minimize the effort, only the symbols that you want to test can be clicked. This is also referred to as the "Happy Path" of the customer, i.e. clicking on the wireframes is deliberately designed to be simple and clear. This incompleteness can motivate customers even more than perfectly styled templates, as they get the feeling that they can really make a difference with their feedback at an early stage.

Mockups

Mockups are already more extensively designed websites. Mockups already use typography, colors, symbols, as it could be visualized in the later design. The basic structure of the control elements is there, but without being fully functional.

Website/Landing Page

A website is created and visitors (traffic) for this website are mobilized (e.g. via Google AdWords, advertising, partner programs). This website (also called "landing page") describes either only the problem or already a possible solution, which can be tried out depending on the stage of development of the product/service offer. The user of this website can register with his contact data for more information or for a newsletter or for a notification when the product is available. Registration measures the conversion rate, i.e. how many visitors convert to actively interested parties.

In addition to registration, it is also possible to evaluate the customer's clicking on certain buttons. The comparison of different versions of a website using so-called A/B testing (see box below) is a widespread method of evaluation. Numerous software tools are available for this purpose, which enable detailed analyses of visitor behaviour. In addition, one should provide recommendation possibilities and evaluate these. It is important to use the appropriate buttons and forms to give clear or multiple redundant requests for action ("call-to-actions") in order to register, obtain more information, download a free copy, etc.

A simplifying variant can be the so-called "fake door" or also "404 page". Here, after a request to click on a button, one is led either to a page where one thanks for the interest and refers to the structure of the offer ("Under Construction") or the forwarding leads to nothing (display: "Page not found"; in HTML this is the so-called "404 Page" error message). This variant is only used to test the interest of the customer: "Fake it till you make it". However, this annoys potential customers.

A/B-Testing (split testing) Two groups (A and B) of users alternately face randomly selected different versions of a website, a prototype or image material. Possible differences in reaction/user behavior are analysed in these (both) groups. The differences between the versions should preferably only show up in one feature/function/activity, otherwise the result will not be unambiguous. These versions should also be available at the same time in order to minimize time influences. Theoretically more than two versions are possible (A/B-n testing). This method is only suitable for larger sample sizes. For the use of websites, there are numerous software tools available to perform A/B testing or to evaluate the results statistically.

Videos

With similar goals, a video can also be created about the (supposed) customer problem/need or the planned product/service offering. In so-called simple explanatory videos, even complex facts can be schematically explained for the customer first and then requested to act in the sense of customer feedback. For the production of such explanation videos there are already comfortable software Tools. The installation of possibilities of the registration and/or forwarding and/or a left to the Website/Landing Page serves the Hypothesentestung. As with the Website/Landing Page, the user behavior can be evaluated in detail using appropriate software analysis tools.

Concierge-MVP

With concierge MVP, a customer order for the test phase is executed manually, which is later to be automated/online in the business model. Eric Ries (2012): 93 coined the term concierge MVP for this. Before a (perfect) automated technical solution is created with a lot of time and money, the principle or offer is tested on the customer's premises. For the manual processing of individual customer orders, this can initially be time-consuming, but one learns a lot. This way, you know exactly how to execute the process, what the customer is asking for, what he is willing to pay, etc.

Wizard-of-Oz-MVP

Same approach as concierge MVP, but the customer does not know that the background process is manual. This means that the customer thinks his order is largely automated. As in the classic film Wizard of Oz, something happens behind a curtain. So here is the approach: "Fake it till you make it!"

Open-Source-Prototypen

For the cost-effective creation of technical prototypes based on hardware/software modules, there are several platforms on the Internet that offer standard modules for specific applications with sensors, actuators, displays and software solutions, etc.

3D-Rapid-Prototyping

Use of 3D printers, laser cutters, digital 3D models, etc.

Crowdfunding

Originally intended primarily for financing at an early stage, crowdfunding also offers the benefit of meaningful customer feedback and the opportunity to come into contact with a variety of early evangelists. The success in attracting funds from small investors, who can also be potential customers, serves to validate the product/service offering. Experience can also be used for pricing purposes. However, this method is more likely to be used in a later development phase.

Business Model Canvas

The Business Model Canvas by Osterwalder/Pigneur (2010) is also suitable for outlining the essential components of a business model vividly and in a condensed form and for discussing them with external persons or developing them further afterwards.

6.3 Visualization and presentation techniques

An essential rule in the Design Thinking process is to make one's own understanding of a situation/problem/need or one's thoughts about possible solutions visible and tangible as quickly as possible in order to receive qualified feedback either internally from the Design Thinking team or, in particular, externally from e.g. customers.

A variety of visualization techniques are available, which are listed in the following table.

Table 36: Visualization type

Visualization type	Tips
line chart	<ul><li>Present developments</li><li>3-4 lines maximum</li><li>With max. 2 lines: Labeling on the lines</li><li>Use different shapes, color</li><li>Axes thicker than single lines</li><li>Draw the zero point</li></ul>
bar chart — comparison	<ul><li>Bar charts for size comparisons</li><li>Display bars in 2-D (no shadows, otherwise it distracts)</li><li>Display bars in 2-D (no shadows, only distracts)</li><li>Use different colours/raster</li><li>Do not enter the name in the bars</li><li>Numerical values above or next to bars</li></ul>
pie chart — sales	<ul><li>Pie chart for ratio of partial quantities to total quantity</li><li>Delimit areas with color or rasterization</li><li>Labelling outside with connecting lines if necessary</li><li>Circle=100 %</li><li>Highlighting by color or pulling out of the circle</li></ul>

6 How to protoype

Venn diagram 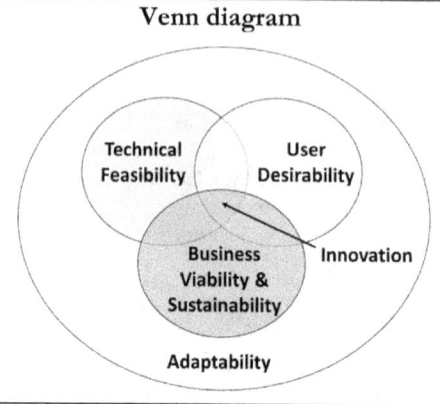	- Use cases of the Venn diagram are e.g. the evaluation of ideas (see diagram above) as well as the representation of different customer needs. - The intersections of the circles symbolise similarities or possible combinations of features/functions/activities that can represent new goals or potentials for new ideas.
Radar Chart/Spiderweb Diagram (polar coordinate diagram) 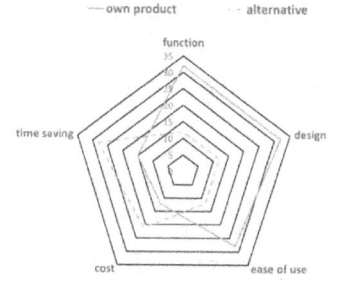	With radar charts, or spider web charts or polar coordinate charts, each evaluation criterion has an axis that has the same numerical values from the inside to the outside. The axes are arranged in a circle. The values of each idea are connected with each other.
2X2 matrix 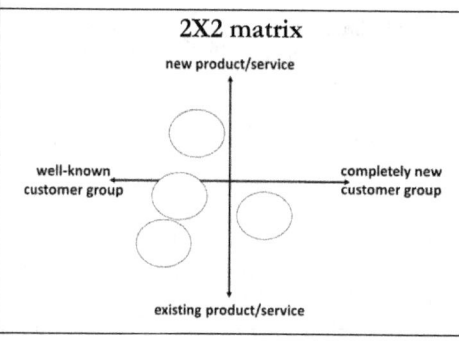	- Classify customer groups/products along two dimensions - Gaps can open up new possibilities

Matrix 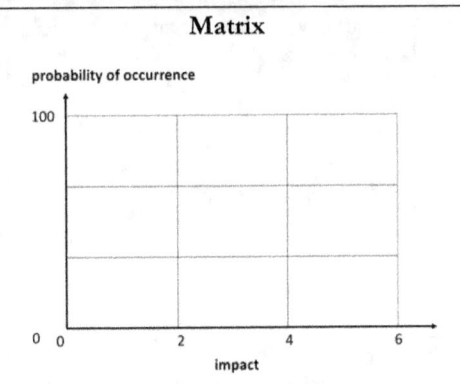	▪ Can be differentiated as 9 or 16 field matrix using two dimensions ▪ Dimensions should be independent of each other
Mind Mapping 	Mind mapping focuses on the topic. It is written in the middle of the sheet and surrounded by a circle. Branches fork outfrom this, which divide and fan out the topic into its individual areas. Keywords are written on the branches. Topics represent the main branches. Details are written to the branches (see chapter 5.3.2.2).
Network Diagram (Concept Mapping/Cognitive Mapping) 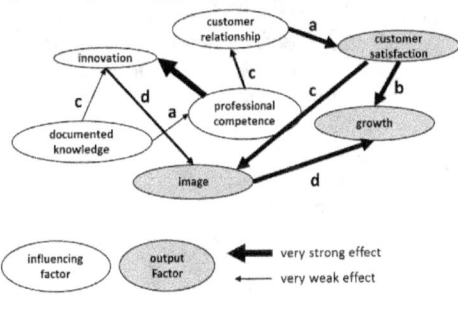	Network diagrams can be used to show correlations in a visualized form. For example, statements by persons, descriptions of situations or features can be related to each other. In contrast to mind maps, the focus here is not on a central term. Connections can simply be terms (in the form of verbs) that describe a context or positive (+)/negative (-) effects. In concept mapping, further characteristics are derived from a generic term or question and set in relation to each other. With cognitive mapping, decision processes can be represented.

affinity diagram

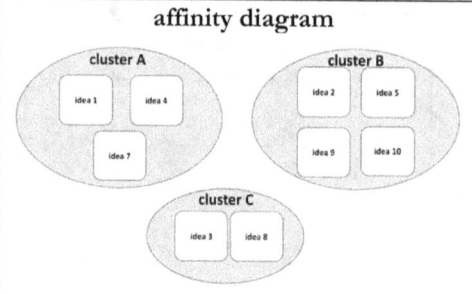

An affinity diagram is used to merge characteristics into individual content-like clusters.
This allows correlations to be recognized, visualized and analysed. First, similar characteristics are clustered and then a cluster category (heading) is determined.

Force Field analysis

supporting factors		inhibiting factors
5	idea	-1
2		-5
4		-3
1		-4

Force field analysis enables the representation of opposing characteristics, e.g. about challenges, tasks, product/service characteristics.
The contrast can be in the form of advantages or positive (best-case scenario) forces vs. disadvantages or negative (worst-case scenario) forces. The strength of these factors can be evaluated by numerical values and/or visually by the thick arrows (see illustration on the left). In this way, reasons and factors that would support or inhibit an innovation can be identified and evaluated.

Semantic Differential (polarity profile)

brand values fully accurate	neutral	brand values fully accurate
authentic		artificial
traditional		modern
young		old
warmly		cold
exciting		homely
expensive		cheap
sociably		alone
clear		cluttered
innovative		standard
classy		ordinary
harmonious		unbalanced
...		...

In the Semantic Differential, opposing pairs of terms face each other. The own evaluation must be positioned between these terms in a seven-step scale, for example.
This results in a polarity profile that can be evaluated on the basis of mean values and scattering measures.

Presentation techniques

At numerous points in the Design Thinking process, the individual intermediate results must be presented for internal communication within the Design Thinking team or for external communication to customers, users, suppliers, etc.. This often involves very short presentations on specific aspects, such as clarifying the understanding of the problem, presenting ideas or explaining and testing a prototype. There are different forms like the Pecha Kucha or an Elevator Pitch (see box below). The feedback on these presentations is used to continue working on the problem, the idea, the prototype etc. and to quickly implement improvements. For the presentation techniques, use the presentation types mentioned above.

Pecha Kucha

Pecha Kucha is a form of short presentation with a clearly defined schedule in which the idea is conveyed in 20 presentation slides, each of which is described in 20 seconds.
www.pechakucha.org

Elevator Pitch:

A presentation lasting 60 to a maximum of 120 seconds, symbolizing an elevator ride with an investor from the first to the last floor, can be structured as follows using the acronym NABC (customer/internal/value/external perspective):

- **N**eed: What is the customer's central need/problem?
- **A**pproach: How should the need/problem be solved? How do you secure a sustainable advantage? Which resources and skills are necessary?
- **B**enefit: How does the customer benefit from the solution? What is the benefit does the company have? Which other partners will benefit?
- **C**ompetition: What are the unique selling points compared to other solutions? How will the competitors react?

In the style of Moore (2014), you can summarize your business idea in one sentence with the following format:

We _____(Company name/Project name) want to _____(What do you want to do?) for _____ (For whom? Customers/users?), who_____want/need/want/have (desire/need/problem/task of the customer) in contrast to _____ (existing/alternative solution) we make _____ (differentiation advantage/USP) in comparison to the solution of _____ (competitor).

In addition, one should – especially in connection with the presentation to investors – also present one's own competencies (very briefly!) and always with reference to the business idea. Why can I/can we successfully implement this idea? What do we lack for this and how will we build up this competence by when or complete it with partners?

Storyboarding

Storyboarding is a method, initially used by Walt Disney for cinema film productions, which schematically visualizes individual scenes of an action (hence also called visual storytelling) and summarizes dialogues or activities of persons in a situation in a keyword manner. Storyboards can be used in Design Thinking to visualize customer activities during problem identification on the one hand, and as a kind of prototype during the solution finding phase on the other, in order to obtain customer feedback. For the development of service offerings, this is a good opportunity for visualization.

How-to do it:

The first thing to clarify is what the storyboard is to be used for:

On the one hand, it can be used at an early stage to gain a better understanding of the customer's problem/need through visualization. In this context (supposed) customer problems can be visualized by storyboards and customers can be shown, who are then asked for a qualified feedback (if the storyboard realistically outlines the problems/activities of the customer, if activities are represented incorrectly, if there is a need for change etc.). The storyboards can also be incomplete and customers are asked to complete them (see below).

On the other hand, it can serve as a kind of prototype to show the customer initial solutions using the storyboard and to ask for feedback (is the solution shown useful from the customer's point of view).

After this clarification individual scenes of a customer action or interaction can be thought up. For example, the main stages of a customer journey (see chapter 3.4.7) can be sketched for structuring. Here, the scene of a customer action could be shown, for example, in interaction with a customer consultant. The persona method (see chapter 4.2) can be used to depict the characters.

The customer action with the representation of problems and/or solution approaches should not comprise more than six to eight scenes, which are schematically sketched in individual small boxes in the size of Post-Its. The sketch consists of only a few elements: Environment, figures (customers, company representatives), speech bubbles, thought bubbles, symbols ("Like It!") and relevant tools (laptop, mobile phone, devices, furniture etc.). A sketched clock can show the respective time. Thought bubbles can be left open at the storyboards, where customers can enter their thoughts themselves (e.g. enter their feelings like pleasure, anger, confusion). Artistic abilities are not necessary here, because it is not about drawing perfection, but the simplest techniques are to be used (see grey box).

The first box can represent the status quo, the last box the ideal state in the future.

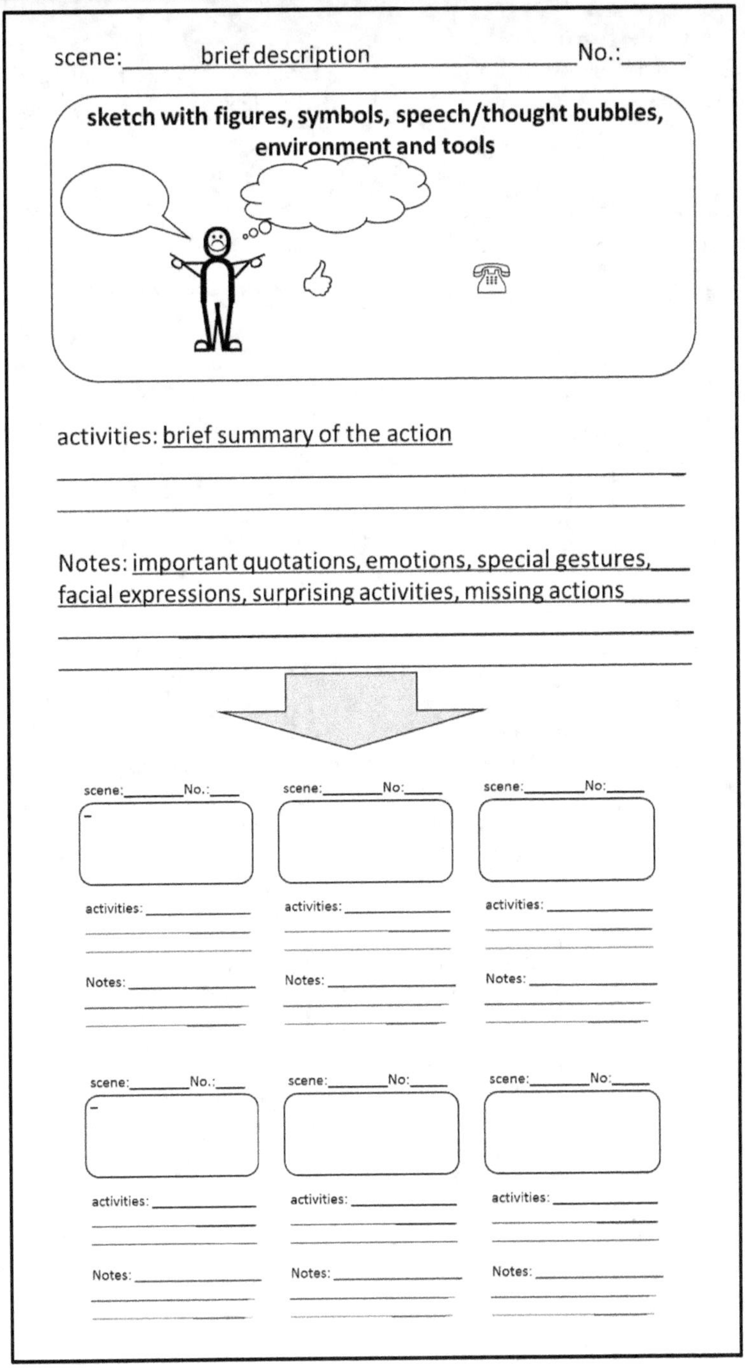

Figure 36: Storyboarding

How to sketch simple figures:

Without great drawing skills, drawings with letters from the alphabet make simple but thoroughly appealing depictions of persons possible. A person is drawn with the following letters:

- **O** for the head
- two **V**s for the legs
- **d** ((as lower case letter) for left pointing hand
- **b** (as lower case letter) for right pointing hand
- **D** (as capital letter) horizontally tilted for shoes

- Inverted **U** for the body
- Twisted **V**s for the arms

Add face with emotions as needed (see below)

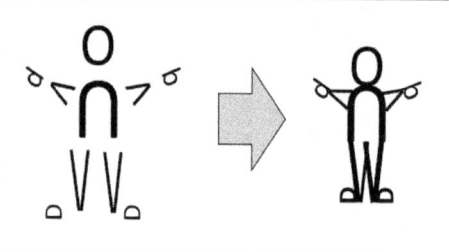

Figure 37: Figures with letters

Table 37: Facial emotions

Gray, Dave / Brown, Sunni / Macanufo, James (2010): Gamestorming: A Playbook for Innovators, Rulebreakers, and Changemakers, O`Reilly Media, Sebastopol/USA.

Rhode, Mike (2012): The Sketchnote Handbook: the illustrated guide to visual note taking, Peachpit Press, Berkeley/USA.

Roam, Dan (2009): The Back of the Napkin (Expanded Edition): Solving Problems and Selling Ideas with Pictures, Penguin Group, London/UK.

Sibbet, David (2010): Visual Meetings: How Graphics, Sticky Notes and Idea Mapping Can Transform Group Productivity, John Wiley & Sons, Hoboken/USA.

Storytelling

The narration of a fictitious or real story, e.g. about a prototypical customer (persona), his daily routine and his problems or needs, can be given to customers with the request for feedback (Is this also the case with you? Is it different? If so, how? What would you add/remove in the story?). This enables the customer to put himself better in a situation and compare it with his situation. The storytelling is presented in more detail in the grey box below.

Storytelling

Storytelling describes in a narrative form as a real (but also fictitious) story the vision/strategy, the benefits or use of an innovation or the successes (best practices) or (typical) mistakes in innovation activities. Storytelling can be used as a kind of prototype test (see chapter 6.2 on the Lean Startup Method) to illustrate an innovative idea to customers and to ask for feedback. Since innovations or innovation-related missions, visions and values can be complex and difficult to grasp, storytelling is a suitable method for communicating innovations in a clear and understandable way. In summary, stories can be...

- communicate the company's values vividly,
- creating sense and meaning for the vision/strategy/innovation,
- provide orientation,
- building and maintaining a culture of innovation,
- motivate and inspire creativity,
- facilitate communication within the company,
- generate and transfer (explicit and implicit) knowledge,
- convince and inspire employees, customers and other stakeholders (e.g. investors) of new ideas,
- develop and establish corporate and/or innovation brands,
- support change processes and
- the loyalty of employees and customers as well as other stakeholders (e.g. investors) to the the company.

The plot of history must ultimately answer the questions of what, why, when, who, where and how it acted, either in the past or for the future. The procedure for the creation of a story is similar to the creation of a communication concept in marketing or can be part of such a concept.

First, the central message of the story (goal) should be defined or the target group determined in very simple words. This can be the mission/vision, the benefit of an innovation or lessons learned from past innovation projects. This central message should always be present at every step. The story should also end with this central message (if necessary with a concrete appeal, call-to-action). The following key questions need to be answered in order to create a central message:

- Who is the target group (reader/listener/viewer) for the message?
- Why should this story be told?
- What should the reader/listener/viewer take with them?
- How will the reader/listener/viewer benefit from the story?
- Is the message important/relevant to the reader/listener/viewer?
- What can the reader/listener/viewer learn from it?
- What should the reader/listener/viewer think, feel, feel or do after the story?

In order to emotionalize the central message, it should address basic needs at the psychological level. People search stories for reward(s). Rewards can manifest themselves in three ways:

6 How to protoype

- **A feeling of safety and security:** People want to overcome fear and insecurity. He looks for stability, stability and balance. He longs for commitment, care, home and tradition.

- **Feeling of excitement:** The person is looking for new stimuli. He wants to be active and break out of the familiar. Instead of boredom, we seek enjoyment, tingling, fun, excitement and variety / surprise.

- **Sense of status and superiority:** We strive to perform at the top. We want to enjoy success and superiority, assert ourselves against others, expand our territory. Therefore man wants to avoid defeats, anger, rage and dissatisfaction.

The story should address some (but far from all) of these three types of rewards (security/security, excitement and/or status/superiority). To build tension, the story should be about a conflict that can manifest itself in a "fight" against fear and insecurity, monotony and boredom, or inferiority and anger. The solution to this conflict consists of alternatives that can be taken. At the end of the story is the happy ending, the positive solution.

Once the message has been defined, the framework for action must be defined, which can be an event from the past or a future development. The action takes place under certain conditions at a certain time and in a certain place, quasi the stage for the staging, also these are to be described, above all if they are of meaning.

For past events:
- Which interesting, beautiful/less beautiful, surprising, problematic, funny, especially positive/negative and/or astonishing events were there?
- Were there conflicts, disagreements, contradictions, etc.?
- What can we learn from them? How should it be better?

For future developments:
- What challenges, opportunities, risks, problems, conflicts, contradictions, surprises can there be (on the way) in the future? And how should we react to them?
- What should the future ideally look like?

Then the characters of the story are to be determined and here above all the main character, who is often the hero in the story. The main character should best be a well-known personality, such as the founder of the company, the inventor of an innovation important to the company, or a "normal" employee. The role of an initial "underdogs" who removes seemingly insurmountable barriers is a popular framework for action (see below).

In addition, there may be other characters such as antagonists, supporters, advisors, cooperation partners and other secondary characters with different roles.

In order to prepare the storytelling, relevant background information on these elements, e.g. interviews with the people actually involved in the story, must be researched, which is relevant in the broadest sense. The person should also be described with their strengths and weaknesses, preferences, character traits, attitudes, etc. in order to identify with them and create an emotional bond. Quotations of the personality can also be well incorporated into the story. In order to better understand the role of the characters, the persona method (see chapter 4.2) or the empathy map (see chapter 3.4.3) can be used to prepare the story.

Fictitious or even only partially fictitious stories should only be used very carefully. Storytelling lives from the authentic telling of real (true) events and characters. In this sense manipulations or too strong transmissions are to be avoided as well. In principle, however, a real fact or a typical plot can also be alienated into a fictitious environment with fictitious characters. Thus personality rights/confidentiality problems can be circumvented. In addition, one can build stronger images. Nevertheless, it must be easy for the reader/listener/viewer to be able to draw conclusions from fiction to their own reality.

The storyline:

In principle, a chronological, theme-oriented or mixed-oriented course of history is possible. In the case of a chronological, time-structured course of events, developmental histories can be used to describe the process. The theme-oriented process focuses on certain topics, problems and values that cannot be structured in time. Particularly complex areas can, if necessary, be told with a mixed-orientation process.

It is important to build up a tension curve, a dramaturgy. They create a tension when they talk about the initial conflicts, defeats, mistakes, barriers, challenges, etc. that have to be overcome. In a chronological sequence, the increasing tension results from the sequence of events; in a theme-centered sequence, the theme can be presented more and more intensively.

The concrete courses of action can be classically structured in three acts:

Act 1: Departure: Something is happening or something must happen (initial situation)

The introduction must attract attention, immediately show the relevance of the topic to the reader/listener/viewer, make him curious, emotionally grab him. Here – as described above – a conflict, a lack situation, missing knowledge, failures can be described. The hero of the story must dare something, must get involved in something foreign, uncomfortable, difficult and free himself from his old/known world. At first he can refuse this challenge or he hesitates and looks for excuses. Initially describing the fears of the hero enables the reader/listener/viewer to identify more strongly.

Then (surprisingly) the initial spark, an aha moment, a motivation boost happens. This can also be done by help/an impulse from another character.

Act 2: The voyage of discovery

The path to overcoming conflict is full of trials, setbacks, problems, barriers, contradictions, etc. Opponents can emerge. These can be in the form of competitors, but also in everyday routines/conventions and habits.

Afterwards we head towards a climax. This climax of the story is the decision for one direction: good or evil. Everything is at stake.

Act 3: Resolution with happy ending

Finally, depending on the above-mentioned framework for action, the conflict is resolved. The opponent is defeated or the deficiency situation is remedied. The reader/listener/viewer receives his reward (see above). At the end, the solution is sketched out, the message of the story is clearly conveyed, an appeal is formulated, hints are given on how to transfer the results to the situation of the reader/listener/viewer. Ideally, the story comes to a symbolic end.

The following recommendations can be made for writing the story:

- Use a pictorial language with pictorial actions, personal thoughts or emotions and metaphors: The use of metaphors is especially recommended for stories.
- Stories should be told in verbs and not in nouns.
- Good stories are simple and focused.
- Good stories have elements of surprise
- Make a reference to the life of the target group, use the language/expressions of the target group.
- Present the main character sympathetically and realistically.

- Use creativity techniques (see chapter 5.2) to create the story: To make the action situation more imaginative, ask yourself the what-if question.

The realisation of the story can be realised as text, radio play or video or as a combination of these possibilities (multimedia). In digital form, the story can also have interactive elements, so that the reader/listener/viewer can get further background information about a different presentation format or even influence the course of the story. In addition, readers/listeners/viewers can use digital media to exchange information and get in touch with the contact persons for the story. However, one must critically assess whether interactivity is possible at all and whether it is desired, especially from the point of view of the "storyteller" but also of the reader/listener/viewer. Passive consumption can make sense.

Newspaper articles from the future

Write a newspaper article that is to appear in the future and describes the ideal situation – either from the perspective of a person (or group of persons) or from the perspective of the company.

Creative Collages

Pictures and excerpts from books, magazines, newspapers, advertising brochures, catalogues or other documents are compiled in the form of a collage as a pattern either in individual or group work in the workshop. The pattern is related to the question/problem and given a title. It should thus inspire new ideas (cf. Michalko (2006)).

Design Scenarios

Design scenarios answer the following questions: How does a service ideally work with a specific persona (also negative scenarios: How could the service be degraded)? The method of service blueprinting (see chapter 3.4.8) can also be used for this.

Role plays

With role plays it is possible to realistically simulate an action/situation in order to be able to put oneself better into the role or situation. Different roles can be assumed by different types of customers and employees. These types can, for example, be developed beforehand with the persona method (see chapter 4.2). In order to simulate the role play as realistically as possible, disguises, props, furniture, devices etc. can be used. The participants can then reflect on what and how they experienced the situation, why they acted as they did and whether they could have acted differently. In addition, there may be an observer who takes notes or photos or records a video of the role play.

Bodystorming

Bodystorming expands role-playing to the extent that the partially playful transfer into a person (e.g. the customer) is at the same time linked to an idea-finding or solution process. It is therefore a kind of combination of brainstorming and role-playing. This is intended to find a solution idea from a different perspective. Bodystorming can be practiced spontaneously or a special situation can be considered, in which the brainstorming takes place, or certain framework conditions of the action can be defined (a kind of script). The main question is how one feels in a certain problematic (challenging) situation and how one wants to solve it ("what would I do now"). The above mentioned other elements from role plays (observers, different role assignments, realistic framework conditions) can be taken over here.

Diary method /Cultural Probes/Experience Sampling

In the context of the diary method, users are asked to write down or record their experiences, thoughts and feelings (cultural probes) about the phenomenon investigated in a diary (can also be in the form of an app or using photos, videos or voice recorder). If a diary is to be maintained over a longer period of time, e-mails or phone calls with the customer can also be made from time to time. Postcards can also be written in addition. The specification of a rough structure for the diary notes is recommended. The specifications can also include open questions (How do you feel today?). What have you experienced? What did you do at a certain time? What was the most exciting moment today? What did you get angry about today? What astonished you? etc.), which should be answered. With the help of a smartphone app, signals can also be given (automatically) that detailed statements can be queried at certain points in time (experience sampling). The current emotional state can be queried (happy, relaxed, etc.). The results from these approaches can then be evaluated (e.g. in the form of a content analysis) and, if necessary, discussed again with the customer.

Graffiti Walls

A so-called graffiti wall is a large blank paper with a pen on which comments about the use/claim of a product/service can be made anonymously by the customer/user directly at the place of action (cf. Martin/Hanington (2012): 96). If necessary, an open question will be asked: How did they perceive the service/location/product? What was good? What annoyed them?. The method is particularly suitable for situations in which a personal interview is not possible or could have an effect on the answer (see chapter 7.2 Interviewer effect).

7
How to test business ideas

7 How to test business ideas

7.1	Test phase	177
7.2	Tips for interviews	179
7.3	Tips for surveys	185
7.4	Kano-Model	188
7.5	Desirability Testing	194

7 How to test business ideas

"Even a disappointment, if it is only thorough and final, means a step forward.."
—Max Planck (translation from German)

"In God we trust, all others must bring data." – W. Edwards Deming

After presenting the main tasks of the test phase (chapter 7.1), tips are given for conducting oral (chapter 7.2) and written surveys (chapter 7.3), which enable early testing of assumptions or prototypes in connection with new business ideas by obtaining customer feedback. A particularly meaningful survey technique is explained with the Kano model in chapter 7.4. Finally, chapter 7.5 introduces Desirability Testing, another method that can provide rapid feedback, especially in workshops with customers.

7.1 Test Phase

Prototype development moves seamlessly into the final phase of testing. After selecting the prototype technology and creating one or more prototypes in the previous phase, the testing of the prototype must be planned and organized with the concrete interaction with the customer/user: How does the customer interact with the visualization/prototype? Who is involved? When, how long and where does this take place? This means that the selection and design of the test methods must be clarified here. The classic test methods explained in the previous section are ideal for testing the prototype:

- On-site interviews
- Customer observation
- Interviews on neutral location
- Phone interviews
- Video-Chats
- Instant Messaging
- E-mails
- Online suvey
- Focus groups /customer clinics/Usability-Tests/Live-Testing
- Eye-Tracking Systems

In the case of radical innovations, characterised by the fact that there is no similar range of products/services on the market, these classic methods often reach their limits because customers' imagination is limited. In order to obtain tacit customer feedback, especially for radical innovations, the methods described in the previous section are particularly useful in addition to the method of customer observation (see chapter 3):

- Drawings and design of models
- Storyboarding
- Storytelling/Comics/Lego Serious Games
- Bodystorming

- Wireframes/Mockups
- Website/Landing Page
- Videos
- Concierge MVP
- Wizard-of-Oz MVP
- Open-Source Prototypes
- 3D-Rapid Prototyping
- Crowdfunding

Before you start testing the prototype, think about how you want to record the customer feedback (voice recorder, camera, etc.) and which criteria you want to use to analyze the customer feedback. The customer's statements on the following basic questions are to be analysed in particular:

- What was positively evaluated?
- What concerns arose?
- What was a surprising message/action from the customer?
- Did emotions come up with the customer, if so, what kind of emotions?
- What suggestions were made?
- What insights and feedback do you get for the idea concept?
- What can be learned from this?

Prioritize this feedback. Try to implement the feedback in the next (improved) prototype.

In addition to the improvement (or rejection) of the prototype or idea, customer feedback could also result in possibilities for variants of the product/service idea:

- Are there any indications in customer feedback that other variants of the product/service are (or could be) in demand?
- In what respect could the idea be varied?
- How extensive would other variants be?
- Are further variants feasible and economically sensible?

Tips for prototype testing:

- Offer multiple prototypes for comparison. In addition to the very promising ideas, you can also deliberately create a prototype for an idea that you would exclude due to (supposed) inefficiency, for example. One also speaks of **Dark Horse prototypes**, developed by Professor Mark Cutkosky, Stanford University, which are very creative, but are also considered too risky. Dark Horse is meant in reference to horse betting, where outsiders sometimes win. This also prevents a too early commitment to certain prototypes, so that the solution space is not unnecessarily quickly narrowed. Especially in the Protype phase, the focus is very (too) quickly on the favourite idea.

- Ask for feedback without comment. Each evaluation on your part can influence the assessment of the customer (so-called observer/interviewer effect).

- Ask the customer to suggest or implement changes to the prototype.

7.2 Tips for interviews

Where and how to find customers for the experiments?

- First, use your own social network (contacts on Facebook, LinkedIn, Twitter etc.) for the survey. Ask for recommendations to friends of friends (so-called "second-degree connections"). To do this, create redirectable mails with your request.
- Use your own employees or colleagues as customers (this is also called "dogfooding", which stands for "eating your own dog food" and means that you use your own products for your own needs).
- If you do not yet have a clear idea of the exact target customers, start broadly, but focus on the potential target group as quickly as possible.
- Think about where you could find potential customers (preferably early evangelists). Where do your customers shop? Where do they spend their free time? Where do they work? A place can be understood as a real place (e.g. cafés, shops, trade fairs, events, concerts) or a virtual place (Facebook and other social networks, specialist forums).
- Search for studies, news articles, reports about your target group and collect statements, contact data or other relevant information.
- In existing companies, customer service is also a very fruitful source. Especially angry customers are very useful here. This means that it is best to integrate hypothesis testing into the customer service process. You should also analyze the top 10 customer complaints every month.
- With already existing similar products or predecessor products, you can also address existing customers directly, whether they would be ready for customer feedback on the above-mentioned hypotheses. Establish a customer advisory board from which you can recruit people for the tests.
- When (cold) addressing – especially unknown people – you should stress that it's not about selling, but about seeking advice and expertise (it's often surprising how many people like to help you despite time pressure because they feel flattered or actually find the problem relevant).
- You have come across particularly interesting customers (so-called "early evangelists") if they are already actively looking for a solution to a problem themselves or are even reporting on initial approaches to a solution.

How do you formulate the right questions?

- Always speak of "I" and do not hide behind a "we" or "our company", even in business contacts. This is the only way to reach a more personal level that allows you to have more in-depth conversations.
- Avoid technical terms! Speak in the customer's language. Better something more colloquial than incomprehensible or misleading.
- Also encourage your interviewee not to answer generally or hide behind a "we", "us" or, in the case of business customers, behind "our company/management", but rather to report from his or her point of view. Ask: How do you personally see this? What does this mean for you in particular? What experience have they gained?
- Always concentrate on certain activities, events or decisions in the present or past. What/how did you do the last time…? How often did you…? How did they decide last time…? What frustrated them? What pleased them? What did they invest a lot of time in? What did they try several times? What is important to them at X? What do they like about X? What do they miss in X? In addition to the What and How questions, the When- and With-Whom questions as well as the Why questions (see below) should also be clarified.

7 How to test business ideas

- Alternatively (but sub-optimally), you can describe the problem, activity or task yourself – especially in the case of rather faltering conversations – and then ask the customer whether he sees/feels a similar situation or whether he has deviations/additions. Here you should be careful not to use suggestive questions (see below).
- As mentioned above, you should not ask hypothetical questions (e.g. how much would you pay for...? how would you decide?). So don't ask if customers would like anything abstract (especially when it comes to innovation, customers lack imagination), but ask what they do or have done in certain situations/occasions. Rather at the end you can ask what you would dream of in certain situations.
- So good questions are about the current situation of the customer and his previous experiences. Ask for stories and examples. If you nevertheless ask for wishes, this should always be related to something that the customer can actually imagine.
- Likewise you should avoid suggestive questions like: Don't you think that...? Do you agree with me that...? Would they not also want that...?
- Yes-no questions are not very helpful, you won't learn much from them and often the answers to the really relevant hypotheses are more complex in order to answer them with simple yes or no.
- Projective questions, which include an indirect question, are also very helpful: The person is not asked about his/her wishes/needs, but should answer from the point of view of a third, similar or known person. For example: For what reasons does your friend use product X? What do you think your acquaintance has bought recently?
- In order to get to the bottom of the causes of customer problems/needs, it is often recommended to ask the why question several times (the so-called 5-Whys technique of the means-end approach, see chapter 4.3.2). However, you should avoid asking up to five why questions in a row during interviews, because constant why questions can have a very aggressive effect and rather create a defensive/blockade behaviour on the part of the customer. If necessary one can ask alternatively to the alternation for the "Why?" and/or "How comes that? It is better to summarize the customer's previous answers in your own words and ask them to tell you more about the situation/problem/need.
- Never accept or take anything for granted: Ask also if you know the supposed reason or take something for granted yourself.

How to conduct interviews correctly

- Make the focus of the interview clear in advance so that you can concentrate on it. Each interview should focus on the following aspects (Alvarez (2014)):
    - **Statements on the concrete hypotheses**
      (either in the sense of confirmation or nonconfirmation)
    - **Surprising statements**
    - **Emotional statements**
      (Emotions expressed by content, choice of words, vocal pitch, gestures or facial expressions. Emotions can show anger, worry, frustration, curiosity, or excitement).
- A good preparation is to practice the interview with colleagues/friends beforehand.
- Before the interview, at least play through the situation in your head yourself. Have a look at the previous information about the person you are interviewing and think about their character, needs, problems etc.

- Do not conduct group interviews à la focus groups, even if this seems very efficient. The so-called Group Think leads to the fact that rather average opinions develop, in order to achieve consensus in the group among other things. The tendencies of the participants to influence each other are simply too pronounced.
- Avoid presenting your concrete business idea right at the beginning. This is not about your self-presentation or selling a (still vague) idea, but about customer feedback and learning from these answers. Stress the importance of the interviewee's (honest) answers and don't be afraid to explicitly ask for advice.
- First describe the problem and ask if the interviewee feels it as such.
- Communicate that the interview only lasts a few minutes (5 to 20 minutes at most). In order to actually keep to this schedule, you must prepare yourself well (see below). You should prioritise your questions and ask them in this order, so that you can test the essential hypotheses at least if you are short of time.
- For the organisation of the interviews it is also helpful to send out electronic calendar entry invitations with your phone number and to set up a reminder on the planned day.
- Taking notes is certainly very helpful for phone interviews, but it can be a hindrance for personal interviews. It is not advisable to use a laptop, as you are also putting up a protective shield for the interviewee. Trays would be more practicable. However, the spatial conditions such as a pad for the notebook may also be missing on site. When taking notes one should also be aware that on the one hand one inevitably pays less attention to the interviewee and on the other hand gesture/mimic is lost or the interview can appear more unnatural.
- In this context the most important tip at all: **Listen, don't talk too much yourself!** 80% of the interviewee should talk and only 20% of the questioner.
- Also pay attention to speech (volume, rhythm, melody, intonation), gestures and facial expressions. Especially contradictions between what is said and how it is said can be interesting for further analysis.
- Recorders should not be used for interviews with strangers. Often the interviewees become more reserved when recording. In addition, it is not a good start if you first ask the interviewee at the beginning of the interview whether he or she is willing to take the interview.
- Another possible interview method would be to perform with two people: One asks, the other takes notes. But this can also have a deterrent effect and is very (cost/time) expensive.
- Be flexible in your conversations: If the customer reports about something very emotionally or describes his futile search for a problem solution, but this problem does not agree with your own original approach, continue to ask for a better understanding. This may lead to a completely new business idea and a "pivot" (see chapter 6.2).
- After the interview you should always allow a little time for follow-up to note down the most important results. You can also ask yourself what went well or bad in the interview. From this one can learn for the next interview
- You can enter the notes electronically (e.g. in Excel in the form of the above hypothesis table, in Google Docs, in Evernote, etc.) or handwritten and use note pads, Post-Its or index cards to write them down. The last two have the advantage that they can also be rearranged and arranged on a wall.
- When taking notes during or – better – after the interview, you can still mark the results with simple symbols in order to identify particularly interesting statements. Particularly important (especially emotional) statements should be quoted as literally as possible. You can also use emoticons to record the type of emotions (anger, worry, frustration, curiosity, or excitement).
- Especially the recording of the intensity and kind of emotions can give important hints. This is also referred to as a "wow test", i.e. how enthusiastic customers are.

- At the end of the interview, you should always ask if you can contact the person again for further questions or if he is interested in being informed at the product launch. In addition, one could also ask whether the interviewee could recommend further persons.
- You will notice that you have led enough interviews to a hypothesis complex if you can recognize a clear answer pattern. The broader your potential customer group is, the more interviews you may have to conduct. In a focused customer segment (which is always recommended at first), five to ten interviews can be enough to identify a clear pattern. This means that the number of interview partners ultimately also depends on the size of the target market. Likewise, the response behaviour to very concrete, focused questions becomes visible more quickly.
- If there are no clear answer patterns even in a large number of interviews, then you should take another critical look at the customer segment (who really are our customers?) or revise your questions/hypotheses (what problems/needs do the customers actually have?) in the sense of concretization.
- But always be sceptical about every statement. Take questionable statements as an opportunity to ask further questions or to confront other people with this statement.
- For structuring and for an efficient and effective interview, you should prepare an interview guideline in advance and adhere to it as far as possible. In the interview guideline, the relevant hypotheses mentioned above are logically listed in question form.
- If the possibility exists and it is not too expensive, it is best to conduct personal interviews ("face-to-face"). If not, the next choice would be a phone interview. Only then should you consider an exchange via electronic media (e-mails, chat).
- Basically, you should never pay your interviewees for it. Paid persons will never openly and honestly tell you their opinions and authentically describe their problems and needs.
- Create a list of your top 3 questions that you would ask in spontaneous meetings with potential customers, investors, business partners, industry experts, scientists, etc. So you are always prepared when talking to interesting people and use them effectively for your own learning (Fitzpartick (2013)).

The following is an interview template based on Alvarez (2014) and supplemented by Pauk/Owens (2013).

Table 38: Template for an interview protocol for hypothesis testing
Source: According to Alvarez (2014) and with the addition of Pauck/Owens (2013)

interview protocol				
hypothesis (assumption):				
interview conducted by:			at:	
information about the interviewee:				
name:		position:		
gender: ☐ ♂ ☐ ♀		age:		
other characteristic traits: (work experience, in the company for X years, leisure activities, usage habits, etc.)				
keywords of the key messages:	notes:			
summary:				

After the so-called Cornell notes by Walter Pauk at Cornell University (Pauk/Owens (2013)), keywords of the core statements are written after the conversation on the left-hand side of the margin, the notes during the conversation are found in the larger right-hand area and the summaries in presentation style are later placed at the bottom as a footer.

The so-called **5R rule** (see Andler (2016)) is helpful when making the notes:

1. **Record:** Write down as much as necessary, as little as possible.
2. **Reduce:** Reduce the conversation by keywords and summaries on the the most important statements. Use keywords instead of whole sentences. Just make sure that you can use the information later.
Instead of writing out whole sentences, you should use bullets, short forms (such as "+" instead of "and"), abbreviations and any symbols when taking notes.
3. **Recite:** Cover an area of the notes you have made and try to remember them in this way. as much as possible. Ask yourself: Are all areas coherent?
4. **Reflect:** Think about what you have remembered.
5. **Review:** Repeat the steps 3 to 5.

Ideally, the Design Thinking process ends with information already being available and prepared for the subsequent steps of implementation and market launch. A documentation of the results and the course of Design Thinking processes that is also comprehensible for outsiders is recommended here. An example is the following idea profile, which summarizes the idea with its essential features as well as an initial evaluation. Only in this way is a seamless and smooth implementation of the results possible. In larger companies, people are often not involved in the Design Thinking process or only selectively in the subsequent implementation of the results. However, it is precisely this transfer of knowledge via minds that would be particularly promising.

Table 39: Ideas Profile
Source: According to Hartschen/Scherer/Brügger (2009), S. 65ff.

Ideas Profile					
name of the idea			No.		
contact person			date:		
brief description of the idea					
Describe briefly (3-4 paragraphs) the core concept of the idea.					
target group					
Describe briefly the target group on the basis of characteristic features, in the appendix you can attach the results of the persona technique (see chapter 4.2).					
customer benefits					
Briefly describe the customer benefit, use the jobs-to-be-done scheme (see chapter 4.3.1).					
opportunities					
Describe briefly the chances of the idea for the company. Use the SWOT analysis for this (see chapter 5.4.3).					
risks					
Briefly describe the risks (see SWOT analysis in chapter 5.4.3).					
short evaluation of the idea					
"Desirability"/ "Utility"	very high ☐	high ☐	mid ☐	low ☐	very low ☐
"Feasibility"	very high ☐	high ☐	mid ☐	low ☐	very low ☐
"Business Viability"	very high ☐	high ☐	mid ☐	low ☐	very low ☐
"Sustainability/Scalability"	very high ☐	high ☐	mid ☐	low ☐	very low ☐
"Strategically"	very high ☐	high ☐	mid ☐	low ☐	very low ☐
overall rating	very high ☐	high ☐	mid ☐	low ☐	very low ☐
cost expenditure	rough cost estimate				
time expenditure	time estimation up to the market launch or up to a certain development step				
milestones	milestones			When?	
implementation plan	What?		Who?		until when?
decision		go ☐		on hold ☐	stop ☐
remarks					
attachments					

7.3 Tips for surveys

In the following some recommendations are given to the contents as well as to the planning and execution of customer surveys. In addition, the tips for conducting (qualitative) interviews should be observed (see chapter 5.4.2 on the Lean Startup method).

Already in connection with the Lean Startup method (see chapter 6.2), numerous tips were given for planning and conducting customer surveys, which, however, are primarily related to personal interviews in an early innovation phase. At this point, additional tips for more extensive (large number) written surveys will be presented. Such surveys particularly require thorough preparation, as the checklist in the following table makes clear.

Table 40: Checklist for written customer surveys

Checklist for planning a customer survey
▪ **Objective planning:** What is the objective of the survey? The objective should be clear and realistic. What is to be investigated (contents of the customer surveys such as benefit characteristic, certain services around the business idea, price)?
▪ **Current situation:** What information about the customer is available so far? (if necessary, key figures such as number of buyers, repurchase rates, number of returns/complaints etc.)? Which information is still missing?
▪ **Target group:** Which and how many target persons must be responsible for missing information? Customers (new customers, regular customers, lost/abducted customers, non customers) users, purchase decision makers (B2B segment)?
▪ **Selection of methods:** How do I survey/which method do I use? In writing, electronically (online/by mail), by telephone? Take their advantages and disadvantages into account.
▪ **Content of the survey:** Which questions arise from the objectives or from the missing information? Which questions create a gain in knowledge? Which questions could improve the business idea? Which questions could provide impetus for more ideas? From which questions could concrete measures be derived? Which mandatory information is required for the evaluation?
▪ **Data collection and analysis methods:** Which questions should I ask with closed or open questions? How can the questions be quantified? Which evaluation scale is appropriate?
▪ **Conduct of the survey:** design of the cover letter, layout of the questionnaire; which Software tool for creation and evaluation should be used? How many people will finally questioned? How is the evaluation carried out?
▪ **Guidelines:** Which internal company and legal guidelines (e.g. data protection, corporate identity) must be taken into account during implementation?
▪ **Survey effort:** What is the effort for implementation and evaluation?
▪ **Follow-up:** By whom, when and how should be followed up, in order to to increase the response rate?
▪ **Communication of results:** How and to whom should the results be communicated? Should results be published? If so, how and in what form?

Tips for planning and implementation a survey

- The length of the questionnaire should be between 5 and 20 minutes. The more questions, the worse the response rate and the more complex the evaluation. As much as necessary, as little as possible.
- Each question should be checked to see whether the objectives can be achieved and whether the questions could be shortened or deleted.
- Consider the contents of the survey, the target group and the effort involved, and consider whether an online, personal, written and/or telephone survey or a survey by app or feedback terminal would be effective.
- A sufficient number (e.g. 20) of completed questionnaires is necessary to obtain statistically relevant statements.
- Use your e-mail contact lists, place the questionnaire on a website or in social networks, use the questionnaire for all interactions with customers.
- Depending on the focus of the survey, the time of the survey should be adjusted accordingly, otherwise the memory of the customer/user will blast.
- Check whether you can run a competition with attractive prizes for the participants and use a picture of the prize in the cover letter.
- Structure the questionnaire logically and clearly.
- Do not formulate suggestive questions. Use a simple, understandable language (even if the survey is aimed at experts), no nested sentences, no repetitions, no extensive explanations and no sub-questions. Do not use negations, but always formulate positively. The questions should not need to be interpreted and should be understandable when read quickly without long reflection. Questions should always refer to only one aspect, otherwise the statements are not unambiguous.
- Use comment and other fields to get more in-depth answers.
- Use different question types:
    - Open questions, for example: "How do you rate the quality of innovation XY?
    - Closed questions with a rating scale (e.g. with a five- or multi-level so-called Likert scale), How satisfied are you with the quality of our products? 1 = very satisfied ... 4 = dissatisfied".
    - Closed questions with rank order, for example: "Arrange in descending order how satisfied you are with the following areas: Product quality, service, price, etc."
    - Multiple Choice (= multiple answers are given and possible)/Single Choice Questions (= multiple answers are given but only one is possible). Multiple Choice has the advantages that it is easy to answer, can be evaluated quickly and facilitates the documentation of the response behaviour, but it does not involve any in-depth analyses (this is particularly relevant in the context of innovation).
- For more variety, vary not only the type of question, but also the rating scale, the implementation in the layout, etc. Use pictures, videos for online surveys and an attractive layout. Try to make your questions entertaining – if possible.
- In an online survey, various interactive elements can also be used, but these must not disturb, distract and influence the result. It is helpful to show how many questions/percentage still have to be answered.

- Use an appealing layout for the cover letter and the questionnaire. Consider the corporate design guidelines in your company. This applies to use such as logo, font/color, background color, header and footer.

- Address customers directly and personally in the cover letter. In the cover letter/conversation, explain the goal of the survey as well as its meaning and emphasize the added value for the customer. Furthermore, the cover letter should be friendly, motivating, name the contact person with the possibility of contact, indicate the amount of time spent honestly, give reference to anonymity/data protection (see below), be short and close with a request for action ("Let's go"). Also give a hint where to get further information (link to an information page).

- Assure the customer of anonymity and sensitive handling of the information (data protection). Already when selecting a survey institute or a survey software, the data protection legal framework has to be observed. Some providers do not always have the same standards here.

- Ask (if necessary with incentives) for more detailed feedback (if necessary by telephone or in person).

- In the case of a larger survey, always carry out a pre-test in order to test the comprehensibility of the questionnaire in advance.

- In a follow-up campaign, try to contact only those customers who have not yet responded (everything else only annoys the customers).

- Clarify during reporting who gets which information in which form and when, and who needs it. In addition to pure evaluation analyses, interpretations (from different areas) may also be necessary. Interdisciplinary workshops to discuss the survey results can also be useful. If you have announced an external publication during the survey, publish the results including the measures taken and, if applicable, the winners of the competition in anonymous, aggregated form.

- Carry out smaller surveys on a regular basis.

www.surveymonkey.com, www.surveygizmo.com

www.qualtrics.com, www.google.com (Google Forms)

www.qualaroo.com, www.zoho.com/survey/

www.clientheartbeat.com, www.surveyplanet.com

www.sogosurvey.com, www.asknicely.com

www.typeform.com, www.survicate.com

www.polldaddy.com, www.getfeedback.com

7.4 Kano Model

The Kano model from the Japanese Noriaki Kano is a way to differentiate customer satisfaction along different types of requirements and to derive priorities for product development from this. The following types of customer requirements are distinguished:

Basics (Must-have):

Customers take these requirements for granted or obvious and often do not even mention them explicitly. They must be available in any case, otherwise the customer is very dissatisfied and changes to the competition.

Linear Satisfier:

Customer satisfaction is proportional to the fulfilment of this requirement. The higher the quality, the higher the satisfaction and vice versa. In other words, if the requirement is met, the customer is satisfied; if it is not met, the customer is dissatisfied.

Delighter:

The customer does not expect these requirements or is not aware of them. This leads to the enthusiasm of the customer. If they are not available, they do not lead to dissatisfaction.

In addition, there are product features that are indifferently evaluated from the customer's point of view ("I don't care") and features that even lead to the rejection of the product if they are present (reverse reaction).

The requirements change with the time by habituation effects: Individual enthusiasm requirements are increasingly expected and accepted by competitors, so that they change into performance requirements and finally into basic requirements.

In addition, indifference zones can often be found within which changes in product feature quality have no influence on customer behavior (cf. Woodruff et al. (1983):. 299). An improvement in performance within this indifference zone therefore does not lead to greater customer satisfaction, but only results in higher costs.

7 How to test business ideas

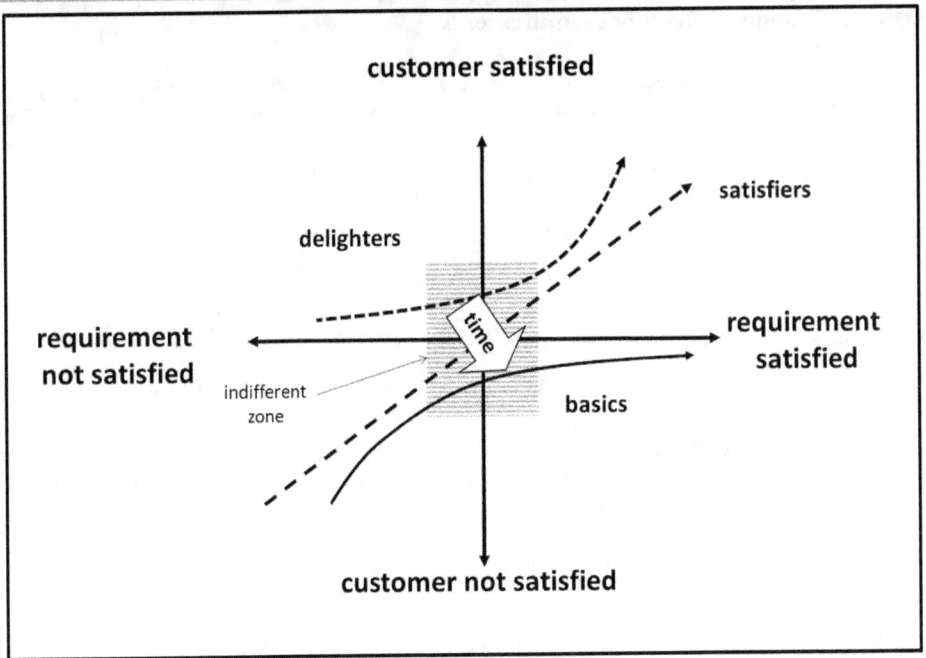

Figure 38: Kano model

How to do it:

The procedure is shown in the following figure, which is explained in the following.

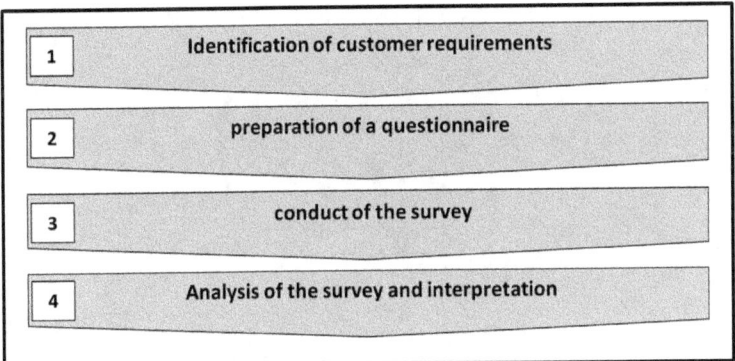

Figure 39: Procedure of the Kano model

❶ Identification of customer requirements

First of all, the right target group should be selected, which preferably has a uniform profile of needs or requirements for the planned products/services (see chapter 6.2 Lean start-up method). The requirements of this target group can be derived from a variety of sources and methods such as surveys, evaluation of complaints and customer service enquiries, focus groups, the customer journey (see chapter 3.4.7) or service blueprinting (see chapter 3.4.8).

It should of course also be noted that not only customers make demands on the product/service, but also, for example, legal requirements, standards, etc. must be taken into account.

❷ Preparation of a questionnaire

The questionnaire consists of two questions per customer requirement, which enable a bipolar evaluation:

- A positively formulated question on the product characteristic (functional question): How would you rate it if the product/service had characteristic X? This means that the existence of the characteristic is valuated.
- A negatively formulated question (dysfunctional question): How would you rate it if the product/service did not have characteristic X? This means that the absence of the characteristic is valuated.

For both questions, the following five identical answers are given (see Figure 42): "That would make me very happy" (coded with the number 1.); "That I assume" (coded with the number 2.); "That I don't care" (coded with the number 3.); "That I could accept" (coded with the number 3.); and "That would bother me a lot" (coded with the number 5.).

When formulating the requirements, one should pay attention to the level of knowledge of the customers, i.e. if end consumers are questioned, one should dispense with technical jargon.

7 How to test business ideas

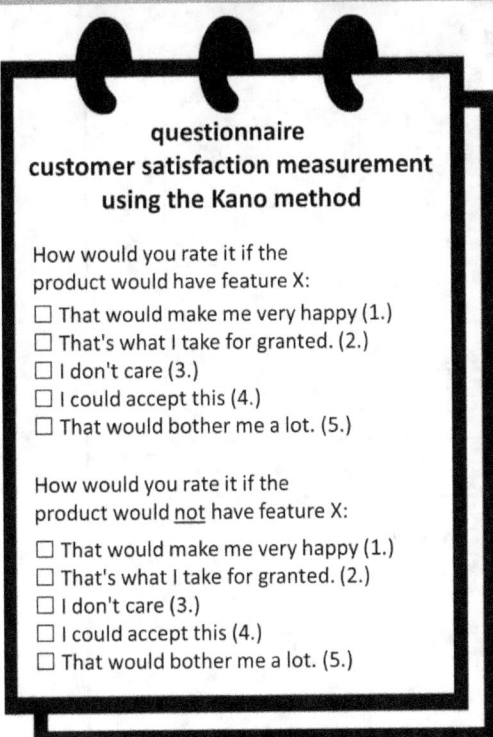

Figure 40: Questionnaire for a customer satisfaction measurement according to Kano

❸ Conduct of the survey

First, the questionnaire should be checked for comprehensibility in a pre-test with selected customers and/or internal employees. The actual survey can be conducted orally with a standardized questionnaire or in the context of a focus group meeting, or in a written form (offline or online). Depending on the complexity of the product, two to three dozen completed questionnaires may be sufficient. Ideally, the survey is carried out from a random sample of the potential target group, which is representative on the basis of predefined criteria (see chapter 4.2 on the Persona method).

❹ Analysis of the survey and interpretation

Depending on the response behaviour to the functional and dsyfunctional question, the result for each characteristic can be classified into the following categories using the evaluation scheme below (see table below): Basic requirement (Must-Have; "M"), Performance requirement (Linear Satisfier, "L"), Enthusiasm requirement (Delighter, "D"), Rejection of the characteristic (reverse/contrary reaction, "R"), indifferent evaluation ("I") and questionable result ("?").

Table 41: Evaluation scheme according to Kano

product feature A		DSYFUNCTIONAL				
		1.	2.	3.	4.	5.
FUNCTIONAL	1.	?	D	D	D	L
	2.	R	I	I	I	M
	3.	R	I	I	I	M
	4.	R	I	I	I	M
	5.	R	R	R	R	?

R: reverse reaction (opposite valuation)
?: questionable result
I: indifferent
M: Must have (Basics)
D: Delighter
L: Linear Satisfier

A questionable result would be an answering behavior "This would make me very happy (1.)" both in the functional question (presence of the characteristic) and in the dysfunctional question (absence of the characteristic). In the case of frequent answers of this kind, the comprehensibility of the questionnaire should be checked in particular. An indifferent answer would not allow a clear classification.

In the results table below, the individual customer evaluations can then be compiled and evaluated according to the categories ("M", "D", "L", "I", "R", "?"). The overall category can be derived from the frequency of the ratings given for a single category. This classification can simply be made according to the majority principle.

If the result is not clear (see table below for characteristic B), one reason may be that the survey addressed a very heterogeneous circle of customers. The more homogeneous the customer group, the clearer the result should be.

Using certain criteria that distinguish different customer segments from each other (e.g. demographic characteristics), the results can therefore also be evaluated differentiated according to customer segments. This makes it possible to determine correlations between customer segments and specific requirement types.

Table 42: Table of results

	M	D	L	I	R	?	sum	overall category
feature A	0	0	0	9	13	3	25	I
feature B	10	3	2	9	0	1	25	M/I
feature C								
feature D								
...								

Finally, the following can be recommended:

- Characteristics leading to rejection should be avoided in any case.
- Basic requirements must be met in any case. However, it is not worth the effort to improve these further, i.e. to exceed them.
- A combination of performance requirements (Linear Satisfier) combined with one or two enthusiasm requirements (Delighters) can be very advantageous to differentiate the offer from the competitors.
- Only relying on one or two enthusiasm requirements (Delighters) without meeting performance requirements (Linear Satisfier) can be problematic in order to achieve lasting competitive advantages. The customer can quickly get used to the surprise effect of the enthusiasm requirements (Delighters).

All in all, the Kano method leads to a better understanding of customer requirements and supports priority setting in product development. In addition, products can be tailored to the different requirements of different customer segments and thus ultimately create competitive advantages.

Nevertheless, one should consider the effort of the method – in particular the execution of the survey – as well as the subjective character of the evaluation by the customer. In addition, customers can often only evaluate features that are understandable, descriptive and/or even tangible for them. These are prerequisites that are not necessarily given for ideas with a radical degree of innovation. Other methods are suitable for this (see Lean Startup method in chapter 6.2). Furthermore, one should not rely exclusively on the customer, since there is a danger that one will only update what already exists and miss out on disruptive developments (Christensen (1997)).

7.5 Desirability Testing

Desirability Toolkit (also known as Microsoft Reaction Card Method) allows you to evaluate ideas/prototypes using a list of adjectives that include positive and negative scores. The customers/users should select three to five cards from a larger number of cards, on each of which an adjective is written, which best characterize the idea from their point of view.

In the list below, based on Benedek/Miner (2010), two to a maximum of three dozen adjectives are to be selected, which appear to be appropriate or relevant to the topic of the idea or the research focus. If, for example, it is only a matter of design questions, the adjectives on functionality should be omitted. The list below can, of course, be expanded to include specific topics. If possible, the adjectives should be presented to the customers/users in a random order, and negative or positive words should be varied. Benedek/Miner (2010) recommend that the card deck contain at least 40% negative expressions.

The evaluation can be based on a frequency distribution, e.g. X% of the participants have chosen the word Y (cf. Martin/Hanington (2012), 64f.) in connection with the Idea/Protypes Z. In addition to the frequency distribution for comparing different ideas/prototypes, it is also possible to differentiate between different groups of participants who represent different persona (see Persona Method in chapter 4.2). This makes it possible to link the frequency distributions with different persona characteristics.

The frequency distribution of the individual adjectives can be visualized with different display types (see chapter 6.3). The Venn diagram, for example, makes it possible to differentiate between adjectives that are mentioned equally frequently as an intersection and adjectives that are mentioned differently from two different ideas/prototypes or groups of participants. A tag cloud (e.g. with www.wordle.net) also visualizes the frequency distribution.

Table 43: Desirability Toolkit
Source: According to Benedek/Miner (2010)

POSITIVE		NEGATIVE	
quality			
advanced	state of the art	old	out of fashion
clear/explicit	comprehensive	vague	incomprehensible
novel/new	creative	known	
effective	efficient	ineffective	inefficient
innovative	disruptive / of high quality	disruptive	of inferior quality
useful	valuable	wasteful	worthless
storable	clean	fragile	
meaningful essential	extraordinary	meaningless	ordinary
relevant	high-performance	irrelevant	underperforming
secure	solid	insecure	unstable
reliable	professional	unreliable / prone to interference	unprofessional
integrated/holistic	technically sophisticated	punctual helpful	too technical
maintenace-free (low maintenance effort)		maintenance-intensive	
challenging	satisfying	unambitious	unsatisfying
ease of use			
accessible	available	inaccessible	lacking
business-like		distracting	
comfortable	flexible adaptable	uncomfortable	inflexible
structured expectable	predictable	unstructured confusing	unpredictable
logically coherent	consistent	illogically incoherent	inconsistent
easy to use	easy to operate	complex difficult	difficult to use
compatible	helpful	incomprehensible	
hands-on	controllable	interfering	uncontrollable
easily applicable		exhausting	
easily responsive	intuitive	rigid	
easy to handle	direct/uncomplicated	erratic	
ergonomical	easily reachable	unergonomical	

social/emotional			
attractive	collaborative	annoying	boring
fascinating	friendly	unattractive	frustrating
amusing	vivid	humorless/too serious	monotonous
thrilling	entertaining	sterile	stressful
inspiring	irresistibly impressive	outdated	
convincing	motivating	doubtful	discouraging
stimulating	trustworthy	dull	questionable
personal	exciting	impersonal	
familiar	inspirational	intimidating	busy
inviting	optimistic	undesirable	pessimistic
supporting	preferable	patronizing	arrogant
calm / relaxed / mild	overwhelming		roh/ungebildet
unconventional		unconventional	
time			
time-saving	fast	slow	time-consuming

In addition, the following statements on the possible behavior of the user are helpful in usability testing:

- Understands the task, but cannot solve it in a reasonable time.
- Understands the goal, but must make several attempts to solve it.
- Aborts the step.
- Ends a step, but not the one that was asked.
- Was surprised.
- Is annoyed, frustrated.
- Must ask.

See also chapter 3.4.4 on cognitive walkthroughs, chapter 3.4.6 on mental models and chapter 3.4.5 on heuristic evaluation.

8

How to implement Design Thinking

8   How to implement Design Thinking

8.1	How to conduct workshops	199
8.2	Workshop methods	199
8.2.1	Card Sorting	200
8.2.2	Gallery method	201
8.2.3	Fishbowl discussion	201
8.2.4	World Café	202
8.2.5	Open Space	202
8.2.6	Barcamps	204
8.3	Requirements for the space	205
8.4	Material requirements	206
8.5	Agility for Design Thinking	207

8 How to implement Design Thinking

„In order to achieve the possible, the impossible must be tried again and again." (translation from German) – Hermann Hesse, German-born poet, novelist

Based on the planning of the Design Thinking project (see chapter 1.3) and the content (chapters 2 to 7), this section contains recommendations for the implementation of Design Thinking projects. Since the Design Thinking process depends on interactive teamwork, tips for the implementation of workshop formats are given first (chapter 8.1) and some workshop techniques (chapter 8.2) are presented. In the following you will find explanations about the creative design of the rooms (chapter 8.3) and the requirements for the required materials (chapter 8.4). Finally, in chapter 8.5, the principles for an agile implementation of Design Thinking are given.

8.1 How to conduct workshops

The following tips are given for preparing and conducting workshops as part of the Design Thinking process:

➤ Send information about the course and goals of the workshop in advance; possibly ask as a kind of "homework assignment" to think about something, to read something, to do something etc.
➤ Use different methods in the workshop and alternate them.
➤ You should also change other factors for reasons of variety and inspiration, such as group vs. individual work, length of work/breaks, rooms, etc.
➤ Use warm-up methods especially for groups whose participants do not all know each other and/or who are interdisciplinary in their subject, who come from different departments, who come from different cultural backgrounds, who are located at different hierarchical levels.
➤ In principle, one should avoid excessive differences among the participants with regard to the hierarchy.
➤ In the beginning, it makes sense to start with brainstorming or brainwriting. Reverse brainstorming, in which one first asks to formulate something negative in order to let off steam, can also be very helpful at the beginning.
➤ Agenda can also be symbolized with drawings (e.g. with the metaphor of a common walk or bicycle ride), so that a first visual stimulus is set.

A thorough preparation is an important success factor. The following must be clarified during the preparation process:

- Clarify the objectives and purpose of the meeting

- Clarify process details (see below)
- Composition of the team
- Clarify moderation, protocol keeping and other roles for the workshop, if applicable.
- Creating technical and spatial conditions
- Compiling presentation documents
- Preparing and copying handouts
- Plan social event after the workshop

The conduct of a workshop can be structured as follows:

(1) Personal/technical introduction
(2) Warm-ups so that participants get to know each other
(3) Clarification of the objectives, the procedure and the rules of the workshop (see chapter 1.1 as well as chapter 5.3.1.1 on brainstorming) with query of the expectations of the participants
(4) Problem clarification (see chapter 2.2)
(5) Idea generation phase (I) (see chapters 5.1 to 5.3)
(6) Pause
(7) Idea generation phase (II) (see chapters 5.1 to 5.3)
(8) Idea evaluation/selection (see chapter 5.4)
(9) Presentation of the results (preparation of the ideas: Summarising, reformulating, structuring (clusters/associations) (see chapter 6.3)
(10) Implementation steps (to do`s)
(11) Critical reflection of the workshop regarding the approach, if necessary (what was good/bad about the workshop?)

As part of the follow-up to the workshop, the focus will initially be on following up the ideas. After the workshop, the ideas can first be subjected to a detailed external and/or internal evaluation and on this basis the ideas can finally be selected. The workshop participants should also be regularly informed about the individual steps involved in implementing the ideas. The follow-up also includes the critical analysis of the workshop itself, which includes the preparation phase up to the details of the process. The lessons learned can be summarised here.

8.1.1 Card Sorting

Card sorting can be used for user-friendly structuring and designation of functionalities or features of a product or service. Card sorting is very similar to the so-called KJ method with an affinity diagram as presented in chapter 6.3. Card Sorting is used in the area of software development and web design so that the menu structure is organised and described in a way that is comprehensible to the user.

However, the principle can be applied to all innovation objects and types. In addition, this method can be used in various Design Thinking phases. For example, (customer) problems or initial solution ideas (possibly together with potential customers/users) can be systematically structured or in a later phase it is tested whether the customer understands the structure as intended. The number of cards should be limited and clear timelines should be adhered to.

According to Ross (2011), there are various card sorting approaches:

- **Open card sorting (the so-called generative approach):**

  The participants of the workshop receive cards with problem areas or solution ideas written on them – if necessary with a short description on the back – and must combine these into categories or generic terms (clustering) and label them. The participants can also be given empty cards to write down and sort further problems/ideas. This shows which problems/ideas logically belong together for the participants. In addition, at least the maximum number or even the number of headings can be specified.

- **Closed card sorting (the so-called evaluating approach):**

  Here the participants of the workshop are not only given a fixed number of headings, but the categories/headings are also already defined in their designations. On this basis, the participants should sort the cards into these categories. This in turn shows whether the participants are sorting the cards as expected.

- **Reverses Card Sorting (also part of the evaluative approach):**

  Here, the participants are tested to see whether they can find the required information within a given structure. If the structure is presented to the participants in full detail, this is referred to as card-based classification evaluation or tree testing. This approach is particularly helpful in a later Design Thinking phase (testing phase) in order to be able to make improvements to the solution idea, e.g. in the form of a prototype.

All approaches can be carried out offline in a real workshop or online using software tools. There are several software solutions on the market for the online version. In addition, the card sorting can take place with one person as an individual work or with several participants in a group of three to a maximum of seven participants, e.g. to experience the group discussions. A further variant in this combination is the modified Delphi Card Sorting (modified Delphi card sorting), which is carried out in several stages according to the Delphi method (see chapter 2.4.4) (see Paul (2008)). Here the first participant starts an open card sorting and this result is then passed on to another participant who can change and supplement this first proposal. This result will then be checked by another participant. This check by other participants will be aborted if several participants do not make any more changes one after the other and thus there is a consensus among the participants on the best structuring.

8.1.2 Gallery method

With the gallery method, developed by the German creativity expert Horst Geschka, the results from the idea generation for visualization can be presented in the form of a poster or on flip charts or pin boards for all participants. After the creation of the "Gallery", all participants can take a tour, as at a vernissage, to look at the results of the others, take notes, ask questions, make suggestions for further processing or implementation.

8.1.3 Fishbowl discussion

In the so-called Fishbowl discussion, an inner and outer circle of chairs is created. The inner circle leads together the discussion to a topic and the outer circle forms the audience. If a listener wants to participate in the discussion, he must either sit down on a free chair in the inner circle or stand behind the chair of a previous fellow discussant, who – if he is talking – is allowed to finish his thoughts and then has to leave the inner circle. The free chair may only be used for one word at a time and must then be left. With the Fishbowl method a discussion can be stimulated and frequent speakers can be regulated.

8.1.4 World Café

The World Café format is a large group moderation method in which a larger number of people (>> 12) exchange ideas in small groups (five to seven people) on a given question, problem or idea at a common (round) café house table. The "owner of the café house" moderates the discussion at the table (as reservedly as possible with his own contributions). After a certain time (30 to 45 minutes), the visitors change tables. The moderator ("café-owner") then informs them about the question/problem/topic of the table and the previous ideas/results of the previous visitors. If necessary, visitors can report on the results/ideas of previous visits to other tables. The World Café will (at the latest) end as soon as each participant has visited all the tables.

The goal is not necessarily ready-made solutions, but an informal exchange in order to gain new perspectives on a topic. Results can, for example, be visualized in the form of a mind map – either on a flip chart or whiteboard, with moderation cards or Post-Its on a metaplan wall, or directly on a paper tablecloth. The last table round should also be used to summarize the results. Finally, the results can be summarized in the large plenum by the "coffee house owners" of the tables and the flip charts or tablecloths can also be displayed as a results gallery (see also the gallery method above for this). If necessary, the moderator of the entire World Café should call for comments and additions in the plenum. The results (ideas/measures) can also be evaluated by each participant attaching glue points to the ideas (dot voting). Finally, the moderator should also ensure who has to complete which ideas/measures by when and with what result.

An important success factor is the right question/problem or the right topic. The question should therefore be thoroughly prepared in advance so that it is inspiring, challenging, worth discussing and not too general but also not too special. You should try to break down the question, problem or topic thematically so that you can work on it in parts at different tables. For example, the topic can first be worked on in the form of an as-is analysis, then one table deals with the target state and another table is dedicated to improvement measures.

A heterogeneous group of participants is helpful for this method, so that different perspectives can be integrated. Likewise one should pay more attention to the selection of the "Café owners" and prepare them for their tasks as moderators. In chapter 8.1 you will find some hints for conducting workshops, which can also be used by the moderators. To loosen up the working atmosphere and spread a café-house atmosphere, coffee, tea, drinks, small snacks and biscuits and cakes can also be offered at supply stations and quiet music can be played in the background. The room and the technical and material equipment should also be considered (see chapter 8.3 and 8.4).

This method can also be integrated into conferences or meetings. In addition to generating ideas, this method can also be used for exchanging knowledge. This is referred to as knowledge cafés. Further Tipps to the World Café/Knowledge Café are e.g. with Brown/Isaacs (2007).

8.1.5 Open Space

Open Space (Owen (2008)) is also a method for large groups (8 to more than 1000 people) that can be used to solve problems and especially in the context of change processes. A very heterogeneous group of participants is advantageous. Since knowledge development or knowledge exchange also takes place here, this method can also be used for knowledge management. Open Space can be a component, for example, of company-wide events, meetings or conferences and can last from a few hours to several days.

The method is characterized by the fact that there is no sequence defined down to the last detail. Rather, only one (lead) topic or special problem/challenge is specified. The self-organisation of the participants and thus their self-responsibility and self-determination is an essential element, which should increase the creativity and motivation of the participants. It contributes to the creation of a sense of we and the acceptance of the ideas, solutions and measures in the subsequent implementation. The participants should be invited to a comprehensive openness for what is happening already during the invitation and the moderation.

In Open Space, there is the law of two feet: if you cannot contribute anything constructive to a group discussion or if you have no interest in a topic, you should leave the room and look for a new group. One also speaks here of the "bumblebees" who go from group to group ("flying from flower to flower") and bring in new ideas, dust off other ideas and carry them to the next group. The "butterflies", on the other hand, are more often to be found in the break area, are points of attraction for other participants and conduct their conversations there on the fringes of the working groups, so that they rather indirectly "fertilize" the working groups.

Although Open Space focuses on the self-organisation of the participants, extensive preparatory planning of the topic (problem/challenge), the premises, the workshop material as well as the organisation of the catering is necessary. An easily accessible venue (e.g. hotel, restaurants) with a sufficient number of seminar rooms of different sizes should be selected depending on the size of the group. Technical equipment (printers, copiers, laptops, beamers, etc.) and materials must also be organised. The individual groups can work in their own rooms or in areas separated by partitions. Seating circles without chairs are preferred. A high flexibility of the furniture as well as a clear arrangement of the rooms/work areas and materials are required (see chapter 8.3). Depending on the size of the group, additional personnel may be required for supervision and catering in addition to the moderator (or even team of moderators) and observer. Conference folder with rough agenda, room plan, background information on the method, name tags can also be helpful, depending on the scope.

The (preferably external) moderator presents the theme and objectives of the open space event, explains the process and the principles of the method (openness, law of two feet). The information on where to find what (rooms, materials, contact persons, etc.) and how to document the results are also explained at the beginning. The moderator should see himself more as a facilitator, who is present when needed, but is very reserved, quasi invisible.

The first step is to subdivide the overriding topic into further sub-topics. Participants are asked to write sub-topics on a sheet of paper and attach them to a blackboard/wall. This blackboard/wall is also the documentation wall of the Open Space method, which is positioned in the large plenum room, the so-called marketplace, and collects all (interim) results after the small group work. The participants themselves and, if necessary, with the support of the moderator, arrange the topics on the documentation wall. The selection or prioritisation of topics does not take place in this so-called market phase. The relevance of a topic is ultimately determined by the number of participants ("coordination with the feet") in the subsequent small group sessions. For each topic, a room is assigned that is clearly visible to all. Interested participants can meet and discuss the topic, goals of solutions/improvements, initial ideas for solutions or measures, etc. in the work areas. It is a good idea for the person with the proposed topic to take over the (initial) moderation of the group. A time budget of 90 to 120 minutes is sufficient, then everyone meets again in the large room. Alternatively, in the case of a large number of topics, several successive periods of time can be defined and attached to the message wall with a clearly visible timetable.

What the small groups discuss, how they discuss, which tools (internet, laptop, flipcharts, building prototypes (see chapter 6)) they use, how long they discuss, all this lies in the self-organisation of the group.

The results are documented by the participants themselves or by silent observers on flipcharts, metaplans, in power-point presentations and/or protocols in writing or by photo. This can be followed by a documentation volume.

Then another round of group work can be started to discuss the priorities and implementation possibilities from the results and, in the best case, to create a to-do list with goals, measures, time and responsibilities. It is ideal if those affected by the implementation already participate in the group. In a large circle, these results are again presented and reflected upon in a final round. It can also be agreed that in a few months one will meet again either in the large group or in small groups to reflect on the implementation results. At the end all participants should meet again in the plenum and with the support of the moderator.

8.1.6 Barcamps

Similar to the open space method, barcamps represent large group activities according to the principle of self-organisation, which are (even) carried out more loosely. At Barcamps, each participant is asked in advance to bring along a topic/contribution/open question/brief presentation or a completely different form of problem presentation/questioning and to offer a working session for it, the so called session. Compared to Open Space, these sessions are only scheduled for 30 minutes. As Barcamps have their origins in the IT sector, software applications such as wikis, blogs and social networks are often used for preparation, working sessions and documentation of results.

8.2 Requirements for the space

Design Thinking Workshops include both group and individual work in different constellations. This requires certain conditions to the premises. Therefore, both common workstations for groups and separate individual workstations should be available. One speaks here of **"We-Spaces"** (for groups or as plenum for all) for open communication and **"Me-Spaces"** for quiet individual work for deeper concentration.

The size of the room (or rooms) should be larger for the participants than for usual room uses, since Design Thinking workshops require a lot of space due to the division into small groups, the use of bulky whiteboards/metaplan walls, collaborative work on prototypes and the desired movement of the participants. It may be advisable to choose different locations, rooms or furniture arrangements for the different design-thinking phases in order to always create new atmospheres (suitable for the respective work).

The premises (or, in good weather, outdoor areas!) may be unusual locations that are rented, or they may be used for their own premises that are either unusually rearranged or have been used for completely different purposes (e.g. warehouses, workshop, corridors, cafeteria). The furnishings in the existing rooms can be arranged accordingly (unusually) (e.g. as reception counters, workshops, station halls, etc.) in order to gain new impressions and provide initial inspiration.

In order to flexibly realize different (small) group constellations that do not disturb each other in their work, movable whiteboard/pin/metaplan walls can also be used as room dividers, whereby the groups can even use the different sides of a corresponding mobile whiteboard/pin/metaplan wall. A wide range of sizes and equipment variants are available in stores, including combined whiteboard/pinn walls. Foam boards are also very flexible and have the advantage over whiteboards because they are very light, e.g. to quickly carry out work on different floors. These are available in different sizes.

The four walls in a room can also be used for thematic structuring. For example, the first wall can contain information about the customer, the second wall contains information about the problems/needs of the customer, the third wall provides information about additional needs, and finally the fourth wall contains illustrations about initial solutions. In the middle, there is space for the collaborative prototyping workspace.

Overall, it is important to note that there are many horizontal and vertical surfaces in the form of large desks/writing surfaces and walls (where windows, doors and white walls can also be used) to attach Post-Its, cards and entire prototypes. A flexible, cost-effective alternative are electrostatic whiteboard films that can be attached to almost any surface.

Also for the flexibility to realize different ways of working, the tables, chairs and boxes should be equipped with castors and as light and stackable as possible. "Normal" meeting rooms with the typical table constellations should be avoided. In principle, the areas for group work are best equipped with bar tables and stools in order to quickly form new groups between the participants and encourage movement. Stools can also be used as storage boxes for materials. There is also a large selection available in the shops.

In the work rooms themselves or better in a separate room, which can be used as a refreshment room with drinks and pastries, comfortable chairs/armchairs or even sofas should be provided to facilitate phases of relaxation or informal exchange.

The rooms should also be equipped with internet (or better Wi-Fi) and especially electricity connections in many places (only use cables and multiple sockets if necessary, as they are a nuisance or a trip hazard). A permanently installed beamer is not necessarily mandatory, as it restricts flexibility in the use of space. White walls are sufficient here without the need for an additional projection screen.

A room with plenty of daylight is conducive. This has the additional advantage that the surfaces of large windows can also be used for attaching notes. At least the work and presentation areas should be well

8 How to implement Design Thinking

illuminated. Good acoustics without echo and reverberation in the rooms are also essential when working in small groups. Finally, warm natural colours on the walls, high ceilings, fresh air and a temperature between 18 and 22 degrees (rather 18 degrees, since the participants in this workshop are often in motion) create a room climate conducive to work.

The necessary materials should be quickly available, well sorted and stowed to avoid chaos. Modular cabinet systems or stools as storage boxes allow a lot of flexibility.

8.3 Material requirements

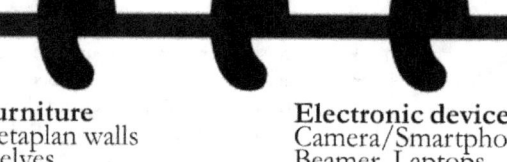

Furniture
metaplan walls
shelves
Bar tables, stools
flip chart, whiteboards
foam boards

Electronic devices
Camera/Smartphone
Beamer, Laptops
Stopwatch, presenter

Writing utensils
Post-Its in different size/color
pens of various types
index cards/moderation cards in various shapes/colours (square, round, oval, cloudy)
paper in different sizes/colours, foils

pins, magnets, adhesives
hot glue, crepe paper, colour dots, adhesive tape
cutter, hammer, saw, wiping cloth, cords fabric,
red/yellow cards, picture material cable ties, tapes,
insulating tapes, pieces of fabric plastic cutlery,
wires, bags, stickers
gong

Protoytpen materials:
clay, modelling clay, Lego bricks, matchbox cars,
figures, polystyrene, aluminium foil, wood
cardboard, scissors, carpet knives, rulers,
measuring tapes, screwdrivers, pliers, nails, screws,
staples, sandpaper, cardboard boxes, for role-
playing games: clothing, magazines/newspapers

⇨ Cartons / Boxes / Cans
    to sort materials (otherwise chaos will occur)

Figure 41: Material List for Design Thinking Workshops

8.4 Agility for Design Thinking

Design Thinking processes exhibit a high degree of uncertainty and complexity. In addition, there are dynamic changes with regard to the questions processed as well as with regard to the implementation. The concrete requirements only become clearer in the course of Design Thinking. In this respect, Design Thinking should be carried out according to an agile project management approach.

The most widespread approach, which will also be briefly presented here with its principles, is Scrum. The term Scrum originates from rugby and was first used by Takeuchi/Nonaka (1986) and made popular by Ken Schwaber. The term rugby stands here for the close, self-organized and self-responsible cooperation in a development team under strict adherence to a few, but clear rules (Scrum refers specifically to the crowding of players during a free kick action in rugby, in which the players spontaneously discuss their further actions, since there are no practiced moves or instructions from the coach).

Scrum projects should be carried out according to a few principles and a few clear rules, which are succinctly summarized in the "The Scrum Guide" by Schwaber/Sutherland (2016) (freely available and highly recommended). The main principles are explained below.

Principle of the incremental, iterative and adaptive process

Scrum is an incremental, iterative and adaptive process. This means that the project tasks are first deliberately broken down into small task packages (increments) and prioritized. These are processed in strictly defined short iterations in order to then adapt the project to the (desired!) upcoming changes – ideally in the form of customer feedback – early, quickly and flexibly. The short, manageable stages (so-called sprints) enable a quick reaction. In contrast to traditional project management or the Stage Gate process, the requirements are not fixed en detail or are not completely specified at the beginning, but are to be understood as changeable. The detailed planning of the project is successively carried out at the right time (see the following principle of just-in-time planning). The fact that changes in requirements (goals) are considered legitimate and even virtually desirable can be advantageous, especially for Design Thinking projects in a dynamically changing market environment. Thus it is accepted in this process that one does not have all information right at the beginning and does everything right immediately.

Prinzip of just-in-time planning

Planning is step-by-step and demand-oriented – just at the right time (just-in-time) when something is due. This means that only the next steps are planned in detail. Traditional project management, on the other hand, tries to fully plan the project in terms of content, time, resources and costs at the beginning. At Scrum, this step-by-step and demand-oriented planning does not mean that a project is ultimately planned less – on the contrary, it means that the planning is done step-by-step. When a step is completed, this and developments outside the project have improved the information base to plan the next step. The planning is delayed until the last responsible moment, in order to allow as much up-to-date information as possible to flow in. This planning process can be illustrated with the pen-pencil rule (Layton 2012): 142): The next steps are bindingly written with a ballpoint pen, whereas the later steps are sketched with a pencil and can easily be changed.

8 How to implement Design Thinking

Principle of communication before documentation

The Scrum process gives priority to communication rather than documentation. The documentation should be reduced to a minimum. Scrum focuses on speed and the early collection of informal customer feedback. Comprehensive and formalized documentation would be a hindrance. If documented, then only for the visualization of direct communication about the future course of the project. Spontaneous discussions and face-to-face meetings are preferred to any other means of communication. This means that the team should ideally work at the same location (collocation) and, if possible, close to the customer/user. The premises should also promote this direct personal exchange (see requirements for the premises in chapter 8.3). Otherwise, video chats (instead of e-mails), instant messaging, collaboration software, etc. should be used.

If results are to be presented, they should be demonstrated in the form of testing a prototype (see Minimal Viable Prototypes in chapter 6.2). The motto is: "Demonstrate instead of present" or: "Write less, Talk more".

Principle of self-organisation

The tasks in the implementation to fulfil the requirements are distributed in the team according to the abilities and competences of the team members themselves (self-organisation). This means that the tasks are not delegated by a project manager to the individual team members, but should be discussed and divided up within the team in the sense of a bottom-up approach.

In addition, the team members do their own work according to the pull principle. This means that the individual team members pull themselves out of the so-called product backlog one after the other and do as much as they think they can do. This is the only way team members can successfully deliver their results.

Principle of compliance with – few – but strictly observable rules

Scrum is based on only a few rules, but these must be strictly adhered to. Within these rules the participants are completely free and responsible for their (self-chosen) tasks. This again includes the principle of **timeboxing**: Each meeting and each task execution (so-called sprints) are strictly limited in time, one speaks here of "Timeboxing". These time limits must never be exceeded. "A deadline is a deadline is a deadline." These strict rules simplify the planning and control of the project as well as the coordination – both within the project team and between individual projects. These rules are known to everyone and everyone knows what they mean. In addition, the uniformly fixed duration should also ensure a constant working rhythm (so-called cadence).

These principles are also helpful for implementing Design Thinking. In this respect, it is recommended that you take a closer look at Scrum. A detailed description of the further Scrum process can be found in Rubin (2012).

9 Glossary

5
5R rule 183

9
9-field thinking 27

A
A Day in the Life 50
A/B-Testing 159
AEIOU 35
affinity diagram 164
agile project management 207
analogy 81, 87, 99, 100
artifact analysis 40
attribute listing 105

B
barcamps 204
behavioral mapping 40
biomimicry .... see bionics
bionics 100
blind spot 15
bodystorming 172
brainstorming 85
brainwriting 90
business model 148
business model canvas 160

C
card sorting 200
cognitive walkthrough 42
collective notebook 91
concierge-MVP 160
Concierge-MVP 178
convergent phase 2
Cornell notes 183
creativity 79
Critical-Incident technique 56, 57
cross-industry innovations 92
crowdfunding 160
cultural probes 173
customer benefit matrix 49
customer experience map 48
customer journey 45, 51
customer orientation 1
customer scorecard ..... see opportunity algorithm
customer touchpoint management 47

D
Dark Horse prototypes 178
Delphi method 22, 96
design scenarios 172
desirability toolkit 194
diary method 173
disruptive innovations 71
divergent phase 2
diversity 2
dot voting 132
double diamond 2

E
early evangelists 147, 179
Elevator Pitch 165
Empathic design 34
empathy map 41, 53, 68
experience sampling 173
eye-tracking system 157

F
fish bone diagram .... see Ishikawa diagram
force field analysis 164
forced relationship 93

G
graffiti wall 173

H
Halo effect 39
Hawthorne Effect .... see interviewer effect
heuristic evaluation 43
Heuristic Ideation Technique (HIT) 105

I
ideation 79
illumination 79

9 Glossary

image boards	*see moodboards*
innovation checklist	114
innovation principles	120
interviewer effect	35, 39, 40
Ishikawa diagram	23

J

job mapping	66
Jobs-to-be-done	33, **65**, 146

K

Kano model	71, 188
KJ method	86

L

laddering	28, **75**
landing Page	159
lead users	33
Lean Startup	144
Lego Serious Games	158
Lotus Blossom	106

M

means-end	**74**, 87
mental models	44
Me-Spaces	205
method 635	*see brainwriting*
Microsoft Reaction Card Method	*...see desirability toolkit*
mind mapping	98, 163
Minimum Viable Product (MVP)	152, 157
mockups	159
moments of truth	48, 52
moodboards	64
morphological box	103
mystery shopping	56

N

NABC	165
Net Promotor Score (NPS)	154
Not-Invented-Here-Syndrom	83

O

observation	33
observer effect	*see interviewer effect*
open source	160
open space	202
Operator Time-Size-Cost	115
opportunity algorithm	72
opus method	132
Osborn checklist	96

P

pair comparison	136
Pecha Kucha	165
persona	46, 53, **62**, 66
personal inventory	*see artifact analysis*
PESTEL	16, 22
pivots	144
POEMS	35
Power-of-Ten	29
prefix method	92
primary effect	39
problem space	2, 4
process	4
provocation technique	93

R

random word technique	92
rapid prototyping	160
recency effect	39
resource analysis	115
Root Conflict Analysis	24
Rosenthal effect	39

S

SCAMPER	*see Osborn checklist*
scoring model	137
scrum	207
Sean Ellis test	154
semantic differential	164
semantic intuition	92
separation principles	119
sequential morphology	104
service blueprinting	51, 56
shadowing	34
silent shopping	*see mystery shopping*
Six Thinking Hats	95
solution space	2, 4
split testing	*Siehe* A/B-Testing
sprints	207
storyboarding	166
storytelling	158, 169
SWOT analysis	135
synectics	99

Systematic Inventive Thinking (SIT) 128

T
think-aloud 38
timeboxing 4, 208
touchpoints 47, 54
trends 20
TRIZ 81, 107

U
user story **64**, 151

V
Venn diagram 162

viral coefficient 155
VUCA 134

W
Walt Disney method 94
We-Spaces 205
wireframe 158
Wizard-of-Oz 160
world café 202

Y
Yes, and 85

10 Bibliography

A

Altschuler, Genrich Saulowitsch (1994): And Suddenly the Inventor Appeared: TRIZ, the Theory of Inventive Problem Solving, Technical Innovation Center, Worcester/USA.

Alvarez, Cindy (2014): Lean Customer Development: Building Products Your Customers Will Buy, O'Reilly, Sebastopol/USA.

Andler, Nicolai (2016): Tools for Project Management, Workshops and Consulting: A Must-Have Compendium of Essential Tools and Techniques, 3rd edition, Publicis Publishing, Erlangen/Germany.

Aerssen, Benno van / Buchholz, Christian (2018): Das große Handbuch Innovation: 555 Methoden und Instrumente für mehr Kreativität und Innovation im Unternehmen, Vahlen-Verlag, München.

B

Baumeister, Dayna (2014): Biomimicry Resource Handbook, Biomimicry 3.8, Missoula/USA.

Benedek, Joey / Miner, Trish (2010): Measuring desirability: New methods for evaluating desirability in a usability lab setting, in: Proceedings of Usability Professionals Association 2002 Conference, Orlando/USA.

Blank, Steve (2006): The Four Steps to the Epiphany: Successful Strategies for Products That Win, K&S Ranch Press, Palo Alto/USA.

Blank, Steve /Dorf, Bob (2012), The Startup Owner's Manual: The Step-By-Step Guide for Building a Great Company, K&S RANCH, Pescadero/USA.

Boyd, Drew / Goldenberg, Jacob (2013): Inside the Box: A Proven System of Creativity for Breakthrough Results, Simon & Schuster, New York/USA.

Brown, Tim (2009): Change by Design – How Design Thinking Transforms Organizations and Inspires Innovation, Harper Collins, New York/USA.

Brügger, Chris / Hartschen, Michael / Scherer, Jiri (2017): simplicity: Starke Strategien für einfache Produkte, Dienstleistungen und Prozesse, 2nd edition, Gabal-Verlag, Offenbach.

Buzan, Tony (2013): Mind Map Handbook: The ultimate thinking tool, HarperCollins, New York/USA.

C

Carlzon, Jan (1989): Moments of Truth, HarperBusiness, New York/USA.

Christensen, Clayton M. (1997): The Innovator's Dilemma: When new technologies cause great firms to fall, Harvard Business School Press, Boston/USA.

Christensen, Clayton M. / Raynor, Michael E. (2003): The Innovator's Solution: Creating and Sustaining Successful Growth, Harvard Business School Press, Boston/USA.

Christensen, Clayton M. / Hall, Taddy / Dillo, Karen / Duncan, David S. (2016): Competing against luck, HarperBusiness, New York/USA.

Cohn, Mike (2004): User Stories Applied: For Agile Software Development, Addison-Wesley Professional, Boston/USA.

Cooper, Robert G. (2011): Winning at New Products: Creating Value Through Innovation, 4th edition, Basic Books, New York/USA.

Cooper, Brant / Vlaskovits, Patrick (2014): The Lean Entrepreneur: How Visionaries Create Products, Innovate with New Ventures, and Disrupt Markets, John Wiley & Sons, Hoboken/USA.

Curedale, Robert (2013): design thinking – process and methods manual, Design Community College, Topanga/USA.

D

Day, George S. (2007): Is it real? Can we win? Is it worth it? Managing risk and reward in an innovation portfolio, in: Harvard Business Review, 85, 12, S. 110 - 120.

De Bono, Edward (1972): PO: A Device for Successful Thinking, Simon & Schuster, New York/USA.

De Bono, Edward (2016): Six Thinking Hats, Penguin Books, London/UK.

Design Council UK (2005): The Design Process, https://www.designcouncil.org.uk/news-opinion/design-process-what-double-diamond, Zugriffsdatum: 11.06.2018.

F

Flanagan, John C. (1954): The critical incident technique. Psychological Bulletin, 51, 4: 327 - 358.

Fritzpatrick, Rob (2013): The Mom Test: How to talk to customers & learn if your business is a good idea when everyone is lying to you, CreateSpace, New York/USA.

Furr, Nathan / Dyer, Jeff (2014): The Innovator's Method: Bringing the Lean Start-up into Your Organization, Harvard Business Review Press, Boston/USA.

G

Gadd, Karen (2011): TRIZ for Engineers: Enabling Inventive Problem Solving, John Wiley & Son, Chichester/UK.

Goller, Ina / Bessant, John (2017): Creativity of Innovation Management, Rotledge, Abingdon-on-Thames/UK.

Gordon, William (1961): Synectics: The development of creative capacity. Harper, New York/USA:

Gray, Dave / Brown, Sunni / Macanufo, James (2010): Gamestorming: A Playbook for Innovators, Rulebreakers, and Changemakers, O`Reilly Media, Sebastopol/USA.

K

Kelley, Tom / Kelley, David (2014): Creative Confidence: Unleashing the Creative Potential within us all, HarperCollins, London/UK.

Kelley, Tom/Littman, Jonathan (2001): The Art of Innovation: Lessons in Creativity from IDEO, America's Leading Design Firm, Crown Business, New York/USA.

Kim, W. Chan/ Mauborgne, Renée A. (2015): Blue Ocean Strategy, Expanded Edition: How to Create Uncontested Market Space and Make the Competition Irrelevant, expanded edition, Harvard Business school Publishing, Boston/USA.

Klein, Gary (2007): Performing a Project Premortem, in: Harvard Business Review. 85, 9, S. 18 - 19.

Koltze, Karl / Souchkov, Valeri (2017): Systematische Innovation – TRIZ-Anwendung in der Produkt- und Prozessentwicklung, 2. Auflage, Hanser Verlag, München.

Kumar, Vijay (2012): 101 Design Methods: A Structured Approach for Driving Innovation in Your Organization, John Wiley & Sons, Hoboken/USA.

Kumar, Vijay / Whitney, Patrick (2003): Faster, Cheaper, Deeper User Research, in: Design Management Journal: 50 - 57.

L

Layton, Mark C. (2012), Scrum For Dummies, John Wiley & Sons, Hoboken/USA.

Levitt, Theodore (1986): The Marketing Imagination, Free Press, New York/USA.

Lewrick, Michael / Link, Patrick / Leifer, Larry (2018): The Design Thinking Playbook: Mindful Digital Transformation of Teams, Products, Services, Businesses and Ecosystems, John Wiley & Sons, Hoboken/USA.

Liedtka, Jeanne / Oglivie, Tim (2011): Designing for Growth: A Design Thinking Tool Kit for Managers, Columbia Univers. Press, New York/USA.

Lindberg, Tilmann / Gumienny, Raja / Jobst, Birgit / Meinel, Christoph (2010): Is There a Need for a Design Thinking Process?, in: Proceedings of Design Thinking Research Symposium 8 (Design 2010), Sydney, Australia, October 2010, pp. 243-254.

M

Martin, John / Bell, Ros / Farmer, Eion (2000): B822 – Technique Library, The Open University, Milton Keynes/USA.

Martin, Bella / Hanington, Bruce (2012): Universal Methods of Design: 100 Ways to Research Complex Problems, Develop Innovative Ideas, and Design Effective Solutions, Rockport Publishers, Beverly/USA.

Maurya, Ash (2013): Running Lean - Das How-to für erfolgreiche Innovationen, O`Reilly Verlag, Köln.

Michalko, Michael (2006): Thinkertoys: A Handbook of Creative-Thinking Techniques, 2. Auflage, Ten Speed Press, Berkeley/USA.

Moore, Geoffrey A. (2014): Crossing the Chasm: Marketing and Selling Disruptive Products to Mainstream Customers, HarperCollins Publishers, New York/USA.

N

Nielsen, Jakob (1994): Enhancing the explanatory power of usability heuristics, in: Proc. ACM CHI'94 Conf., April 24-28, Boston/USA, S. 152-158.

Nielsen, Jakob (1995): Severity Ratings for Usability Problems. https://www.nngroup.com/articles/how-to-rate-the-severity-of-usability-problems/, date of access: 18.10.2018.

O

Olsen, Dan (2015): The Lean Product Playbook: How to Innovate with Minimum Viable Products and Rapid Customer Feedback, John Wiley & Sons, Hoboken/USA.

Orloff, Michael (2010): Inventive Thinking through TRIZ: A Practical Guide, 2nd edition, Springer, Berlin/Germany.

Osterwalder, Alexander / Pigneur, Yves (2010): Business Model Generation: A Handbook for Visionaries, Game Changers, and Challengers, John Wiley & Sons, New York/USA.

Osterwalder, Alexander / Pigneur, Yves / Bernarda, Gregory / Smith, Alan (2014): Value Proposition Design: How to Create Products and Services Customers Want, John Wiley & Sons, Hoboken/USA.

Owen, Harrison (2008): Open Space Technology: A User's Guide, 3rd edition, Berrett-Koehler Publishers, Oakland/USA.

P

Pauk, Walter / Owens, Ross J.K. (2013): How to Study in College, 11. Auflage, Cengage Learning, Wadsworth/USA.

Paul, Celeste Lyn (2008): A Modified Delphi Approach to a New Card Sorting Methodology."PDF Journal of Usability Studies, 4, 1, Seite 7 - 30.

Plattner, Hasso / Meinel, Christoph / Weinberg, Ulrich (2009): Design-Thinking, mi-Wirtschaftsbuch, München.

Puccio, Gerard J. / Murdock, Mary C. / Mance, Marie (2011): Creative Leadership: Skills That Drive Change, 2nd edition, Sage Publications, London/UK.

R

Reichheld, Frederick F. (2003): The number one you need to grow, in: Harvard Business Review, 12: 47 - 54.

Reynolds, Thomas J. / Gutman, Jonathan (1984): Advertising is Image Management: Translating Image Research to Image Strategies, in: Journal of Advertising Research, 24, 1, S. 27 - 38.

Reynolds, Thomas J. / Gutman, Jonathan (1988): Laddering theory, method, analysis, and interpretation, in: Journal of Advertising Research, 28, S. 11 - 31.

Rhode, Mike (2012): The Sketchnote Handbook: the illustrated guide to visual note taking, Peachpit Press, Berkeley/USA.

Ries, Eric (2012): Lean Startup, Redline Verlag, München.

Roam, Dan (2009): The Back of the Napkin (Expanded Edition): Solving Problems and Selling Ideas with Pictures, Penguin Group, London/UK.

Ross, Jim (2011): Comparing User Research Methods for Information Architecture, in: https://www.uxmatters.com/mt/archives/2011/06/comparing-user-research-methods-for-information-architecture.php; date of access: 15.10.2018.

Rubin, Kenneth S. (2012): Essential Scrum: A Practical Guide to the Most Popular Agile Process (Addison-Wesley Signature): A Practical Guide To The Most Popular Agile Process, Addison-Wesley Professional, Boston/USA:

S

Schlicksupp, Helmut (2004): Ideenfindung, 6. edition, Vogel Business Media, Würzburg/Germany.

Schwaber, Ken / Sutherland, Jeff (2016), The Scrum Guide, in: http://www.scrumguides.org, Zugriffsdatum: 12.09.2017.

Shostack, Lynn G. (1984): Designing Services That Deliver, in: Harvard Business Review, 01/1984.

Sibbet, David (2010): Visual Meetings: How Graphics, Sticky Notes and Idea Mapping Can Transform Group Productivity, John Wiley & Sons, Hoboken/USA

10 Bibliography

Silverstein, David / Samuel, Philip / DeCarlo, Neil (2012): The Innovator's Toolkit: 50+ Techniques for Predictable and Sustainable Organic Growth, 2. Edition, John Wiley & Sons, Hoboken/USA.

Souchkov, Valeri (2005): Root Conflict Analysis (RCA+): Structured Problems and Contradictions Mapping, ETRIA Conference TRIZ FUTURE 2005, Graz, Austria, November 11-13, 2005.

Stickdorn, Marc / Schneider, Jakob (2013): This Service Design Thinking, BIS Publishers, Amsterdam/The Netherlands.

T

Takeuchi, Hirotaka / Nonaka, Ikujiro Harvard (1986), The New New Product Development Game, in: Harvard Business Review, 64, 1, Boston/USA.

Tognazzini, Bruce (2014): First Principles of Interaction Design (Revised & Expanded), https://asktog.com/atc/principles-of-interaction-design/; Date: 18.10.2018.

U

Ulwick, Anthony W. (2005): What customers want, McGraw Hill, New York /USA.

V

Vulling, Ramon / Heleven, Marc (2017): Not Invented Here – cross-industry innovation, 3rd edition, BIS Publishers, Amsterdam/The Netherlands.

W

Wake, Bill (2003): INVEST in Good Storys, and SMART Tasks, in: http://xp123.com/articles/invest-in-good-Storys-and-smart-tasks, date of access: 12.09.2017.

Wallas, Graham (1926): Art of Thought, Harcourt, Brace and Company, New York/USA.

Wharton, Cathleen /Rieman, John /Lewis, Clayton /Polson, Peter (1994): The Cognitive Walkthrough Method: A Practitioner's Guide, in: Nielsen, Jacob /Mack, Robert L. (Hrsg.): Usability Inspection Methods, John Wiley & Sons, Inc., New York/USA.

Woodruff, Robert B. / Cadotte, Ernest R. / Jenkins, Roger L. (1983): Modeling Consumer Satisfaction Processes Using Experience-Based Norms, in: Journal of marketing research, 20, 3: 296 - 304.

Y

Young, Indi (2008): Mental Models: Aligning Design Strategy with Human Behavior, Rosenfeld Media, New York/USA.

www.ingramcontent.com/pod-product-compliance
Lightning Source LLC
Chambersburg PA
CBHW051307220526
45468CB00004B/1245